CW01376640

Palgrave Socio-Legal Studies

Series Editor
Dave Cowan
School of Law
University of Bristol
Bristol, UK

The Palgrave Socio-Legal Studies series is a developing series of monographs and textbooks featuring cutting edge work which, in the best tradition of socio-legal studies, reach out to a wide international audience.

Editorial Board
Dame Hazel Genn, University College London, UK
Fiona Haines, University of Melbourne, Australia
Herbert Kritzer, University of Minnesota, USA
Linda Mulcahy, University of Oxford, UK
Carl Stychin, University of London, UK
Mariana Valverde, University of Toronto, Canada
Sally Wheeler, Australian National University College of Law, Australia.

More information about this series at
http://www.palgrave.com/gp/series/14679

Jackie Gulland

Gender, Work and Social Control

A Century of Disability Benefits

palgrave
macmillan

Jackie Gulland
Edinburgh, UK

Palgrave Socio-Legal Studies
ISBN 978-1-137-60562-7   ISBN 978-1-137-60564-1   (eBook)
https://doi.org/10.1057/978-1-137-60564-1

© The Editor(s) (if applicable) and The Author(s), under exclusive license to Springer Nature Limited 2019
The author(s) has/have asserted their right(s) to be identified as the author(s) of this work in accordance with the Copyright, Designs and Patents Act 1988.
This work is subject to copyright. All rights are solely and exclusively licensed by the Publisher, whether the whole or part of the material is concerned, specifically the rights of translation, reprinting, reuse of illustrations, recitation, broadcasting, reproduction on microfilms or in any other physical way, and transmission or information storage and retrieval, electronic adaptation, computer software, or by similar or dissimilar methodology now known or hereafter developed.
The use of general descriptive names, registered names, trademarks, service marks, etc. in this publication does not imply, even in the absence of a specific statement, that such names are exempt from the relevant protective laws and regulations and therefore free for general use.
The publisher, the authors and the editors are safe to assume that the advice and information in this book are believed to be true and accurate at the date of publication. Neither the publisher nor the authors or the editors give a warranty, expressed or implied, with respect to the material contained herein or for any errors or omissions that may have been made. The publisher remains neutral with regard to jurisdictional claims in published maps and institutional affiliations.

Image credit: Alamy E6320R

This Palgrave Macmillan imprint is published by the registered company Springer Nature Limited
The registered company address is: The Campus, 4 Crinan Street, London, N1 9XW, United Kingdom

For Julian, Malcolm and Duncan

Acknowledgements

The research for this book was funded by a Leverhulme Trust Early Career Fellowship (ECF-2012-178) based in the School of Social and Political Science at the University of Edinburgh. This funding enabled me to visit archives and carry out the bulk of the research. Much of the material which I used for this book can only be accessed by visiting an archive or library. I am grateful to the Institute of Historical Research for its excellent course on Methods and Sources for Historical Research which introduced me to the London archives. The University of Edinburgh Library, the National Library of Scotland and the archives listed in the Appendix have been vital in providing access to a wealth of material. I am grateful to the staff of these institutions for their professional skills in making this material available. Other material is available digitally but is supported by library and information services. I am grateful for the access available through the University of Edinburgh, the National Library of Scotland and Edinburgh City Libraries. The University of Edinburgh Library enabled me to access some hard-to-find published material through the inter-library loans service. At a time when the digital age marks all that is fashionable in research, I cannot emphasise too strongly the value of archives and libraries in making this book possible.

This book draws on ideas from several disciplines, including law, history, social science and disability studies. I have benefited greatly from feedback and supportive comments from the conference organisers and participants at events organised by the Law and Society Association, the Socio-Legal Studies Association, the Social Policy Association, the Social History Society, the Women's History Network, the European Social Science

History conference, the British Sociological Society, the Medical Sociology Conference, ESPAnet, Citizens Advice Scotland, a workshop on the "Politics of gender, work and value", and seminars organised at the University of Edinburgh in social policy, gender history and empirical legal studies. The Disability Research Network at the University of Edinburgh has been important in reminding me of the continuing struggles of disabled people today. I was fortunate to take part in several events which helped me to think more creatively about my research: a "pop-up museum of legal objects", organised by the SLSA, a workshop on creative methods in social research at the Morgan Centre at the University of Manchester and events organised by the Beltane Public Engagement project at the University of Edinburgh. Academic and voluntary sector colleagues on Twitter have contributed to my thinking on a wide range of subjects related to the research. I have contributed blog posts for the Legal Treasure Project, Dangerous Women and Challenge Poverty Week. I am grateful to the hosts of these blog sites and to David Oulton at the University of Edinburgh for setting up the blog site for this project: Constructing Incapacity for work.

I am grateful to staff at Palgrave Macmillan and to Dave Cowan for support and advice in bringing the book to publication. Several anonymous readers have provided constructive comments on the book at various points in its development. I would like to thank them for their time, detailed comments and advice.

Over the course of this project, I have shared teaching and academic-related work with many colleagues in the School of Social and Political Science at the University of Edinburgh, particularly those in social work, and in the School of Applied Social Science at the University of Stirling. They are too many to name but I thank you all for this wider collegiality and for understanding that sometimes my head was in this book. The following academic colleagues in a variety of institutions have provided specific advice or mentoring in relation to this research and have helped me through some challenging times. This has ranged from comments on my initial funding application to the Leverhulme Trust, reading versions of book proposals or advice on specific social security, legal and historical issues, to the indispensable encouragement and moral support which has kept this project and my confidence in it on track over several years. Thank you to:

Mike Adler, Isobel Anderson, Sarah Anderson, Ruth Bailey, Hayley Bennett, Kate Bradley, Julie Brownlie, Jochen Clasen, Sharon Cowan, Sarah Craig, Viv Cree, Emma Davidson, John Devaney, Ciara Fitzpatrick, Isabel Fletcher, Mark Freeman, Simon Halliday, Bernard Harris, Neville Harris, Louise Jackson, Sue Kelly, Vicki Lens, Michael Lipsky, Audrey MacDougall,

John Macnicol, Gráinne McKeever, Mary Mitchell, Fiona Morrison, Tom Mullen, Amanda Perry-Kessaris, Heather Rae, Adrian Sinfield, Mark Simpson, Kat Smith, Ellen Stewart, David Turner, David Webster, Jay Wiggan, Sharon Wright, Valerie Wright.

Writing about social change can be challenging while watching the world and family change around you. Families also provide links to the future. My sons, Malcolm and Duncan Goodare, have become adults over the course of this project and have been a constant source of inspiration, music and wise advice. This book is dedicated to them and to my husband, Julian Goodare. He has provided boundless advice, encouragement and motivation. Together we continue to discover the connections between history, law, social science and everyday life.

This book stems from a long-standing interest in social security and disability rights which dates back to my work as a welfare rights adviser and disability information officer in the 1980s and 1990s. The organisations that I worked for and the people that I worked with and advised in those years are part of what has made this book possible. This book uncovers the stories of people who struggled with the benefits system in the past. They did not know that their experiences would be stored in archives to be uncovered decades later. I have tried to maintain an ethical respect for the intimate details of their lives and I hope that the book will help to redress some of the injustices which they experienced and which their successors continue to experience today.

January 2019   Jackie Gulland

Contents

1	Introduction	1
2	From National Insurance in 1911 to Employment and Support Allowance	23
3	Only Those Unconscious or Asleep: Definitions of Incapacity for Work	33
4	The Necessity of Questioning the Doctor: Medical and Other Evidence	53
5	Bridge Toll Attendants and Driving a Quiet Horse: The Labour Market and Structural Barriers to Work	79
6	Fit for the Ordinary Work of the Home: Women and Domestic Work	109
7	Not Incapable of Playing Bingo: Ideas About "Work" in Incapacity Benefits	135
8	Immoral Conduct: Moral Regulation in Incapacity Benefits	155
9	Unacceptable Snooping: Sick Visitors and Other Methods of Surveillance	183

10 Conclusion	203
Appendix Sources and Methods	211
References	217
Index	231

Abbreviations and Acronyms

BAMS	Benefits Agency Medical Service
CPAG	Child Poverty Action Group
DHSS	Department of Health and Social Security
DIG	Disability Income Group
DLA	Disability Living Allowance
DMO	District Medical Officer
DSS	Department of Social Security
DWP	Department of Work and Pensions
ESA	Employment and Support Allowance
HNCIP	Housewives Non-Contributory Invalidity Pension
NCIP	Non-Contributory Invalidity Pension
NFU	National Farmers' Union
NHIC	National Health Insurance Commission
NHIJC	National Health Insurance Joint Committee
NHS	National Health Service
NIAC	National Insurance Advisory Committee
OPCS	Office of Population Censuses and Surveys
PIP	Personal Independence Payments
RMO	Regional Medical officer
SDA	Severe Disablement Allowance
UPIAS	Union of Physical Impaired Against Segregation
WCA	Work Capability Assessment
WCML	Working Class Movement Library

Table of Cases

Court Cases

Heard v Pickthorne and others (1913) KB 3 299	56
Stated Case in a dispute under section 90(1) of the National Health Insurance Act 1924 between Hannah O'Brien and the Scottish Catholic Insurance Society for the Opinion and Judgment of the First Division of the Court of Session	169
Sutton v New Tabernacle (Old Street Congregational) Approved Society (1924) 1 KB 494	156, 164, 186, 207

Post-War Reported Commissioners' Decisions	
CWS 2/48KL	149
CS 499/50KL	142
CWS 25/50KL	144, 145
R(S)11/51	1, 3, 4, 5, 15, 16, 44, 45, 46, 83, 120, 121, 122, 123, 124, 131, 136, 137, 139, 143, 196, 208
R(S)17/51	120, 122, 131, 196
R(S)22/51	140, 142
R(S)24/51	80, 83
R(S)20/52	104, 149, 197
R(S)21/52	176, 177
R(S)24/52	70
R(S)33/52	142

R(S)2/53	174, 175, 178
R(S)8/53	103
R(S)9/53	141
R(S)10/54	93
R(S)24/54	102, 103
R(S)6/55	177
R(S)8/55	150
R(S)4/56	63
R(S)3/57	124, 125, 152, 176
R(S)4/60	64
R(S)2/61	141
R(S)8/61	103
R(S)1/72	103
R(S)2/78	43
R(S)4/78	129
R(S)5/78	129
R(S)7/78	129
R(S)6/79	129
R(S)2/80	146
R(S)3/81	43, 44
R(S)2/82	43, 83, 93, 95, 136
R(S)7/83	177
R(S)6/85	94, 95, 136
R(S)1/87	177
R(IB)1/03, 2001	130, 150
Upper Tribunal Decisions	
M v SSWP (ESA) (2012) UKUT 376 (AAC)	48
CE/811/2013 (2013) UKUT 518 (AAC)	105
JC v SWWP (ESA) (2013) UKUT 0219 (AAC)	48
SI v SSWP (ESA) (2014) UKUT 308 (AAC)	49

Table of Statutes

Disability Discrimination Act 1995	28
Equality Act 2010	28, 96, 104
Health and Social Security Act 1984	37
National Health Insurance Act 1924	169
National Health Insurance Act 1918	164
National Health Insurance Act 1928	114
National Health Insurance and Contributory Pensions Act 1932	114
National Insurance Act 1911	3, 23, 24, 25, 34, 37, 56, 111, 136, 157, 158, 170
National Insurance Act 1946	1, 23, 26, 34, 37, 120, 136, 174, 175
National Insurance Act 1971	37
Social Security (Incapacity for Work) Act 1994	28, 34, 38, 46
Social Security Act 1975	34, 37, 127, 136
Social Security Act 1985	38
Social Security and Housing Benefits Act 1982	38
Welfare Reform Act 2007	28, 35, 38, 47
Welfare Reform Act 2009	178
Welfare Reform Act 2012	35
Workmen's Compensation Act 1897	100, 160

1

Introduction

Incapacity for Work

> A person is incapable of work within the meaning of the National Insurance Act 1946, Section 11(2)(a)(ii) if, having regard to his age, education, experience, state of health and other personal factors, there is no work or type of work which he can be reasonably expected to do. By 'work' in this connection we mean remunerative work, that is to say, work whether part-time or whole time for which an employer would be willing to pay, or work as a self-employed person in some gainful occupation. (R(S)11/51, para 5)

This statement comes from the leading case law on the interpretation of "incapacity for work" in the disability benefits system in the UK from the 1950s until the 1990s. The statement comes from the decision on an appeal to the then National Insurance Commissioners, from a woman, Mrs E,[1] who had claimed Sickness Benefit and been refused. Mrs E's case was important because it recognised the social element in assessing whether someone was "incapable of work". The stress on "age, education, experience … and other personal factors" as well as "state of health" recognised that it is not possible to make a purely medical assessment of a person's capacity for work. This is in marked contrast to assessments for Employment and Support Allowance today, which rely on a rigid medical assessment of claimants' functional capacities to do such things as carrying a carton full of liquid or pressing a button on a telephone keypad. More than sixty years after Mrs E's appeal, relentless changes to the UK social security system have made it more difficult for people with health issues or

---

[1] I refer to Mrs E, rather than using her full name. For details of my approach to anonymity and other ethical matters, see the Appendix.

© The Author(s) 2019
J. Gulland, *Gender, Work and Social Control*, Palgrave Socio-Legal Studies,
https://doi.org/10.1057/978-1-137-60564-1_1

impairments to qualify for support. From the introduction of "objective medical tests" under Incapacity Benefit in the 1990s to work-related conditionality in Employment and Support Allowance in recent years, these changes have been designed to reduce the number of people eligible for benefit and have made the act of claiming more humiliating and stressful. Incapacity benefit claimants have joined the ranks of the untrustworthy poor: people who must be managed and coerced into the labour market. While the current discourse of scroungers and hard-working families is questioned by radical, critical and academic writers, the history of people attempting to claim incapacity benefits is often lost.

The book explores how the definition of incapacity for work and mechanisms for social control of benefit claimants has changed over a hundred years, starting with the UK's first national insurance Sickness Benefits in 1911. While the political history of disability benefits has been well documented, this book takes a different approach, seeking to understand the interaction between legislative change, policy implementation and front-line decision making on incapacity for work. Valverde asks socio-legal scholars to look at both the "technical" legal interpretation of law and the "social" (2009, p. 154). In this book, I look at both the legislation and case law on the development of the meaning of incapacity for work over a hundred years but also how that worked when viewed through a sociological lens. At every stage, the debate about incapacity benefits has been located within assumptions about disability, gender and the meaning of work, using mechanisms of social control to regulate the lives of claimants. In this introduction, I will look at these concepts and I will explain the sources used for this book. First of all, it is useful to return to the case of Mrs E.

Sweeping the Path: The Case of Mrs E

One morning in early November 1950 Mrs E was sweeping the path outside her house. Mrs E was a married woman in her late forties who had worked in factories in her youth and then as a paid carer. During the Second World War, she returned to factory work until a heart condition and problems with her leg led her to claim Sickness Benefit. That November, a sick visitor, employed by the new Ministry of National Insurance, visited her house and spotted her sweeping the path. The sick visitor reported Mrs E as fit for work. She was referred for a medical examination, and her benefit was stopped. Mrs E appealed to a local tribunal, which agreed that she was fit for work, and then to the National Insurance Commissioners. Mrs E's case was important for its interpretation of incapacity for work but also because her story illustrates a number of issues which I will return to throughout the book. The interpretation of incapacity for work in 1951 reflected debates about how to assess people's eligibility for incapacity benefits since the introduction of the first UK state Sickness Benefit under the 1911 National Insurance Act. Within six months of the first payments from the 1911 scheme an inquiry was launched into "excessive claims " (NHIJC 1914). The inquiry investigated these excessive claims, concerns that people might be cheating, worries about the status of doctors' certificates, what to do about people who may be working while claiming benefits, how to treat unpaid work, fears about creating dependency on benefits, how to check whether people were making sufficient effort to return to the labour market, the extent to which disability could, or should, exempt some people from looking for work, what kinds of work people should be expected to do. In 1914, policy makers were particularly troubled by women's claims for incapacity benefits. Married women, such as Mrs E forty years later, were subjected to particular scrutiny regarding their unpaid domestic work in the home. In the early twentieth century, people could be refused benefit or sanctioned if their health issues were related to alcohol or perceived immoral sexual behaviour. Although some of the more clearly gendered and moralistic assumptions may have changed in a hundred years, many of the concerns raised in 1914 are still important today.

When I began the research for this book, I knew that R(S)11/51 would be important in understanding the post-war development of incapacity benefits. My research led me to the National Archives in London and to case files for some of the early post-war Commissioners' decisions. Here, I found the papers for R(S)11/51, discovered Mrs E's name and saw that her story had wider significance (case files in PIN 62/1354 and CT11/43).[2] The archive files contain copies of the original medical certificate signed by Mrs E's doctor, evidence submitted by the National Insurance Office, Mrs E's original letter of appeal, the decision of the lower level tribunal and the final Commissioners' decision. The papers relating to Mrs E's appeal are an example of what Robinson has described as the physicality of archives: "the shock of archival discovery comes with an intense jolt of recognition – whether it be a handwritten note, a lost photograph or a peculiarly fitting fact" (Robinson 2010, p. 514). These additional papers told me more about this important case than the written judgement by the Commissioners reveals. Mrs E was a married woman whose benefit had been stopped because she had been observed doing housework. The local decision makers considered housework to be work for the purposes of Sickness Benefits, therefore excluding her from benefit and reflecting pol-

---

[2]For details of archives, see Appendix.

icy makers' concerns going back to 1911. The Commissioners in R(S)11/51 disagreed, marking an important turning point in assessing married women's claims for benefit. Furthermore, Mrs E's benefit was stopped after a sick visitor spotted her sweeping the path, an example of the role of sick visitors in carrying out surveillance of benefit claimants. The case file also includes Mrs E's own evidence, which helps to show how she understood the definition of incapacity and explains why she was sweeping the path "The place was so dirty for shame's sake I was putting water on the path and was in the act of sweeping off when the sick visitor came". The archive file provided me with a crucial document that led me to understand the meaning of decision makers' obsession with housework. The submission from the local office argued that claims by married women should be treated differently from claims by men or single women because married women were not really in the labour market. This explained how the whole debate about married women and housework both in the early twentieth century and into the post-war period had little to do with capacity for work as such. The debate was about attachment to the labour market. If married women were able to do housework, this was evidence that they were housewives rather than workers. The Commissioners in R(S)11/51 disagreed with this interpretation of the law but that was not the end of it. Mrs E's case had a considerable impact on decision making and policy in the early 1950s. It led to volumes of discussion within the Ministry of National Insurance about how to deal with married women, how to police their claims effectively without carrying out a "witch hunt". It led to a surveillance exercise intensifying the role of the sick visitor service to check up on women's housework (for more discussion of married women and housework, see Chapter 6 and of surveillance by sick visitors, see Chapter 9). Mrs E's case was also important in showing the connections between the 1946 National Insurance Scheme and the old 1911 National Insurance Scheme. The post-war Beveridgean National Insurance Scheme is usually considered to be break from the past but there are references in this case to appeal hearings from the early twentieth century. The decision refers to a case from 1919, concerning a man with a spinal injury who could no longer work as a butcher and an appeal from 1921, concerning a woman's capacity for housework (R(S)11/51, para 7). One of the Commissioners in 1951 was Archibald Safford, who had also acted as an adjudicator for appeals under the old National Insurance Scheme. R(S)11/51 was pivotal, both in establishing the case law on incapacity benefits from the 1950s until the 1990s, but also in looking back to the ideas and debates from the 1911 Sickness Benefit scheme. It also confirmed that work meant paid work and that it was necessary to consider whether an employer would be likely to be willing to pay the person to do that work. The case is important for its dismissal of the relevance of the labour market and for its firm line on the implications of housework in assessing capacity for work. The papers in the archive files provide insight into the significance of the case at the time, as well as information about married women's claims to benefit, the role of sick visitors, the views of ordinary claimants and their doctors. These elements of the debate on the meaning of incapacity for work in R(S)11/51 are central to this book. Mrs E's final comment, in her appeal to the tribunal, shows how her case is more than just a piece of sterile case law: "I would like to point out that I would sooner be able to go to work than have this humiliation. This is all I can say". The archive papers are a reminder that all of this case law concerns real people. In this book, my focus is on these real people and their struggles to assert their rights to benefits. The remainder of this chapter looks at some of the key theoretical issues which permeate the discussion: disability, gender, work and social control. The chapter ends with a discussion of the sources for the research and an outline of the rest of the book.

Disability

The term "disability benefits" is usually used in the UK to describe "extra costs" benefits such as Attendance Allowance and Personal Independence Payments, while "incapacity benefits" usually mean "out of work" benefits for people who are unable to work because of a health issue or impairment. This book focusses on the "out of work" incapacity benefits. Disability and incapacity are not the same thing but these terms are used as shorthand to categorise benefit claimants. Categories are important in social security benefits, and policy makers must find a cost-effective way of allocating claimants to these categories (Mashaw 1983; Stone 1984). Categorisation as "incapable of work" is humiliating but is essential in order for people to access social security resources. Debates about incapacity benefits usually rely on an assumption that incapacity for work can be measured objectively, relying on an individualised medical model of disability. In this book, I address the issue of disability and incapacity for work using a social model of disability. Critical disability theorists and disabled people's organisations have long criticised individual models of disability because such models ignore the ways in which people are disabled by society. The social model of disability has been described as a "British model" in contrast to a minority identity model developed in the United States (Grue 2015, pp. 35–36). I won't dwell on the differences hypothesised between these models but will focus on the British social model as one which focusses on the role of societal barriers in created disability. The social model considers how people with impairments are disabled by society and focusses on the barriers which prevent people from participating fully in society. This perspective was developed in the 1970s by the Union of Physically Impaired Against Segregation (UPIAS), which made an important distinction between "impairment", those medicalised aspects of a person's physical or mental status and "disability", which is what causes that person to be excluded from society because of external or societal barriers (UPIAS and Disability Alliance 1976). This key distinction between impairment and disability comes from a document published jointly by the UPIAS and the Disability Alliance, a document which represents a disagreement between the two organisations about the best way to tackle the disablement created by society. The Disability Alliance, led by the poverty campaigner, Peter Townsend, promoted the idea of campaigning for a comprehensive disability income scheme to compensate for disabled people's lack of access to the labour market (for a development of this, see Disability Alliance 1987) while the disability activists leading UPIAS contested this view, arguing instead for a radical restructuring of society which would enable disabled people to participate fully in the labour market. Political histories of the development of disability policies describe this debate in more detail. For brief accounts, see Walker (2010) and Thomas (2011).

The distinction between impairment and disability articulated by UPIAS has been crucial to the development of the social model of disability because it situates the problem in society rather than in the individual. Disabled people's organisations have long criticised the individual model of disability because it ignores the ways in which people are disabled by society and relies on medicalised notions of "normality" (Grue 2015; Hughes 2015). Using the social model of disability, French and Swain (2012) outline how society creates different kinds of barriers for people with impairments. They list structural barriers, environmental barriers and attitudinal barriers. Structural barriers include the underlying norms, ideologies and power structures which create and reinforce power structures and notions of "normality". Examples of these include the ways in which many disabled children have traditionally been excluded from mainstream education or the ways in which assumptions about what is normal have excluded people with mental impairments or intellectual disabilities from mainstream society. Environmental barriers include physical barriers such as steps, lack of ramps, adequate space, accessible information, audio and sign language, assumptions about the time needed to do things and lack of resources for personal assistance. These are often the easiest to identify and in some ways the easiest to address although in practice they remain as major barriers. Attitudinal barriers include adverse attitudes and behaviour towards disabled people. These are commonly experienced by disabled people. Crucially, these three barriers interact, so that power structures and negative attitudes can often lead to the relatively simple environmental barriers not being addressed, or environmental barriers prevent people from accessing mainstream society thus making it more difficult to address the attitudinal and structural barriers. The importance of the social model of disability is that it focusses on these barriers rather than the supposed lack of capacity or ability of individual people with impairments. The distinction between "impairment" and "disability" is now well understood in writing on disability but it can also conceal an additional assumption: that medical diagnosis of individual impairments is equivalent to objective fact. Medical diagnosis is a contested area, and one that itself is embedded in the social inequalities of people's lives, leading to different diagnostic practices based on assumptions about social class, gender, age and ethnicity (Pryma 2017; Sherry 2016). There is difference between disability and illness. People who claim incapacity benefits are usually thought to be "ill", rather than disabled. This is certainly true for people making short-term claims for benefits. For longer-term claimants, the distinction is much less clear cut, since the definition of incapacity for work is so entwined with barriers to employment. Definitions of disability have tended to consider disability and illness to be separate and there is a continuing debate even within the disability movement as to whether or not "chronic illness" is the same as impairment (Grue 2015, p. 103).

Incapacity benefits, by definition, are problematic for a social model because they imply that individual incapacity can be identified. A social model approach would ask what barriers there are in the workplace and in society more generally which make it difficult for this person to earn a living. Barnes (2000) has argued that a social model approach recognises that disability and impairment cannot be separated from the "social organisation of work" (p. 444). Benefits systems are inherently individualistic. They compensate claimants for an individual failure to find work, or to earn enough to meet an established minimum. They create categories of deservingness, based on age, disability or status as an approved job seeker into which claimants must be placed in order to qualify for benefits. Some approaches to assessment recognise wider societal disadvantages but the focus is primarily on individual failings. So a social model of disability would not usually be able to design a benefit which paid people a wage replacement benefit solely because of their impairment. The conflict between the UPIAS and the Disability Alliance in the 1970s reflected just this debate.

Stone's work on the development of the "disability category" in benefits systems does not take a social model approach but she does recognise that mechanisms for categorising benefit claimants must be able to distinguish between those who should be expected to be in the labour market and those who "have legitimate reason for receiving social aid" (Stone 1984, p. 118). Stone observes that the category of incapacity carries with it an inbuilt assumption that claimants will attempt to cheat and therefore that it needs "a means to detect deception" (Stone 1984, pp. 22–23). This creates a difficulty for policy makers, who must find a cost-effective way of distinguishing between the "genuinely" ill and the malingerers. Stone's book describes how that legitimation became associated strongly with medical expertise. Foucault's work shows such categories are the creation of discourse and that they concern power relations. He argues that the medical examination is both a ritual in "pinning down" the details of an individual's life and confirming the individual as the object of power (Foucault 1977, p. 192). In another work, Foucault invites the questions: "Who is speaking? Who is accorded the right to use this sort of language …Who derives from it his own special quality, his prestige, and from whom in return does he receive if not the assurance, at least the presumption that what he says is true?" (Foucault 1972, p. 50).

These insights from Foucault and from the social model of disability show that categories such as incapacity are social constructions presented as facts. The concept of incapacity for work relies on the power of medical professionals who are deemed to be sufficiently expert to make judgements on people's claims to incapacity. By definition this leads to the downgrading of claimants' own knowledge and, Hughes argues, to the treatment of disabled people as people who "cannot do things for themselves" (Hughes 2015, p. 83). Thus a person's claim to incapacity for work requires the claimant to subject themselves to the medical gaze of expert knowledge, which then creates the claimant's status as either capable or incapable of work as an objective fact. Policy makers' continued search for more objective measures of incapacity endorses the idea that such a measure is possible and that therefore incapacity for work is an objectively measurable state. The insights from disability studies and the social model of disability question that assumption. This book uses these insights to interrogate the ways in which incapacity for work has been interpreted over a hundred years.

Gender

A number of writers have looked at the concept of disability in relation to the history of social security benefits (e.g. Borsay 2004; Hampton 2016; Macnicol 2013; Mashaw 1983; Stone 1984), but there are few examples where the intersections of disability and gender are discussed. Gender is an important lense through which to consider the problem of defining people as incapable of work. As Hunter (2013) reminds us, "a failure or refusal to engage with gender and intersectional differences … presents a limited and potentially damaging vision of the world as it might be" (p. 218). While it might appear from a medical model of disability that disability and health is not gendered, from a social model it clearly is. In this book, I will argue that we cannot look at the concept of incapacity for work without looking at the concept of work. When we think about work, we immediately recognise the gendered nature of the concept. We must also recognise that the whole concept of a welfare state based on wage replacement benefits is a gendered construct. It both defines who is entitled to resources in gendered ways and reinforces gendered assumptions about work and caring roles (Lister 2003).

Students of social policy learn early on in their studies that the classic British welfare state was based on a male breadwinner model of social security, which assumed that married women would be financially dependent on their husbands' earnings and that social security contributions and payments should follow this pattern, giving women little entitlement to benefits in their own right (Lister 1994; Orloff 2010; Rowlingson 2009). This model of social security is often exemplified by quoting William Beveridge: "The attitude of the housewife to gainful employment outside the home is not and should not be the same as that of the single woman: she has other duties" (Beveridge 1942, para 114). The male breadwinner model has been widely critiqued, both for its failure to recognise the complexity of family life in Beveridge's time and for its failure to adapt to fundamental changes in the family and the workplace over the late twentieth century (Baldwin and Falkingham 1994; Daly and Rake 2003; Land 1994, 2009). Analysis of the early twentieth-century development of the welfare state has also noted the ways in which women were disadvantaged by structural assumptions about women's role in the labour market, often excluding them from benefit systems altogether or making less favourable provisions (Pedersen 1993; Thane 1991). More recently, women's claims for incapacity benefits have been recognised as an object of study in their own right, leading to an argument in the early twenty-first century that there was a "feminisation of incapacity benefits" (Kemp and Davidson 2009, p. 591) and to studies attempting to understand the gendered patterns of claims for incapacity benefits (Beatty et al. 2009, 2010).

Studies of the welfare state often include discussions of gender, usually meaning women, but rarely discuss men. Studies of unemployed men have pointed to the ways in which men's unemployment can be perceived as a loss of masculinity unless clearly framed within a rights-based system of interruption of regular employment (Willott and Griffin 1996; Levine-Clarke 2015).

Writers in disability studies have shown how the relationship between social class, gender and manual labour creates an image of masculinity which is a challenge to working-class disabled men (Borsay 2004). Disabled feminists such as Shildrick (1997) have pointed to the lack of gender analysis in much disability studies writing. There has been very little research however on the gendered nature of decision making on claims for incapacity benefits in the past, in relation to either men or women. Butler's influential work questions whether traditional gender categories are helpful at all (Butler 2006) and there are important debates which arise from this. However, Butler also recognises that gender categories are both created and reinforced by the law. Social security systems are prime examples of this. This book attempts to uncover the ways in which expectations of gendered behaviour among incapacity benefit claimants have affected definitions of incapacity for work.

Work

The concept of incapacity for work requires a definition of work. Bauman notes that work is not a neutral concept: it carries a strong moral underpinning (Baumann 2005). Our welfare systems are saturated with the idea of paid work as morally superior to other activities but social inequalities control access to paid work. As Weeks points out: "work, including its absence, is both important to and differently experienced within and across lines of class, gender, race and nation" (Weeks 2011, p. 18). Sociologists of work have usually been interested in the organisation of work within the workplace, access to work within the labour market or with the ways in which different types of paid and unpaid work are valued within economic and social systems (Grint and Nixon 2015). Pahl's writing on the divisions of labour explores how work can only be understood as a socially relational concept. It cannot be understood in isolation (1984, p. 128). Yet the concept is at the heart of categorising incapacity benefit claimants as either "capable" or "incapable" of such activity. Feminists of course have highlighted the many problems with valuing paid work above all other types of activity, emphasising the issue of unpaid work in the home. Weeks (2011, pp. 65–67) usefully distinguishes between two strands of feminist thought on this matter: on the one hand, some feminists have argued for equal access to the paid labour market as the key to women's equality; while others have argued for the recognition and value of unpaid domestic work as the key. This has sometimes been described as a "wages for housework" model and relies on producing economic costings for the value of domestic labour (Grint and Nixon 2015, p. 29). In practice, many Western societies have partially achieved this by the outsourcing of domestic labour to low-paid working class and migrant women, freeing up middle-class women to enter the formal labour market. Feminist sociologists, such as Glucksmann, use historical data to show that women's working lives in the twentieth century cannot be easily divided by binary divisions of paid work/unpaid work or public/private sphere (Glucksmann 2000). Glucksmann argues that much of women's activities in the twentieth century can be conceptualised as "informal economic activity" (p. 157) where money may, or may not, have exchanged hands in return for domestic labour including looking after children, laundry, cleaning and cooking. Because administrative frameworks, such as the census or the welfare state, have difficulty in conceptualising such activities, this kind of women's work has often been ignored by economists or other analysts attempting to account for patterns of work. More recently feminist legal academics have argued that the definition of work should be expanded to include unpaid work when writing about traditional labour law (Brodie et al. 2016; Busby 2011; Fudge 2016). Weeks (2011) and other "post-work" theorisers such as Frayne (2015) have looked beyond traditional sociologies of work to begin to imagine worlds where the labour market and the commodification of domestic work does not dominate discussions of the meanings of work. Frayne (2015) also stresses the ethical centrality of the term "work". The word is imbued with assumptions about responsibility, respectability and freedom from dependence. Work is usually assumed to mean paid work, to be carried out in the public realm and to be separate from the private sphere. Recent discourse on "work/life balance" suggests that work can be separated from life. Feminists have long challenged this assumption. On the other hand, twenty-first-century assumptions about work, combined with technological changes and concepts of employability, mean that control and surveillance of work-related behaviour increasingly invades our "non-work" time (Frayne 2015, p. 75). Frayne criticises some sociologists for reinforcing the work ethic by treating work "unquestionably as normal" (p. 106).

Disability theorists have also tackled the problem of the work ethic. Disability activist organisations such as the UPIAS have long argued for equal access to the workplace for disabled people (UPIAS and Disability Alliance 1976). Writers have pointed to the disabling barriers which make disabled people less likely to access paid work (Bambra 2011; Barnes 1991, 2012; Barnes and Mercer 2005; Roulstone and Prideaux 2012). While these arguments draw attention to serious discriminations in society and in the workplace, they have also helped to feed the "work first" social policies that arise in today's Employment and Support Allowance and other activation regimes. Critics have noted that, while such work-first policies may help to tackle discrimination, they can also lead to further exclusion and the raising of disabling barriers for people who struggle to enter the labour market, while creating further divisions of "deserving" and "undeserving" disabled people which benefit no-one (Bambra 2011; Grover and Piggott 2010). In parallel with the feminist approach to unpaid work, some writers have drawn attention to the importance of "body work" and the challenges of the everyday which take up time for many disabled people (Barnes and Roulstone 2005), while recognising that many disabled people also have caring and domestic responsibilities of the kind emphasised by feminist writers. Recent developments in the provision of self-directed support, enabling disabled people to employ their own support staff, have also raised questions of whether acting as employers in this way constitutes work (Prideaux et al. 2009). As with the argument which Weeks makes in relation to feminist approaches, this can produce two potentially incompatible approaches: a focus on equality in the workplace or recognition of unpaid work, both of which depend on the work ethic for their legitimacy. Frayne argues that "we need to reinvent the term work to describe a far wider range of activities than paid employment and we need to dispel the false dichotomy which says that a person is either working or doing nothing of any value" (p. 233). A Marxist analysis of the concept of work and the idea of the reserve army of labour provides a helpful explanation for what happens to disabled people as the labour market fluctuates but cannot fully explain the relationship between disabled people and work (Roulstone 2012). In the area of incapacity benefits the question of what does, and does not, constitute work raises different questions. This book looks at how decision making on incapacity benefits has defined work and how that has varied by disability, gender and social class. The necessity for defining work in incapacity benefits systems is closely connected to benefits systems as mechanisms of social control, acting to tie workers to the workplace, women to the home and disabled people to exclusion.

Social Control

While the idea of the welfare state as a mechanism for the social control of labour has been central to writing on unemployment, social assistance and benefits for lone mothers (Dean 2000; Gilliom 2001; Handler 2004; Piven and Coward 1972), it has been much less developed in relation to claimants of disability or incapacity benefits. Unemployment benefits in the UK have always been conditional on at least a minimal work-seeking requirement. Recent retrenchments in welfare states have seen an increase in this conditionality for job seekers and an extension of work-related conditionality to new groups of claimants, including claimants of incapacity benefits, lone parents and carers. The extension of work-related conditionality to claimants of Employment and Support Allowance in the UK has led to important new research on the new social control of disability benefit claimants (Dwyer 2016; Dwyer and Wright 2014; Patrick 2011; Patrick et al. 2011; Watts et al. 2014). It is important however to recognise that work-related conditionality is only one form of conditionality in access to benefits. This can be best understood by considering what Clasen and Clegg (2007) have called "levels" and "levers" of conditionality, where they argue that all welfare payments are conditional at least in the sense of being conditional on claimants meeting a "category" requirement: for example that they are unemployed (unemployment benefits), incapable of work (incapacity benefits), over a certain age (retirement pensions) or parents (child benefits). Benefits are also likely to have a circumstance requirement, for example contribution conditions (for social insurance benefits) means-testing (for means-tested benefits), as well as residence and citizenship requirements. "Conduct" conditionality is a third category which relates to conditions of behaviour, for example work-seeking activity. These levers can be moved to extend or restrict availability of welfare payments to and from different groups, while the cash value of payments can be changed by moving the levels of benefit. This definition of conditionality, which is much wider than the behavioural conditionality which is usually associated with welfare benefits, shows how the availability of welfare payments can be changed by moving the levers. Using this definition of conditionality, the category lever and the circumstances levers have changed for claimants of incapacity benefits throughout the twentieth century, affecting people's rights to benefit.

Stone's work has been important in recognising the role of medical power in creating and enforcing these categories (Stone 1984). It is equally important to see how this category forming affects people's status as deserving of support and how this is a form of social control. By changing the discourse and legal definition of incapacity, policy makers have categorised claimants as ineligible for incapacity benefits and thus required to engage in job seeking behaviour in order be eligible for state support, or as eligible but required to meet a discursive expectation of disabled behaviour. Some of these changes in the category levers in statutes have redefined incapacity for work, particularly in the late twentieth and early twenty-first centuries, through the introduction of Incapacity Benefit in the 1990s and its successor Employment and Support Allowance in 2008. But the levers also operate beyond the level of the statute, in the interpretation and street-level implementation of the legislation. Lipsky's work on street-level bureaucracy (Lipsky 2010) has been used many times to explore the day-to-day realities of welfare decision making in relation to late twentieth- and early twenty-first-century welfare policies (e.g. Wright 2003; Brodkin and Marston 2013; Brodkin and Majmunder 2010). This book shows how using historical sources to look at the street-level decisions made by front-line bureaucrats can reveal the day-to-day effect of changing the levers of conditionality.

Sources for the Book

The book is based on an analysis of documents concerning the implementation of incapacity benefits schemes in the UK across the twentieth century.[3] My starting point for the research was the discovery of records of appeal hearings against refusals of Sickness and Disablement Benefit for the period 1913–1923, which were published in a series of volumes by the National Insurance Commissions and the Ministry of Health (NHIC [England] 1915a, b, 1916, 1917, 1919; NHIC [Ireland] 1916; Ministry of Health 1923). These volumes provide the decisions on over two hundred appeals from the very early days of the 1911 National Insurance Scheme. They were published in order to provide guidance on the administration of the scheme (NHIC 1915, p. iv). Although they did not constitute case law in the formal sense, later decision makers did use these published cases as sources of guidance on interpretation of the law (Foster and Taylor 1937; Lesser 1939; Ogus and Barendt 1978, p. 159). Records of a further hundred and twenty decisions for the period 1927–1929 are held in the National Archives. The archive records were not published and were not, to my knowledge, publicly available at the time. These records of appeal decisions form the main sources for the early twentieth century as they provide detailed discussion of the ways in which claims for incapacity benefits were contested. Alongside these individual appeals I have also analysed official reports, civil service files from the interwar Ministry of Health and papers relating to the Scottish and Irish administration of the 1911 scheme. I have also been able to gain insight into the street-level administration of this interwar scheme through looking at the archives of some individual Approved Societies which kept records at this level. There were two major investigations into the early twentieth-century scheme: in 1914 and 1926 (NHIJC 1914; Lawrence 1926). The reports from these investigations and the evidence contained in their appendices have provided key information on ideas about incapacity for work at these times. The Committee of Inquiry in 1914 consisted of representatives of the National Insurance Commission, Approved Societies, trade unions and medical professionals. It met for seven months, hearing oral evi-

---

[3] For details of the main incapacity benefit schemes, including changes to names of benefits and mechanisms for appeal, see Chapter 2.

dence from ninety-four witnesses and considering fifteen hundred pages of written evidence. One of the members of the committee was Mary Macarthur, representing the Women's Trade Union League. She wrote a dissenting memorandum to the final report which is particularly interesting from a gender and working-class perspective, which I refer to in later chapters. The Royal Commission in 1926 and its appendices provide detailed discussion of the scheme and its operation once it had settled down in the period after the First World War.

For the period after 1948, I have used information from the Beveridge Report and its appendices, civil service archives for the post-war Ministry of Pensions and National Insurance and its successors. Case papers for postwar National Insurance Commissioners' decisions are held in the National Archives and these give insights into the background of key cases such as the case of Mrs E in R(S)11/51. Since these contain personal information, they are usually closed for fifty years. I was able to research case papers for these decisions up until the mid-1960s. A search of the online British Newspaper Archive using the term "sick visitor" led me to some additional material on some of the more colourful reactions to sick visiting. Source material for the later twentieth century and early twenty-first century comes from a variety of archive and online government and third sector documents and research by other academics. My thinking on this book has also been influenced by my own experience of working as a welfare rights adviser in the 1980s and 1990s and by research that I carried out into the introduction of Incapacity Benefit in 1995 (Gulland 1996) and on Employment and Support Allowance in 2010 (Gulland 2011).

The sources for this book therefore come from both archive and published material. The Appendix provides details of the main sources, including a list of all archives cited. All of the cited published material, including online sources, is listed in the bibliography. I consulted some of the older publications in archives and libraries. I have listed these as published sources where publication details were available. If publication details were not clear, I have listed them as archive sources. I approached these documentary sources, not as records of established facts, but as socially constructed records of events which, in themselves, may reveal important information about the power struggles and discursive strategies used by the participants. I have therefore tried to get beneath the formal narratives presented in the records and to use them to try and understand the unwritten codes and assumptions in making decisions about incapacity for work and the moral discourses revealed in documents. I recognise that most of the accounts that I have used have been written by those in positions of power and reflect their perspective. Social security and welfare hearings are important mechanisms of administrative justice and may act as symbols of claimants' rights. However, there is also considerable research which shows that people attempting to assert these rights often find themselves subjected to humiliating and degrading procedures and attitudes (Adler and Gulland 2003; Fletcher et al. 2016; Lens 2015; Munger 2004). Sometimes the accounts of appeal hearings include the words of claimants, in letters or references to their verbal contribution to an appeal case. These have been mediated and preserved by the process of the archive but provide an insight into some claimants' views of their experiences. These voices are often hidden from historical accounts of welfare state development which focus primarily on legislation and political processes. I have tried to use these accounts in a way which is respectful of the people attempting to claim their rights within an often demeaning and disrespectful system. For details of my approach to ethics and anonymity, see the Appendix.

Structure of the Book

The structure of the book is thematic rather than chronological. Chapter 2 provides a description of the incapacity benefits scheme created by the National Insurance Act 1911 and the mechanisms for appeal against refusals of benefits in the early twentieth century, followed by a brief outline of the main changes to incapacity benefits over the following hundred years. Chapter 3 provides an outline of the key legislation and case law regarding the definition of incapacity for work and how that has changed between 1911 and today. Tracking key changes in the statutory definition of incapacity, the chapter discusses the shifting boundaries between "sickness" and "disability", illustrated by case law, detailed information in appeal cases and background material in policy makers' records. Chapter 4 looks at the different types of evidence that have been used to decide whether or not someone was incapable of work, both at the front line and in appeals. In Chapter 5, the argument considers the role of the labour market in assessments of incapacity for work. Chapter 6 focusses on women's unpaid work in the domestic sphere. It traces the development of an obsession with housework from the earliest debates about the 1911 scheme and continuing into the 1950s after the decision in R(S)11/51. The chapter includes a discussion of the peak of obsession with housework with the doomed Housewives Non-Contributory Incapacity Benefit in the 1970s, and its discriminatory test of "normal household duties". Chapter 7 turns to the nature of work. Social security legislation and policy documents rarely attempt to define work except in a very technical sense (by defining the number of hours a person must work or not work, or the level of income which work produces). These technical definitions in our welfare systems usually assume that work means paid work. This chapter explores how the incapacity benefits systems, front-line decision makers, case law and claimants themselves have conceptualised work. Chapter 8 considers moral regulation in the incapacity benefit schemes, starting with the heavily moralising approaches in the early twentieth century, where claimants could be sanctioned for perceived moral failings in their sexual conduct, alcohol use or participation in criminal activities. This heavy moralising tailed off in the later twentieth century to be replaced with new moral imperatives regarding willingness to work and new attempts to discipline claimants for failure to manage their own health. Chapter 9 concerns the mechanisms of surveillance and checking which have been used to govern benefit claimants, through the sick visiting system, intrusive medical examinations and the disciplinary "network of writing" described by Foucault (1977, p. 189). Chapter 10 provides a conclusion to the book, returning to the key themes of disability, gender, work and social control.

References

Adler, Michael, and Jackie Gulland. 2003. *Tribunal Users' Experiences, Perceptions and Expectations: A Literature Review*. London: Council on Tribunals. http://webarchive.nationalarchives.gov.uk/20100910235604/http://www.council-on-tribunals.gov.uk/publications/577.htm.

Baldwin, Sally, and Jane Falkingham. 1994. *Social Security and Social Change: New Challenges to the Beveridge Model*. Hemel Hempstead: Harvester Wheatsheaf.

Bambra, Clare. 2011. *Work, Worklessness, and the Political Economy of Health*. Oxford: Oxford University Press.

Barnes, Colin. 1991. *Disabled People in Britain and Discrimination*. London: Hurst and Company/BCoDP.

———. 2000. 'A Working Social Model? Disability, Work and Disability Politics in the 21st Century'. *Critical Social Policy* 20 (4): 441–57.

———. 2012. 'Re-thinking Disability, Work and Welfare'. *Sociology Compass* 6 (6): 472–84.

Barnes, Colin, and Alan Roulstone. 2005. '"Work" Is a Four-Letter Word; Disability, Work and Welfare'. In *Working Futures? Disabled People, Policy and Social Inclusion*, edited by Alan Roulstone and Colin Barnes. Bristol: Policy Press.

Barnes, Colin, and Geof Mercer. 2005. 'Disability, Work and Welfare: Challenging the Social Exclusion of Disabled People'. *Work, Employment & Society* 19 (3): 527–45.

Bauman, Zygmunt. 2005. *Work, Consumerism and the New Poor*. 2nd ed. Buckingham: Open University Press.

Beatty, Christina, Steve Fothergill, Donald Houston, and Ryan Powell. 2010. 'Bringing Incapacity Benefit Numbers Down: To What Extent Do Women Need a Different Approach?' *Policy Studies* 31: 143–62.
Beatty, Christina, Steve Fothergill, Donald Houston, Ryan Powell, and Paul Sissons. 2009. 'A Gendered Theory of Employment, Unemployment and Sickness'. *Environment and Planning C: Government and Policy* 27 (6): 958–74.
Beveridge, Sir William. 1942. *Social Insurance and Allied Services*. Cmnd. 6404. London: HMSO.
Borsay, Anne. 2004. *Disability and Social Policy in Britain Since 1750: A History of Exclusion*. Basingstoke: Palgrave Macmillan.
Brodie, Douglas, Nicole Busby, and Rebecca Zahn, eds. 2016. *The Future Regulation of Work: New Concepts, New Paradigms*. London: Palgrave.
Brodkin, Evelyn, and Gregory Marston. 2013. *Work and the Welfare State: Street-Level Organisations and Workfare Politics*. Washington: Georgetown University Press.
Brodkin, Evelyn, and Malay Majmunder. 2010. 'Administrative Exclusion: Organizations and the Hidden Costs of Welfare Claiming'. *Journal of Public Administration Research and Theory* 20: 827–48.
Busby, Nicole. 2011. *A Right to Care? Unpaid Work in European Employment Law*. Oxford: Oxford University Press.
Butler, Judith. 2006. *Gender Trouble*. Abingdon: Routledge.
Clasen, Jochen, and Daniel Clegg. 2007. 'Levels and Levers of Conditionality: Measuring Change Within Welfare States'. In *Investigating Welfare State Change: The Dependent Variable Problem in Comparative Analysis*, edited by Jochen Clasen and Nico Siegel. Cheltenham: Edward Elgar.
Daly, Mary, and Katherine Rake. 2003. *Gender and the Welfare State*. Oxford: Polity.
Disability Alliance. 1987. *Poverty and Disability: Breaking the Link: The Case for a Comprehensive Disability Income Scheme*. London: Disability Alliance Educational Research Association.
Dean, Hartley. 2000. 'Managing Risk by Controlling Behaviour: Social Security Administration and the Erosion of Welfare Citizenship'. In *Risk, Trust and Welfare*, edited by Peter Taylor-Gooby. Basingstoke: Macmillan.
Dwyer, Peter. 2016. 'Citizenship, Conduct and Conditionality: Sanction and Support in the 21st Century UK Welfare State'. In *Social Policy Review 28: Analysis and Debate in Social Policy, 2016*, edited by Menno Fenger, John Hudson, and Catherine Needham, 41. Bristol: Policy Press.
Dwyer, Peter, and Sharon Wright. 2014. 'Universal Credit, Ubiquitous Conditionality and Its Implications for Social Citizenship'. *Journal of Poverty and Social Justice* 22 (1): 27–35.
Fletcher, Del Roy, John Flint, Elaine Batty, and Jennifer McNeill. 2016. 'Gamers or Victims of the System? Welfare Reform, Cynical Manipulation and Vulnerability'. *Journal of Poverty and Social Justice* 24 (2): 171–85.
Foster, William Justus, and FG Taylor. 1937. *National Health Insurance*. 3rd ed. London: Sir Isaac Pitman and Sons Ltd.

Foucault, Michel. 1972. *The Archaeology of Knowledge (Trans Alan Sheridan)*. London: Tavistock.

———. 1977. *Discipline and Punish: The Birth of the Prison (Trans Alan Sheridan)*. London: Allen Lane.

Frayne, David. 2015. *The Refusal of Work: The Theory and Practice of Resistance to Work*. London: Zed Books.

French, Sally, and John Swain. 2012. *Working with Disabled People in Policy and Practice*. Basingstoke: Palgrave Macmillan.

Fudge, Judy. 2016. 'A New Vocabulary and Imaginary for Labour Law'. In *The Future Regulation of Work New Concepts, New Paradigms*, edited by Douglas Brodie, Nicole Busby, and Rebecca Zahn. London: Palgrave.

Gilliom, John. 2001. *Overseers of the Poor: Surveillance, Resistance, and the Limits of Privacy*. Chicago: University of Chicago Press.

Glucksmann, Miriam. 2000. *Cottons and Casuals: The Gendered Organisation of Labour in Time and Space*. Durham: Sociology Press.

Grint, Keith, and Darren Nixon. 2015. *The Sociology of Work*. 4th ed. Cambridge: Polity Press.

Grover, Chris, and Linda Piggott. 2010. 'From Incapacity Benefit to Employment and Support Allowance: Social Sorting, Sickness and Impairment, and Social Security'. *Policy Studies* 31: 265–82.

Grue, Jan. 2015. *Disability and Discourse Analysis*. Farnham: Ashgate.

Gulland, Jackie. 1996. 'Weighing up the Bag of Potatoes Test: Tribunals and Incapacity Benefit (Unpublished MSc Dissertation)'. Edinburgh: University of Edinburgh.

———. 2011. 'Ticking Boxes: Understanding Decision Making in Employment and Support Allowance'. *Journal of Social Security Law* 18: 69–86.

Hampton, Jameel. 2016. *Disability and the Welfare State in Britain: Changes in Perception and Policy 1948–79*. Bristol: Policy Press.

Handler, Joel F. 2004. *Social Citizenship and Workfare in the United States and Western Europe*. Cambridge: Cambridge University Press.

Hughes, Bill. 2015. 'What Can a Foucauldian Analysis Contribute'. In *Foucault and the Government of Disability*, edited by Shelley Tremain, 2nd ed. Ann Arbor: University of Michigan Press.

Hunter, Rosemary. 2013. 'The Gendered "Socio" of Socio-Legal Studies'. In *Exploring the 'Socio' in Socio-Legal Studies*, edited by Dermot Feenan. Basingstoke: Palgrave Macmillan.

Kemp, Peter, and Jacqueline Davidson. 2009. 'Gender Differences Among New Claimants for Incapacity Benefit'. *Journal of Social Policy* 38: 589–606.

Land, Hilary. 1994. 'The Demise of the Male Breadwinner—In Practice But Not in Theory: A Challenge for Social Security Systems'. In *Social Security and Social Change: New Challenges to the Beveridge Model*, edited by Sally Baldwin and Jane Falkingham. Hemel Hempstead: Harvester Wheatsheaf.

———. 2009. 'Slaying Idleness Without Killing Care: A Challenge for the British Welfare State'. In *Social Policy Review 21*, edited by K. Rummery, Ian Greener, and Chris Holden. Bristol: The Policy Press.

Lawrence, Charles. 1926. *Report of the Royal Commission on National Health Insurance.* Cmd. 2596. London: HMSO.

Lens, Vicki. 2015. 'Welfare Law'. In *The Handbook of Law and Society*, edited by Austin Sarat and Patricia Ewick. Chichester: Wiley Blackwell.

Lesser, Henry. 1939. *The National Health Insurance Acts 1936-1938 with Explanatory Notes, Reported Cases, Decisions of the Minister of Health and Statutory Rules and Orders.* London: Stone and Cox Ltd.

Levine-Clark, Marjorie. 2015. *Unemployment, Welfare and Masculine Citizenship: So Much Honest Poverty in Britain 1870–1930.* Basingstoke: Palgrave Macmillan.

Lipsky, Michael. 2010. *Street Level Bureaucracy: Dilemmas of the Individual in Public Services.* 30th Anniversary Expanded Edition. New York: Russell Sage Foundation.

Lister, Ruth. 1994. '"She Has Other Duties"—Women, Citizenship and Social Security'. In *Social Security and Social Change: New Challenges to the Beveridge Model*, edited by Sally Baldwin and Jane Falkingham. Hemel Hempstead: Harvester Wheatsheaf.

———. 2003. *Citizenship: Feminist Perspectives.* 2nd ed. Basingstoke: Palgrave Macmillan.

Mashaw, Jerry. 1983. *Bureaucratic Justice: Managing Social Security Disability Claims.* New Haven: Yale University Press.

Macnicol, John. 2013. 'The History of Work Disability'. In *Disability Benefits, Welfare Reform and Employment Policy*, edited by Colin Lindsay and Donald Houston. London: Palgrave.

Ministry of Health. 1923. *Reports of Decisions on Appeals and Applications Under Section 67 of the National Insurance Act 1911 and Section 27 of the National Insurance Act 1913, Vol 2—Part I.* London: HMSO.

Munger, Frank. 2004. 'Rights in the Shadow of Class'. In *The Blackwell Companion to Law and Society*, edited by Austin Sarat. Oxford: Blackwell.

National Health Insurance Commission. 1915. *National Insurance Acts Handbook for the Use of Approved Societies (English Edition).* London: HMSO.

National Health Insurance Commission (England). 1915a. *Reports of Decisions on Appeals and Applications Under Section 67 of the National Insurance Act 1911 and Section 27 of the National Insurance Act 1913.* Cd. 7810.

———. 1915b. *Reports of Decisions on Appeals and Applications Under Section 67 of the National Insurance Act 1911 and Section 27 of the National Insurance Act 1913 Part II.* Cd. 8040. London: HMSO.

———. 1916. *Reports of Decisions on Appeals and Applications Under Section 67 of the National Insurance Act 1911 and Section 27 of the National Insurance Act 1913 Part III Cd. 8239.* London: HMSO.

———. 1917. *Reports of Decisions on Appeals and Applications Under Section 67 of the National Insurance Act 1911 and Section 27 of the National Insurance Act 1913 Part IV Cd. 8474.* London: HMSO.

———. 1919. *Reports of Decisions on Appeals and Applications Under Section 67 of the National Insurance Act 1911 and Section 27 of the National Insurance Act 1913 Part V Cmd. 134.* London: HMSO.

National Health Insurance Commission (Ireland). 1916. *Reports of Decisions on Appeals and Applications Under Section 67 of the National Insurance Act, 1911 and Section 27 of the National Insurance Act, 1913*. Dublin: A Thom.

National Health Insurance Joint Committee. 1914. *National Health Insurance. Report of the Departmental Committee on Sickness Benefit Claims Under the National Insurance Act*. Cd. 7687. London: HMSO.

Ogus, Anthony, and Eric Barendt. 1978. *The Law of Social Security*. London: Butterworths.

Orloff, Ann Shola. 2010. 'Gender'. In *The Oxford Handbook of the Welfare State*, edited by Francis G. Castles, Stephan Liebfried, Jane Lewis, and Christopher Pierson. Oxford: Oxford University Press.

Pahl, Ray. 1984. *Divisions of Labour*. London: Blackwell.

Patrick, Ruth. 2011. Disabling or Enabling: The Extension of Work-Related Conditionality to Disabled People. *Social Policy and Society* 10 (3): 309–320.

Patrick, Ruth, Patience Seebohm, and Lawrence M. Mead. 2011. 'The Wrong Prescription: Disabled People and Welfare Conditionality'. *Policy & Politics* 39 (2): 275–91.

Pedersen, Susan. 1993. *Family, Dependence, and the Origins of the Welfare State: Britain and France, 1914–1945*. Cambridge: Cambridge University Press.

Piven, Frances Fox, and Richard A. Cloward. 1972. *Regulating the Poor: The Functions of Public Welfare*. New York: Vintage.

Prideaux, Simon, Alan Roulstone, Jennifer Harris, and Colin Barnes. 2009. 'Disabled People and Self-directed Support Schemes: Reconceptualising Work and Welfare in the 21st Century'. *Disability & Society* 24 (5): 557–69.

Pryma, Jane. 2017. '"Even My Sister Says I'm Acting Like a Crazy to Get a Check": Race, Gender, and Moral Boundary-Work in Women's Claims of Disabling Chronic Pain'. *Social Science & Medicine* 181 (Supplement C): 66–73.

Robinson, Emily. 2010. 'Touching the Void: Affective History and the Impossible'. *Rethinking History: The Journal of Theory and Practice* 14: 503–20.

Roulstone, Alan. 2012. 'Disabled People, Work and Employment'. In *Routledge Handbook of Disability Studies*, edited by Nick Watson, Alan Roulstone, and Carol Thomas. Abingdon: Routledge.

Roulstone, Alan, and Simon Prideaux. 2012. *Understanding Disability Policy*. Bristol: Policy Press.

Rowlingson, Karen. 2009. 'From Cradle to Grave: Social Security and the Lifecourse'. In *Understanding Social Security*, edited by Jane Millar, 2nd ed. Bristol: Policy Press.

Sherry, Mark. 2016. 'A Sociology of Impairment'. *Disability & Society* 31 (6): 729–44.

Shildrick, Margrit. 1997. *Leaky Bodies and Boundaries: Feminism, Postmodernism and (Bio)Ethics*. London: Routledge.

Stone, Deborah. 1984. *The Disabled State*. Philadelphia: Temple University Press.

Thane, Pat. 1991. 'Visions of Gender in the Making of the British Welfare State: The Case of Women in the British Labour Party and Social Policy 1906–1945'. In *Maternity and Gender Policies: Women and the Rise of the European Welfare States 1880s–1950s*, edited by Gisela Bock and Pat Thane. London: Routledge.

Thomas, Carol. 2011. 'Disability: Prospects for Inclusion'. In *Fighting Poverty, Inequality and Injustice: A Manifesto Inspired by Peter Townsend*, edited by Alan Walker, Adrian Sinfield, and Carol Walker. Bristol: Policy Press.

Union of Physically Impaired Against Segregation, and Disability Alliance. 1976. *Fundamental Principles of Disability*. London: UPIAS. http://disability-studies.leeds.ac.uk/files/library/UPIAS-fundamental-principles.pdf.

Valverde, Mariana. 2009. 'Jurisdiction and Scale: Legal "Technicalities" as Resources for Theory'. *Social & Legal Studies* 18 (2): 139–57.

Walker, Alan. 2010. 'Disability'. In *The Peter Townsend Reader*, edited by Alan Walker, David Gordon, Ruth Levitas, Peter Phillimore, Chris Phillipson, Margot Salomon, and Nicola Yeates. Bristol: Policy Press.

Watts, Beth, Suzanne Fitzpatrick, Glen Bramley, and David Watkins. 2014. *Welfare Sanctions and Conditionality in the UK*. York: Joseph Rowntree Foundation.

Weeks, Kathi. 2011. *The Problem with Work: Feminism, Marxism, Antiwork Politics, and Postwork Imaginaries*. Durham: Duke University Press.

Willott, Sarah, and Christine Griffin. 1996. 'Men, Masculinity and the Challenge of Long-Term Unemployment'. In *Understanding Masculinities*, edited by Mairtin Mac an Ghaill. Buckingham: Open University Press.

Wright, Sharon. 2003. 'The Street-Level Implementation of Unemployment Policy'. In *Understanding Social Security*, edited by Jane Miller. Bristol: Policy Press.

2

From National Insurance in 1911 to Employment and Support Allowance

Introduction

This chapter provides an outline of the main changes to incapacity benefits from 1911 until 2018. It summarises the provisions of the National Insurance Act 1911, including the governance of the scheme through a system of Approved Societies, regulation by central government and mechanisms for appeal. The foundation of the post-Second World War welfare state brought about changes to the incapacity benefits scheme through the National Insurance Act 1946. This set the scheme on a wholly statutory basis with a new network of decision making and appeals mechanisms. An expansion of benefits for disabled people in the 1970s introduced higher payments for long-term claimants of incapacity benefits and new benefits for people who had been unable to accrue national insurance contributions. Although these benefits extended payments to those who had previously been excluded from the mainstream system, they also introduced a new twist in the gendered nature of decision making through the highly discriminatory Housewives Non-Contributory Invalidity Pension (HNCIP). Contraction in the welfare state brought Incapacity Benefit in the 1990s and Employment and Support Allowance in 2008. This chapter describes these main changes to the incapacity benefits systems in the UK across the twentieth century.

The National Insurance Act 1911

The starting point of the research for this book is the National Insurance Act of 1911. This Act introduced a nationwide, rights-based national insurance scheme which provided members of the scheme with access to a doctor under the panel doctor system and a right to Sickness Benefit for the first six months if they were unable to work due to ill health, followed by Disablement Benefit after six months, paid at a reduced rate. Unlike the later Beveridgean National Insurance scheme, which was state-run, the 1911 scheme was administered by "Approved Societies", independent voluntary or private bodies which ran the scheme on behalf of the state. These Approved Societies consisted of ten thousand separate Societies, including Friendly Societies, with roots in the nineteenth century, Societies based on trade unions and private insurance companies such as the Prudential Approved Society. Societies varied considerably in size and culture, from the tiny Juvenile Improved Order of the Total Abstinent Sons of the Phoenix Sick and Burial Friendly Society, which had eighty-one members, to the dominant Prudential Approved Society, which had over three million members in 1918 (Watson 1922, Appendix). For further details of the Approved Society system, see Harris (2004) and Beveridge (1942). Some Societies were based in particular industries or geographical locations or had religious affiliations. Some admitted both men and women while others were open to only men or only women. Despite this considerable variation, the scheme introduced by the National Insurance Act 1911 was heavily regulated and the definition of incapacity for work, decision making, medical assessments and appeals soon began to resemble the later twentieth-century social security systems with which social security scholars are more familiar today. Whiteside has described the Approved Society system as "Private agencies for public purposes" (Whiteside 1983), reflecting the fact that the Societies, although operating as independent organisations in competition with each other for members, were running a statutory scheme which was heavily regulated by central government. The system set up by the National Insurance Act 1911 continued until 1948 although there were important amendments and consolidating Acts in the 1920s and 1930s, reflecting increases in claims as a result of economic recession. The changes in the 1920s and 1930s were very important in moving the "circumstances" levers of conditionality described by Clasen and Clegg (2007). There were restrictions on the contribution conditions, making it more difficult to for people with irregular patterns of employment to claim benefits, and there were significant changes in the rules for married women's access to benefits. These were combined with adjustments to the "levels" of benefit, making cuts to the amount of money available to claimants (Foster and Taylor 1937; Thane 1996; Whiteside 1987). The introduction of new pensions for blind people and the reduction of the state pension age from seventy to sixty-five also affected entitlement to incapacity benefits (Borsay 2004).

However, the basic "category" lever, the definition of incapacity for work, did not change over this period.

Appeals Under the National Insurance Act 1911

One of the ways in which the scheme was regulated was in the system of appeals which enabled dissatisfied claimants to take their appeals to an independent adjudicator. Initially, these appeals were heard by National Insurance Commissioners. From 1920, responsibility for the national insurance scheme passed to the Ministry of Health in England and Wales, the Board of Health in Scotland and (from 1922) the Ministry of Labour in Northern Ireland. These bodies took over responsibility for administering the appeals procedure. Before appealing to these independent bodies, claimants had first to negotiate the labyrinth of the internal appeals processes run by the Approved Societies. Although guidance was provided on good practice in appeals procedures (NHIC 1912), there was considerable variation in practice. For example, an inquiry in 1914 noted that some Societies required a deposit before an appeal could be heard and that some appeals were taking too long (NHIJC 1914). By 1926, it was noted that eighty per cent of Societies were following the Ministry of Health's model rules which consisted of a single internal appeal, followed by an appeal to the Ministry, but that some still had two or three levels of internal appeal (Lawrence 1926, pp. 90–101).

Archive evidence from the papers of the Societies themselves suggests that claimants were rarely successful at internal appeals. There are some examples of internal appeals in the records of the Ideal Benefit Society (PIN 24/74, PIN 24/80)[1] and the Leek Textile Federation (TU/SILK/7/3, WCML). These glimpses into the internal appeal procedures of Societies suggest that it was not common for internal appeal bodies to overturn initial decisions but that it was possible if the claimant could produce convincing evidence to support their appeal. Claimants' ability to do this would depend on their understanding of the system and the willingness of their doctors or other credible witnesses to support their case. At the independent appeal hearings, the adjudicators[2] were appointed initially by the National Insurance Commissioners. After 1920 when the Ministry of Health took over the procedure, appeals in England and Wales were heard by referees who were legally qualified (Ministry of Health 1921, p. 154). These were all men. Despite being unable or unwilling to recruit any

---

[1]Archive sources are from the National Archives in London unless otherwise specified. See Appendix for full details of archive sources.
[2]The names for the adjudicators at appeal hearings changed over the course of this period. I will use the term adjudicators in the book for simplicity.

women as adjudicators, the Ministry of Health ensured that there was always a woman at each hearing, either in the form of the medical specialist, or failing that, a lay specialist (correspondence in PIN 4/5). Usually, the Ministry of Health was able to find women doctors to act as medical assessors. When it wasn't possible to find a woman doctor, female lay assessors sat in on the cases. Men's cases all appear to have had male medical assessors. Appeals in Scotland and Northern Ireland were slightly different and the Scottish appeal body included at least one woman as an adjudicator. Other people at the hearings could include legal representatives of the claimants and Societies, as well as witnesses called by either side, often including claimants' doctors and medical referees, called on behalf of the Societies. These appeal cases did not create case law in the way that future appellate decisions did but they were clearly influential in policy and decision makers' thinking and were cited by legal commentators into the 1930s (Foster and Taylor 1937). For further details of the appeals procedures, see Gulland (2018). The records of these appeal hearings provide key insights into the day-to-day decision making on benefits.

The National Insurance Act 1946 and the Post-war Welfare State

Incapacity benefits were included in the major changes brought about by the proposals from the Beveridge Report (Beveridge 1942) and the introduction of a new national insurance scheme through the National Insurance Act 1946. This Act dispensed with the reduced rate Disability Benefit and provided for a single Sickness Benefit, which could be paid indefinitely so long as claimants met the contribution conditions and continued to be defined as incapable of work. For detailed discussions of the provisions of the National Insurance Act and their significance, see Borsay (2004), Harris (2000), Lowe (1993), and Timmins (1995). The main differences, for the purpose of this book, were that the insurance scheme was brought under state control and that the scheme was extended to include most of the working population. The new National Insurance scheme was introduced at the same time as the introduction of the National Health Service, cutting the tie between insurance contributions and entitlement to health care. These changes were significant in the administration of the scheme and in public perceptions of its purpose. However, the definition of incapacity for work did not change significantly and other chapters will show that there was a considerable continuity in the practices of decision makers, with policy guidance often based on the interwar scheme. The appeals procedure changed with the introduction of National Insurance

Appeal Tribunals and the creation of an appellate level of National Insurance Commissioners whose decisions could create case law (Buck et al. 2005; Micklethwait 1976; Safford 1954). Although there have been many changes to the names and procedures for appeal tribunals since 1948, the basic principle of a right to appeal against a decision on benefits and the establishment of case law from higher appellate decisions continued through the many benefit changes over the twentieth century. Claimants' rights of appeal were curtailed with the introduction of "mandatory reconsideration" in 2013. This introduced a new level of internal review of decisions before claimants could appeal, leading to a dramatic reduction in the number of cases reaching appeal hearings. For details of this and other changes to social security appeal hearings, see Mullen (2016).

The Creation of New Benefits for Disabled People in the 1970s

The 1970s saw an expansion of benefits for disabled people (for details, see Borsay 2004; Hampton 2016). This expansion included the introduction of a higher rate Invalidity Benefit for people who were claiming incapacity benefits on a long-term basis and new non-contributory incapacity benefits for people who had been unable to accrue National Insurance contributions. Invalidity Benefit did not significantly change the definition of incapacity for work, although the recognition of the need for a long-term benefit may have changed attitudes to benefit claimants. The new non-contributory benefits did not change the definition of incapacity for work for men and single women, but did, significantly, for married women, in the rules for HNCIP. These rules are discussed in detail in Chapter 6. The 1980s brought further changes with the abolition of HNCIP and its replacement with Severe Disablement Allowance, the introduction of Statutory Sick Pay for claimants in work and retrenchment in the welfare state generally with the neoliberal policies of the Thatcher government. These policies led to a devaluing of national insurance benefits and an increase in means-testing (Harris 2000; Jones and Lowe 2002). These changes and the increased means-testing did not change the definitions of incapacity for work, since the rules for means-tested incapacity benefits, such as Supplementary Benefit and Income Support, were piggy-backed onto those for the main national insurance benefits. They did, however, change the other levers and levels of benefits conditionality, changing access to benefits for many claimants.

Incapacity Benefit and a New Medical Test

A major change to the definition of incapacity for work was introduced with Incapacity Benefit under the Social Security (Incapacity for Work) Act 1994. Incapacity Benefit was framed as a response to growing numbers of people claiming and remaining on Invalidity Benefit in the 1990s and a concern that too many people (particularly older working-class men) were being parked on Invalidity Benefit instead of claiming the less generous Unemployment Benefit. Analysts agreed that this was a likely explanation for at least some of the increase in claims, since there had been a move by policy makers, trade unions and employers to encourage older men to treat Invalidity Benefit as an early retirement pension when health issues or social barriers made it difficult for them to find work (Disney and Webb 1991; Holmes et al. 1991; Lonsdale 1993). Incapacity Benefit brought in a new definition of incapacity for work, discussed in Chapter 3, a significant movement of the category levers of conditionality and the beginnings of a new hardline attitude towards incapacity benefit claimants.

Employment and Support Allowance

If Incapacity Benefit moved the category levers of conditionality in access to incapacity benefits, this was nothing compared to Employment and Support Allowance, brought in by a Labour Government under the Welfare Reform Act 2007. Employment and Support Allowance redefined benefit claimants as having "limited capability for work" rather than as "incapable of work". Employment and Support Allowance was introduced with the intention, not only of reducing the number of eligible claimants, but also of changing expectations about who should work (Gregg 2008). There was an implicit assumption that anti-discrimination legislation (the Disability Discrimination Act 1995, subsequently the Equality Act 2010) should have removed the disabling barriers which prevented many disabled people from accessing the labour market (Bonner 2008). Employment and Support Allowance created two categories of claimants: those who have "limited capability for work", who are subject to work-seeking conditionality and associated sanctions for failing to comply, and those who have "limited capability for work-related activities" who are entitled to benefit without any work-focussed conditionality. Chapter 3 discusses these new definitions in more detail. Employment and Support Allowance made significant changes to both the category and the conduct levers of conditionality. These have been compounded by cuts in the availability of the contribution-based element of Employment and Support Allowance, thus increasing the number of claimants subject to means-testing, combined with restrictions on the scope and level of means-tested benefits. The more recent introduction of the means-tested Universal Credit will bring more claimants into the net of conditional means-testing. For information about the key changes and the effects of conditionality, see Adler (2018), Geiger (2017), Bonner (2008), Dwyer (2016), Dwyer and Wright (2014), Grover and Piggot (2010), Patrick (2011), Patrick et al. (2011), and Watts et al. (2014). For the purposes of the argument in this book, which concerns the definition of incapacity for work, the focus is on the mechanisms for defining what is now called "limited capability" for work.

References

Adler, Michael. 2018. *Cruel, Inhuman or Degrading Treatment? Benefit Sanctions in the UK*. Basingstoke: Palgrave Pivot.
Beveridge, Sir William. 1942. *Social Insurance and Allied Services*. Cmnd. 6404. London: HMSO.
Bonner, David. 2008. 'Employment and Support Allowance: Helping the Sick and Disabled to Return to Work?' *Journal of Social Security Law* 15(4): 123–50.
Borsay, Anne. 2004. *Disability and Social Policy in Britain Since 1750: A History of Exclusion*. Basingstoke: Palgrave Macmillan.
Buck, Trevor, David Bonner, and Roy Sainsbury. 2005. *Making Social Security Law: The Role and Work of the Social Security and Child Support Commissioners*. Aldershot: Ashgate.
Clasen, Jochen, and Daniel Clegg. 2007. 'Levels and Levers of Conditionality: Measuring Change Within Welfare States'. In *Investigating Welfare State Change: The Dependent Variable Problem in Comparative Analysis*, edited by Jochen Clasen and Nico Siegel. Cheltenham: Edward Elgar.
Disney, Richard, and Steven Webb. 1991. 'Why Are There So Many Long Term Sick in Britain'. *Economic Journal* 101: 252–62.
Dwyer, Peter. 2016. 'Citizenship, Conduct and Conditionality: Sanction and Support in the 21st Century UK Welfare State'. In *Social Policy Review 28: Analysis and Debate in Social Policy, 2016*, edited by Menno Fenger, John Hudson, and Catherine Needham, 41. Bristol: Policy Press.
Dwyer, Peter, and Sharon Wright. 2014. 'Universal Credit, Ubiquitous Conditionality and Its Implications for Social Citizenship'. *Journal of Poverty and Social Justice* 22 (1): 27–35.
Foster, William Justus, and FG Taylor. 1937. *National Health Insurance*. 3rd ed. London: Sir Isaac Pitman and Sons Ltd.

Geiger, Ben Baumberg. 2017. 'Benefits Conditionality for Disabled People: Stylised Facts from a Review of International Evidence and Practice'. *Journal of Poverty and Social Justice* 25 (2): 107–28.

Gregg, Paul. 2008. *Realising Potential: A Vision for Conditionality and Support.* London: DWP.

Grover, Chris, and Linda Piggott. 2010. 'From Incapacity Benefit to Employment and Support Allowance: Social Sorting, Sickness and Impairment, and Social Security'. *Policy Studies* 31: 265–82.

Gulland, Jackie. 2018. 'Appellant Knowledge and Representation in Early Twentieth Century Sickness Benefit Tribunals' (Unpublished paper).

Hampton, Jameel. 2016. *Disability and the Welfare State in Britain: Changes in Perception and Policy 1948–79.* Bristol: Policy Press.

Harris, Bernard. 2004. *The Origins of the British Welfare State: Society, State, and Social Welfare in England and Wales, 1800–1945.* Basingstoke: Palgrave Macmillan.

Harris, Neville. 2000. 'Beveridge and Beyond: The Shift from Insurance to Means-Testing'. In *Social Security Law in Context*, edited by Neville Harris. Oxford: Oxford University Press.

Holmes, Phil, Mauricea Lynch, and Ian Molho. 1991. 'An Econometric Analysis of the Growth in Numbers Claiming Invalidity Benefit: An Overview'. *Journal of Social Policy* 20 (1): 87–105.

Jones, Margaret, and Rodney Lowe. 2002. *From Beveridge to Blair: The First Fifty Years of Britain's Welfare State 1948–98.* Manchester: Manchester University Press.

Lawrence, Charles. 1926. *Report of the Royal Commission on National Health Insurance Cmd. 2596.* London: HMSO.

Lonsdale, Susan. 1993. 'Invalidity Benefit an International Comparison'. London: DSS Analytical Services Division, Social Research Branch.

Lowe, Rodney. 1993. *The Welfare State in Britain Since 1945.* Basingstoke: Macmillan.

Micklethwait, Robert. 1976. *The National Insurance Commissioners.* Hamlyn Lectures. London: Stevens. https://socialsciences.exeter.ac.uk/law/hamlyn/lectures/archive.

Ministry of Health. 1921. *Second Annual Report of the Ministry of Health, 1920–1921.* Cmd. 1446. London: HMSO.

Mullen, Tom. 2016. 'Access to Justice in Administrative Law and Administrative Justice'. In *Access to Justice: Beyond the Policies and Politics of Austerity*, edited by Ellie Palmer, Tom Cornford, Yseult Marique, and Marique Guinchard. Oxford: Hart Publishing.

National Health Insurance Commission. 1912. *National Insurance Act 1911 Model Rules.* London: HMSO.

National Health Insurance Joint Committee. 1914. *National Health Insurance. Report of the Departmental Committee on Sickness Benefit Claims Under the National Insurance Act.* Cd. 7687. London: HMSO.

Patrick, Ruth. 2011. 'Disabling or Enabling: The Extension of Work-Related Conditionality to Disabled People'. *Social Policy and Society* 10 (3): 309–320.

Patrick, Ruth, Patience Seebohm, and Lawrence M. Mead. 2011. 'The Wrong Prescription: Disabled People and Welfare Conditionality'. *Policy & Politics* 39 (2): 275–91.

Safford, Archibald. 1954. 'The Creation of Case Law Under the National Insurance and National Insurance (Industrial Injuries) Acts'. *Modern Law Review* 17: 197–210.

Thane, Pat. 1996. *Foundations of the Welfare State*. 2nd ed. London: Longman.

Timmins, Nicholas. 1995. *The Five Giants: A Biography of the Welfare State*. London: HarperCollins.

Watson, Alfred W. 1922. *National Health Insurance. Report by the Government Actuary on the Valuations of the Assets and Liabilities of Approved Societies as at 31st December 1918*. Cmd. 1662. London: HMSO.

Watts, Beth, Suzanne Fitzpatrick, Glen Bramley, and David Watkins. 2014. *Welfare Sanctions and Conditionality in the UK*. York: Joseph Rowntree Foundation.

Whiteside, Noel. 1983. 'Private Agencies for Public Purposes: Some New Perspectives on Policy Making in Health Insurance Between the Wars'. *Journal of Social Policy* 12: 165–94.

———. 1987. 'Counting the Cost: Sickness and Disability Among Working People in an Era of Industrial Recession, 1920–1939'. *Economic History Review* XL: 228–46.

3

Only Those Unconscious or Asleep: Definitions of Incapacity for Work

Introduction

> To argue that sickness benefit can only be paid when incapable of work, meaning incapable of any kind of work, is to argue that sickness benefit can only be paid when the person is unconscious or asleep, and consequently, all the quarter of a million people who are this week drawing sickness benefit are not entitled to it. (NHIJC 1914, Appendix, para 27126)

These are the words of Sidney Webb, the social reformer and Fabian intellectual, in his evidence to the inquiry into "excessive claims" for Sickness Benefit in 1914. Sidney Webb's argument that Sickness Benefit should only be paid to those who were unconscious or asleep was not a proposal that should be reflected in policy but a rhetorical mechanism to draw attention to the question of what was meant by incapacity and what was meant by work. Although Webb did not use the language of the late twentieth century, he was explaining that the term "incapacity for work" is a social construction. He was right to point out that a literal understanding of "incapacity for work" could only apply to a very small number of benefit claimants, since almost everybody is capable of doing something. The problem is that not everything that a person could do would count as work and crucially, not everything would enable them to earn a living. The ability to do work which would enable people to earn a living is heavily socially constructed by the society in which they live, the barriers created by that society and by the specific social circumstances of individuals. This chapter looks in detail at the legal and practical definition of incapacity for work across the twentieth century, showing how these social structures have affected ideas about "incapacity" and about "work".

Statutory Definitions

Despite the difficulty identified by Sidney Webb, the legislative form of what constituted incapacity for work changed little across the twentieth century. The original National Insurance Act of 1911 specified that claimants of the new Sickness or Disablement Benefit must be "rendered incapable of work by some specific disease or by bodily or mental disablement" (National Insurance Act 1911, 8(c)). This definition was firmly based in an individual medical model of disability. The focus was on the individual and his or her "disease or disablement". There was nothing in the legislation to suggest that there was any societal element to a person's capacity to work and the implication was that a person's incapacity could be assessed and evidenced by medical expertise, leaving benefit decision makers to interpret the detail. The definition of incapacity for work in the 1911 National Insurance Act did not specify the form of initial claim but at this stage in the development of health services in the UK, this would usually be a medical certificate from a panel doctor, paid for through the same National Health Insurance Scheme. The doctor's initial medical certificate has remained the basis for claims for incapacity benefits across the twentieth century and into the twenty-first century. Chapter 4 discusses the doctor's medical certificate and other sources of evidence of incapacity in more detail.

Thirty-five years later, the 1946 National Insurance Act used almost identical language to that in 1911. A claimant would qualify for Sickness Benefit under the Act if they were (or were deemed to be): "incapable of work by reason of some specific disease or bodily or mental disablement" (National Insurance Act 1946, S11(2)(a)(ii)). The insertion of the phrase "deemed to be" enabled benefit to be paid to people in certain specific circumstances when they were not, strictly speaking, incapable of work but could be treated as if they were, for example if they had an infectious disease which led to them being excluded from the workplace for public health reasons. The statutory definition did not define incapacity or work and remained the same through updating legislation in 1975, when, for the first time, the definition included a definition of work, as "work which the person can reasonably be expected to do" (Social Security Act 1975, S17(1)(a)). This reflected case law on the definition of work but still relied on an individual medical model, tempered by some recognition of the social context in which it would make it "reasonable" for a claimant to access the labour market. Changes to benefits in the 1990s almost entirely dispensed with the social context of work, with the introduction of points-based medical assessments for Incapacity Benefit (Social Security [Incapacity for Work] Act 1994), although still using some of the original language of

1911. To qualify for Incapacity Benefit, a claimant had to be incapable of work but their incapacity was defined "by reference to the extent of a person's incapacity by reason of some specific disease or bodily or mental disablement to perform such activities as may be prescribed" (S5). This was a major change from focussing on "work" to focussing on "activities" but still retained some concept of work within its overarching rationale. The emphasis, however, had moved firmly into an entirely individualised medical assessment of claimants' impairments, removing all references to the social context of the workplace.

Even in its latest form, Employment and Support Allowance (ESA) has a basic requirement that the claimant has "limited capability for work" (Welfare Reform Act 2007, 1(3)(a)), while the means-tested Universal Credit makes specific provisions for reduced work-seeking conditionality for people who have "limited capability for work" (Welfare Reform Act 2012 19(2)(a)). These new provisions constitute a break with the past but the principle has stayed essentially the same: that claimants must prove their individual incapacity or limited capability for work, based on a medical assessment. Case law, particularly in the later twentieth century, helped to refine the statutory definitions, while official guidance provided decision makers with advice on how the law should be interpreted. Such guidance has never been considered to be legally binding but gives a clear message from policy makers as to how they expect decisions to be made. Street-level interpretation of how this has been understood by day-to-day decision makers provides a more nuanced understanding of what this statutory definition has meant in practice. Interpretation of the legislation has concentrated on the several key issues, some of which I will discuss in this chapter, while others are discussed in more detail later in the book. One important point concerns the difference, if any, between sickness and "disability".

Sickness, Disability and the Six-Month Guideline

Sickness and disability are not the same. It is quite possible for someone to be "sick" in the sense of being unwell and unable to do their current job for short periods of time, while also having a long-term impairment. They may be disabled using the social model definition of disability, but their sickness is likely to be short term. Similarly a person may well be disabled using the social model definition and may have difficulty accessing the labour market while being perfectly well in the sense that they are not ill. Some people may have a chronic illness, which is different from having a short-term illness. There is debate among activists and theorists as to the most useful way of understanding impairment and chronic illness within a social model of disability. Grue argues that the concept of chronic illness is squarely based in the tradition of medical sociology while the disability movement has had more difficulty deciding where to draw a line between long-term illness, impairment and disability (Grue 2015, pp. 51–53). For example, Carol Thomas shows how the different traditions of medical sociology and disability studies have come to different understandings of the issue of chronic illness by using either a "social deviance" or a "social oppression" approach (2007, p. 178).

These distinctions between "sickness", "impairment", "disability" and "chronic illness" matter in the political debate about disabled people's rights but the terms are often confused in the debate about incapacity benefits. Incapacity benefits were designed, at the outset, as short-term benefits for people normally in the labour market who were unable to work because of a short-term illness. They were designed to tide people over until they became well enough to work. The term "period of interruption in employment" was key to the complex rules regarding linking claims when people had short periods back at work between periods of sickness (Bonner et al. 1991, p. 30). This reasoning behind the payment of incapacity benefits shows the clear link between attachment to the labour market and entitlement to benefit. It assumes a typical, probably male, worker, who may be ill for short periods but is expected to return to work. The theory is much less effective where the claimant has a more tenuous attachment to the labour market, because of unemployment, gendered caring responsibilities, barriers to the labour market through discrimination or long-term chronic health issues.

Incapacity benefits in the UK have tended to distinguish between sickness and disability by focussing on the length of time that a claimant has been unable to work, using guidelines which have treated the first six months of a claim as a claim of "sickness", while longer-term claimants have sometimes been labelled as "disabled" (e.g. in the 1911 scheme). The operation of a six-month guideline to distinguish between short- and long-term claims has been fairly consistent but has been more to do with monitoring claims than it has been with understanding the social barriers which create "disablement". In fact, the terms "sickness" and "disability" have been used more or less interchangeably in benefits decision making. The statutory definitions of incapacity for work for short- and long-term claims have usually been similar, if not identical. However, in practice, the monitoring and conditionality applied to long-term claims has usually been much stricter.

Under the 1911 scheme, a distinction was made between short-term sickness and longer-term claims by the provision of Sickness Benefit for the first twenty-six weeks of a claim, and Disablement Benefit for those continuing to claim after that period (National Insurance Act 1911, 8(c)). In theory, Disablement Benefit could continue indefinitely, but was not intended as a pension and was not available to people who had never worked or who had an incomplete record of national insurance contributions. As a deterrent to overclaiming, it was paid at half the rate of Sickness Benefit. The statutory definition of incapacity was the same for both benefits although front-line decision makers usually applied stricter definitions for Disablement Benefit.

The benefit scheme introduced by the 1946 National Insurance Act did not distinguish between short-term and long-term claims, allowing indefinite payment at a standard rate of Sickness Benefit. There was no separate claim for a longer period although, after one year, a claimant would only qualify if they had a more complete national insurance contribution record (National Insurance Act 1946, S12(2)). This change to the scheme, allowing extension of benefit beyond six months at the same rate as for short-term claims, reflected the view of Beveridge in his report of 1942, that "To reduce the income of an unemployed or disabled person, either directly or by the application of a means test, because the unemployment or disability has lasted for a certain period, is wrong in principle" (Beveridge 1942, p. 57). As with the 1911 scheme, there was no statutory difference in the definition of incapacity for longer-term claims, but again, longer-term claimants were usually subject to stricter tests and increased surveillance.

Under the National Insurance Act 1971 (confirmed in the Social Security Act 1975), longer-term claimants became eligible for Invalidity Benefit after 168 days of sickness, this time paid at a higher rate as a recognition of the higher costs of long-term incapacity (Social Security Act 1975, 15(1)). The two non-contributory benefits, Non-Contributory Invalidity Pension (NCIP) and Housewives Non-Contributory Invalidity Pension (HNCIP) introduced by the Social Security Act 1975, s36, made incapacity benefits available to people who had been unable to accumulate national insurance contributions through participation in the workforce. These benefits, along with their replacement, Severe Disablement Allowance (SDA) (Health and Social Security Act 1984, s11), were available only to people who had been incapable of work for 196 days. There had been a change in attitude from paying a reduced rate as a disincentive to claiming under the 1911 scheme, to paying the higher rate Invalidity Benefit as a recognition that long-term exclusion from the labour market led to higher costs. The introduction of NCIP, HNICP and SDA represented a perception that there were some disabled people who might never be able to accumulate a record of labour market participation, although these benefits were paid at a lower rate. These benefits were a nod towards the disability income scheme envisaged by the Child Poverty Action Group and the

Disablement Income Group although far from comprehensive in the way that campaigners had envisaged. For an in-depth discussion of the political debate and introduction of these changes in the 1970s, see Disability Alliance (1987), Hampton (2016), and Walker (2010). The new benefits also carried particular assumptions about disabled people, notably married women, who were subjected to additional tests under the notorious HNCIP (for more details see Chapter 6). The new benefits introduced in the 1970s and 1980s were paid to people after approximately six months of sickness, marking a distinction between short-term sickness benefits and longer-term disablement benefits. In the 1980s, Statutory Sick Pay became the main route to incapacity benefits for short-term sickness absences for people in work. Statutory Sick Pay was payable initially only for eight weeks (Social Security and Housing Benefits Act 1982, s3) although this was extended to 28 weeks in 1985 and continues to be payable for the first 28 weeks for those in work (Social Security Act 1985, s18). The six-month guideline continued with the introduction of Incapacity Benefit in the 1990s, with the application of the "own work" test for the first 194 days, for claimants who had a recent record of employment, followed by the "all work test". The "all work test" was applied immediately to those who did not have a recent record of employment (Social Security [Incapacity for Work] Act 1994, S171B (1)). ESA broke this pattern using instead a period of "assessment" for the first thirteen weeks of a claim, followed by potential higher allowances for those meeting work-seeking conditions or allocated to the "support group" (Welfare Reform Act 2007, S2). So the use of six months as a guideline for long-term sickness has now been removed except for people who are in work when they first become unable to work, who may still be entitled to Statutory Sick Pay for the first 28 weeks. The principle, introduced in the 1970s, of paying people at a higher rate in recognition of the higher costs of long-term health issues, has been abandoned in the recent removal of the higher rate of benefit and of restricting non-means-tested ESA to one year for many people claiming ESA. Long-term eligibility for non-means-tested ESA and the higher rate of means-tested ESA is now payable only to those in the "Support Group", who are categorised as being the most disabled. This means that many claimants of ESA are paid at the same rates as unemployed people, with no recognition of the additional costs of long-term sickness or disability (Low et al. 2015).

This brief outline shows that the general principle of treating claimants differently for the first six months of a claim for incapacity benefits can be found across almost all the UK incapacity benefit schemes until the introduction of ESA in 2008. This six-month rule did not coincide entirely with the concepts of "sickness" and "disability", as understood by decision makers and policy makers, let alone how they might be understood within a social model of disability. Instead the principle acted as guideline for those who were considered to have straightforward claims, that is, the typical worker, with a long record of employment and an apparently short-term health issue, from which they were expected to recover. There has always been a debate, which continues today, about whether people claiming shorter-term sickness benefits or employer-based sick pay are shirking. Generally, policy on state incapacity benefits has not been too concerned with short-term claims by people in work. However, there has always been an increased level of surveillance for those whose claims did not match the model of a regular worker with a short-term health issue. Additional control mechanisms were used for claimants known to have a history of frequent short claims for benefit, particularly during holiday periods, where there had been previous investigations for fraud, or those holding medical certificates indicating particular medical conditions. Other people who were subjected to this more intense surveillance included people who had irregular working histories, people who looked as if they might become long-term claimants and married women (see also Chapters 6 and 9). Although the statutory definition of incapacity for work did not differentiate these groups of claimants, this additional surveillance for some groups provides a clear example of the way in which the definition of incapacity for work has been closely associated with assumptions about participation in the labour market.

Control Measures for Short-Term Claims

Statutory definitions of incapacity for work did not usually differentiate between short-term and long-term claimants, or between sickness and disability. However, case law, appeal cases and guidance on the administration of benefits show that there were differences in practice in the assessment of short-term and long-term claims. Evidence from the early implementation of the 1911 scheme shows the debate emerging. The inquiry in 1914 recommended the principle of following an "own occupation" test for most claimants of Sickness Benefit, illustrating this with a hypothetical example where it would be inappropriate to expect claimants to seek alternative work while unable to do their usual job:

> A labourer with a crushed foot may be pronounced to be physically not incapable of playing the cornet or the drum at the local music hall; a farm labourer with a cold may be physically able to assume the part of an accountant, but in either case, apart from the fact that such occupations cannot be obtained for odd days

or broken periods, he will usually be debarred by his previous training from thus varying the monotony of his life during times of sickness. (NHIJC 1914, p. 32)

However, the inquiry continued, there would come a point at which it would be clear that the claimant had ceased to have a usual occupation, "for example where an engine-driver is probably forever debarred from the footplate owing to minor epilepsy, the problem… is to decide whether he ceased to be an engine-driver" (NHIJC 1914, p. 33). The inquiry concluded that claims for Sickness Benefit should be normally considered against the claimant's ordinary occupation, while recommending a tougher test for Disablement Benefit. There would need to be special rules "when it becomes apparent that [a claimant] will not be able, ever… to follow his previous occupation" recognising that this did not "correspond exactly with the distinction between Sickness and Disablement Benefit" (NHIJC 1914, p. 69).

This reference to "special rules" is an explicit reference to the need for increased surveillance of claimants at risk of a longer break from the labour market even after a short time on benefit. The inquiry did not lead to any change in the statutory definition although evidence from the appeals cases shows that Societies and appeal adjudicators did apply a stricter test for longer-term claimants. An example of this can be found in a case from 1917, where Mr B claimed Sickness Benefit after being discharged from the army with a partial war disablement pension. He was not entitled to a full war pension since his main impairment was caused by rheumatism. The Society paid Sickness Benefit for one month but then stopped it on the grounds that Mr B was fit for light work. It was established that Mr B was not fit for active service, so the test of his incapacity was for other work. When Mr B appealed, the adjudicators considered the various pieces of medical evidence and concluded that the Society's view was correct and that he was capable of work (Case 113, NHIC England 1919, p. 270). This case shows that the test of "usual occupation" could be dispensed with when it was clear that the claimant would not be able to return to their usual work, even before the six-month period had elapsed. In a later case from 1920, Mrs H claimed Sickness Benefit after she became unable to work after 27 years working as a tile presser, described in the appeal decision as "an arduous occupation". Her Society paid her benefit for a few months but, after a referral to a medical referee, decided that she was fit for alternative work. When she appealed, the adjudicators considered the conflicting medical evidence but decided that she was incapable of work and eligible for benefit (Case 2/14, Ministry of Health 1923, p. 42). Although Mrs H was successful in her appeal, the test that the Society and the adjudicators applied was whether she was fit for any work, not just whether she was fit for her previous long-term employment. These cases confirm the principle, outlined in the 1914 inquiry, that the usual occupation test did not correspond directly with the boundary between Sickness and Disablement Benefit. Most of the appeal cases concern people who had been claiming benefit for more than six months, suggesting that the general principle of applying a lighter touch to the first few months of a claim was being followed by Societies, unless there was some other evidence of possible malingering or uncertainty about the claim.

As the scheme became established, evidence from the Ministry of Health to the Royal Commission on National Health Insurance in 1926 confirmed this practice on short- and long-term claims:

> The rule now generally recognised is that in the earlier stages of the illness they should be totally incapable of following their ordinary occupation... then of course if after a certain time it appears to the society that a member will never be able to resume his own occupation, the society must apply its mind afresh to the question. (Lawrence 1926, Minutes of Evidence Vol 1, para 281, Evidence given by Sir Walter Kinnear, Ministry of Health)

By the 1930s, guidance from the Ministry of Health confirmed that the statutory definition was open to interpretation by individual Societies and emphasised that the "ordinary work" rule should be applied in most cases of short-term sickness:

> If in such cases there is a likelihood that the insured person, though unfit at the time for his ordinary employment, will become fit within a reasonable time to return to it, he must be pronounced "incapable of work" and no question of fitness for other work needs to be or should be considered. (Ministry of Health, *Handbook for Regional Medical Officers* (undated but probably 1930) para 152, in MH62/201, underlining in original)

The principle of using a tougher test of incapacity for work once the claimant's impairment or health issue appeared to be long term was also emphasised in guidance to Societies:

> If it becomes clear in the course of the illness that there is no reasonable prospect of the member again becoming fit for his ordinary occupation, a rather different criterion of incapacity should be applied. The Society should then consider whether the member's physical and mental condition is such that he is capable of performing other remunerative work of such a character as a man (sic) of his training education and experience could reasonably be expected to undertake. (Ministry of Health 1933, paras 389–391)

The 1946 National Insurance Scheme carried considerable continuity from the previous scheme. In the Beveridge Report, usually considered to be relatively generous in its approach, William Beveridge noted "The measures for control of claims to disability benefit - both by certification and by sick visiting - will need to be strengthened… Special attention should be paid to the prevention of chronic disability by intensified treatment advice and supervision" (Beveridge 1942, p. 58). Although Beveridge used the term "disability benefit" in the 1942 report, this became Sickness Benefit once the plan took legislative form. Beveridge's use of the term "chronic disability" is used disparagingly to stress the conditionality inherent in the scheme, that people should normally be in the labour market and that benefits should normally cover only short-term illnesses. Those with longer-term health conditions were expected to adapt to their new position and look for different kinds of work. Civil servants who were working on the plans for the 1946 National Insurance Scheme discussed the previous legislation and outlined the issues raised in the interpretation of incapacity for work. These detailed discussions can be found in a file in the National Archives (PIN 35/78). This file contains an eight-page memo on "The problem of the interpretation of the expression "rendered incapable of work by some specific disease or bodily or mental disablement". This memo outlined the issues:

> Incapacity for work is not, as is sometimes assumed, a particular physical or mental condition the existence of which at any given moment of time is definitely ascertainable by a doctor, by means of a medical examination … The determination of whether a person can properly be said to be incapable of work is question of opinion or judgment based on the application of criteria; it is not a question of fact. (Memo, dated September 1945, from A. I. Miller to W. A. H. Hepburn Ministry of National Insurance, para 2, in PIN 35/78)

This memo is notable in recognising that incapacity for work could not be decided purely on medical grounds and that there was room for considerable interpretation and even "opinion". Explaining the "usual" work rule for most short-term claims, the memo went on to say that there would be particular difficulties in assessing capacity for work for people who had been out of the labour market at the time of claim. The memo then discussed the practice, under the 1911 scheme, of assessing claimants against their capacity for any work, rather than just their usual work in these circumstances. This memo provides a link between the guidance under the 1911 scheme and the guidance from the Ministry of National Insurance, under the post-war scheme. A draft circular to local National Insurance Offices in 1949 emphasised the importance of checking up on dubious claims early on:

> Many people, without any intention of malingering, are too prone to go sick and to remain away from work longer than is strictly necessary, while others, who may have been ill, may tend to settle down too easily to a protracted absence from work. There are also men or women who are inclined to chronic invalidism. (Draft circular on the Control of Claims to Sickness or Injury Benefit, 25 November 1949, in PIN 35/37)

This guidance became embedded in the post-war Ministry of National Insurance practices of initiating a visit by a sick visitor after set lengths of time, where certain aspects of the claim suggested that claimants were "settling down to protracted absence". Although the practice of sick visiting was soon replaced by references to Regional Medical Officers (see Chapter 4), advice about what to do with short-term claims became well established in guidance. This guidance confirmed that claimants should usually be assessed against their capacity for their usual jobs unless there were specific circumstances to suggest that "it becomes clear in the course of the illness that there is no reasonable prospect that the claimant will again become fit for his ordinary occupation" (Ministry of Pensions and NI 1960, para 504).

Over the following decades, case law established that claims for benefit should usually be considered in relation to the claimant's "usual job" in the short term (R(S)2/78 and R(S)2/82, cited in Bonner et al. 1991, p. 24). In R(S)2/78, the question concerned whether it was reasonable for the claimant, Mr C, a 48-year-old furniture salesman, to consider looking for alternative work after six months incapacity for his usual job. The Commissioner considered that the key legal test was what was "reasonable" in any particular case.

> Reasonableness rather than any specific measure of time is the crucial matter. It is not normally reasonable in the case of short-term incapacity, to expect a claimant to change his occupation. If incapacity is continued, it may become reasonable to do so. (R(S)2/78, para 8)

In the decision, the Commissioner considered previous case law and concluded that there had never been any attempt to place an explicit time limit on the "normal work" rule but that it was clear that six months was being used as an administrative guideline by the DHSS. As a result, there were very few cases reaching the Commissioners where people had been refused benefit before six months of claiming. In this case, the Commissioner considered that it was reasonable for the claimant to consider other work after six months. This principle was confirmed in R(S)3/81, where the claimant attempted to argue that it was unreasonable to be expected to seek new type of work after eighteen months. The Commissioner disagreed and argued that the administrative use of the six-month guideline was "something of a concession" to enable claimants to return to their original workplaces rather than have to find a new job (R(S)3/81, para 10).

This use of the term "concession" implies that people with a closer attachment to the labour market were being treated differently from those who did not have this clear pattern of regular work. Administrative DHSS guidance in the 1980s used identical wording to the guidance from the 1960s and included standardised letters to claimants' doctors, which would be sent once a Medical Officer had certified a claimant as "partially fit for work" (Form RM10LW in DHSS 1981, Appendix 16).

The standardised control actions listed in the DHSS guidance provided a guide to the length of time that people with particular medical conditions were likely to be unable to continue in their previous job, although the guidance was based on the medical condition, not the job. After these periods, claimants should be investigated either by a referral to a sick visitor or to the Regional Medical Officer. It is clear from this guidance that this control mechanism was designed not only to catch possibly fraudulent claims but also to check up on people who should be returning to work.

Generally speaking, however, the main focus of disputes about incapacity for work concerned people who were not short-term sick. Instead, the focus was on longer-term claimants. As Sidney Webb argued in 1914, it is difficult to imagine a person who can literally do no work. If it had been established that a claimant should no longer be assessed against their usual work or if they had no usual work, the difficulty then remained with assessing what work people should be expected to do and what social aspects of their capacity should be considered.

The Relevance of Social Barriers in Defining Capacity for Work

The definition of incapacity for work relied on a medical model of individual "disease or disablement". This was understood, in the short term, to mean a claimant's inability to carry out their usual job. Longer-term claims for incapacity benefits required at least some consideration of wider social factors and a consideration of what was reasonable. To understand the way in which capacity for work was assessed for most long-term claims it is useful to return to the leading National Insurance Commissioners' decision from 1951 which established the case law on the definition of incapacity for work. R(S)11/51 emphasised the necessity to consider social factors in assessing capacity for work. This decision was incorporated into everyday decision making through guidance issued to decision makers throughout the second half of the twentieth century, with almost identical wording appearing in both DHSS guidance to local offices and to medical assessors. This definition continued until the changes brought about by the Incapacity Benefit reforms of 1994 (Wikeley 1995, p. 523) but it also reflected some of the thinking on the interpretation of rules for Sickness and Disablement Benefit in the first half of the twentieth century. This is clear from an analysis of early appeal decisions and from the reference in R(S)11/51 to the practice in the earlier Sickness Benefit scheme:

> This view of the correct approach to the problem is, we think, consistent with the decisions of Referees under the earliest of the former Insurance Acts, who had to interpret similar words. (R(S)11/51, para 7, citing Ministry of Health 1923)

Although the National Insurance Commissioners in the 1950s referred only to the published appeal cases, this view of the interpretation of incapacity can be found across several other documents in the first half of the twentieth century. There are examples of this interpretation of incapacity for work scattered through the appeals decisions and guidance, starting in 1917, in a report which included an early summary of the National Insurance Commission's view:

> An insured person who is unfit to resume his former occupation should be regarded as incapable of work and entitled to sickness or disablement benefit when his physical condition is such that although not incapable of all work, there is no available remunerative work of any kind which it would be reasonable for him to undertake. (NHIC (JC) 1917, p. 119)

Although this reference to "reasonableness", dating back to 1917 and continuing until the 1990s, suggests an awareness of social barriers in accessing work, it was restated on several occasions that incapacity for work should not be confused with unemployment. Benefits systems in the UK have always attempted to keep the boundary between incapacity and unemployment clear and yet a reasonable assessment of a person's capacities ought to take account of the likelihood of them actually getting a job. Chapter 5 considers this question in more depth.

Incapacity Benefit and the "Objective Test"

All of this was swept away in the 1990s with the introduction of Incapacity Benefit in an attempt to cut down on the numbers of people claiming benefits. The government response to the perceived problem was to bring in an entirely new test of incapacity, which, instead of looking at what a person could reasonably do, would provide an "objective" test of claimants' medical conditions. In the new Incapacity Benefit assessment, the Social Security (Incapacity for Work) Act 1994 still defined incapacity for work as "a day on which a person is incapable of work" (30c (1)(a)) but introduced a two-part test to decide who would qualify. The "own occupation" test, which applied for the first 196 days of a claim, for those who had recently been in work, followed previous legislation, requiring that the claimant was "incapable by reason of some specific disease or bodily or mental disablement of doing work which he could reasonably be expected to do in the course of the occupation in which he was so engaged" (171b (2)). However, after 196 days, and, significantly, for anyone who had not recently been in work, claimants were required to take an "all work test" which measured "the extent of a person's incapacity by reason of some specific disease or bodily or mental disablement to perform such activities as may be prescribed" (171C (2)(a)). This test introduced a medical assessment by a Benefits Agency doctor, who would allocate points for different levels of impairment and a minimum threshold which claimants had to reach to qualify. Although the claim was still reliant on an initial certificate of incapacity from the claimant's GP, the role of the GP became marginalised and almost all of the social factors highlighted by R(S)11/51 were disregarded. Instead the All Work Test focussed on "medical impairment" and included assessment of such capacities as ability to walk, to stand unsupported, to hear, to speak and to carry out a range of quite bizarre tasks such as putting on a hat, turning on a tap or carrying a bag of potatoes (Schedule to Regulation 6(1)(b) 24 of the Social Security (Incapacity for Work) (General) Regulations 1995, SI 1995 No. 311). These tests had been developed from the tools used by the Office of Population Censuses and Surveys (OPCS) to estimate the numbers of disabled people in the country (DSS 1994, p. 11). The use of the OPCS assessment explains some of the more obscure elements in the All Work Test, such as carrying potatoes or turning on taps, since it was intended not to assess individual capacity for work, but functional limitations in everyday life. The OPCS report explained that these measures would not be appropriate for "the assessment of individuals" because they were designed for a quite different purpose (Martin et al. 1988, p. 59). The OPCS surveys themselves had also been criticised by disability scholars for their focus on individual impairment rather than the social barriers which disable people (Barnes 1991, pp. 24–25).

Any element of a social model of disability was removed by the new tests for Incapacity Benefit, although it did contain some social assumptions about impairment and disability by including a fairly long list of people who would be exempt from the All Work Test because their medical conditions were considered sufficiently serious to excuse them from additional medical testing. These included people with severe mental health conditions, high personal care needs, complex learning disabilities, those who were registered blind and people with a range of other severe physical or mental impairments (Regulation 10, Social Security (Incapacity for Work) (General) Regulations 1995. SI 1995 No. 311). It was recognised at the time that these impairments might not exclude a claimant from capacity for work but that "it would be unreasonable to expect the person to be, or to become, capable of work" (DSS 1994, p. 16). It was also recognised that the All Work Test itself did not measure incapacity for work but that it measured the "the point at which a person *should not be expected to work* for benefit purpose" (DSS 1994, p. 35, my emphasis). This view was emphasised by the Minister for Social Security in a Commons debate on the rules: "We all know of people who are blind or use a wheelchair but who are perfectly capable of, and do, full-time work. We do not think those people *should be required to register for work* if they need to claim social security benefits" (William Hague, *Hansard*, 2 February 1995, col 1239, my emphasis).

This shows that, despite the allegedly objective nature of the medical tests introduced by Incapacity Benefit, and its clear foundation in a medical model of disability, the system still included considerable social assumptions about who could or, crucially, *should* work in order to be eligible for social support.

Employment and Support Allowance and Increasing Conditionality

The regulatory role of the All Work Test as an indicator of who should and should not be expected to work was confirmed in the exemptions from the test but it was the successor to Incapacity Benefit which brought overt labour market conditionality into the system. For all its contrast with the previous Invalidity Benefit system, Incapacity Benefit failed in its main purpose, which was to reduce the numbers of successful claims for benefit. Although Incapacity Benefit had changed the definition of incapacity for work dramatically and introduced new hurdles for claimants, the number of people claiming and receiving benefits continued to grow in the early twenty-first century, leading to new calls for change and the introduction of the even harsher ESA (National Audit Office 2010).

ESA, introduced in 2008 by the Welfare Reform Act 2007, kept the points-based assessment but with a tightening of the criteria for the now renamed Work Capability Assessment (WCA). Like the test for Incapacity Benefit, the test is based on a series of descriptors which outline a range of functional impairments (either physical or mental). Each descriptor carries a range of points (between six and fifteen) which, if they add up to fifteen or more, classify a claimant as having "limited capability for work" (The Employment and Support Allowance Regulations 2013). The WCA was tougher than the All Work Test and very few people can claim exemption from the test. The list of people with severe impairments exempt from the WCA was reduced to a bare minimum of those with a terminal illness, those receiving specific invasive therapies and hospital inpatients (Reg 20, Social Security The Employment and Support Allowance Regulations 2008, SI 2008 No. 794). A summary of the changes can be found in Bonner (2008). Everyone else was to be subjected to medical assessment against the WCA descriptors, greatly expanding the range of people for whom the GP's medical judgement was deemed insufficient. Crucially, the WCA also has an additional function of distinguishing between claimants who are fit for work and therefore not eligible for ESA, as having "limited capability for work" and therefore subject to conditionality in work activity, or as having "limited capability for work-related activity" with no conditionality attached.

Similar to Incapacity Benefit, the points-based system for ESA uses an entirely medical model of disability, awarding points for functional capacity, based on impairment, such as inability to "mobilise", to "stand unassisted", "picking up and moving or transferring by the use of the upper body and arms". Elements of the real world of work or of the disabling barriers which people encounter appear to be almost wholly disregarded. The rewording of the mobility element from assessment of ability to "walk" to the assessment of ability to "mobilise", was, in some respects a nod to twenty-first century understandings of disability, since it recognised that wheelchair users might be very well able to get about, without necessarily being able to "walk" (Rahilly 2010). Other descriptors changed the test from ability to see or hear to the ability to navigate safely or to communicate. However this rewording did not in itself recognise that the ability of a mobility-impaired person to get around is wholly dependent on barrier-free environments and access to appropriate equipment. Since its introduction, continuing controversy has led to changes to the original test, including case law which has questioned the purely medical approach. For example the question of mobilising was addressed when claimants were told that they could mobilise by using wheelchairs. In one case, it was decided that this was unreasonable, given that the claimant lived in an upstairs flat but in other cases that it was reasonable to expect a claimant to use a wheelchair, even when they did not currently use one (M v SSWP (ESA) (2012) UKUT 376 (AAC) and JC v SWWP (ESA) (2013) UKUT 0219 (AAC), cited in Bonner et al. 2013, p. 1069). A decision by a three Upper Tribunal judges in 2014 (SI

v SSWP (ESA) (2014) UKUT 308 (AAC)) concluded that a range of factors should be taken into account, including that "the work capability assessment is not to be divorced from the real world of work and the claimant does not actually have an employer, the test must be applied on the basis that the notional employer from whom the claimant might obtain employment has a modern workplace and is prepared to make reasonable adjustments in order to enable the claimant to be employed" (para 76), that it would not normally be relevant whether or not the claimant could use a wheelchair in their home and that it could usually be assumed that a wheelchair would be available if the claimant needed one. In the end, the test would be whether or not it is reasonable for the claimant to use a wheelchair at work in order to "mobilise". The case law is discussed in some detail in Hooker et al. (2017, pp. 1250–1251). The ongoing legal debate about the extent to which a claimant should or could or might be able to use a particular piece of equipment or adaptation to enable them to meet the tests in the ESA Work Capability Assessment suggests that the assessment is not as objectively medical as it appears at first sight. Decisions about a claimant's functional capabilities are subject to at least some recognition of the social realities of people's lives.

Although disability campaigners initially welcomed the assumption built into ESA that everyone can work, the reality of the harsh medical assessment, combined with the failure of the test to lead to improved employment prospects for disabled people, soon turned this initial enthusiasm into serious criticism (Harrington 2010; Shakespeare et al. 2017). A review of the WCA in 2014, while endorsing its principles, did note that it was "somewhat arbitrary" and that it "gives a false impression of scientific validity" (Litchfield 2014, p. 37). It also confirmed continuing mistrust of the system by claimants and claimants' organisation, who did not perceive the system as fair.

Conclusions

This chapter has shown how the definition of incapacity for work has changed since 1911. The statutory definition changed little between 1911 and 1995, requiring only that a claimant was "incapable of work by some specific disease or by bodily or mental disablement". As Sidney Webb noted in the quotation at the beginning of this chapter, a literal interpretation could lead to almost nobody qualifying for benefit. Case law, government guidance and everyday control mechanisms provided a more nuanced interpretation where claimants would be treated differently depending on whether they were making a short-term claim while ill or a had a longer-term health condition which might lead to them being out of the labour market in the long term. Case law in the 1950s led to social factors such as a claimant's past work experience and education being taken into account in the assessment of their capacity for work. Concerns about increasing numbers of claims for incapacity benefits and a general retrenchment in welfare spending in the late 1980s and 1990s led to the principle of points-based medical assessments with the introduction of Incapacity Benefit, which continues in a similar form today with Employment and Support Allowance.

The move to "objective" medical testing for Incapacity Benefit and Employment and Support Allowance demonstrates two things. Firstly it relies on a discourse that objectivity can be achieved by individual medical assessments, without any attention to social factors in assessing capacity for work, when that is clearly not the case. Secondly, such testing makes no difference to claimants' chances of actually finding work. This fundamental shift in incapacity assessments has led to numerous criticisms but it tends to create an impression that the assessments in the past were better. Perhaps they were but they were certainly not unproblematic. The rest of this book explores some of the issues arising in the everyday practices of decision making in incapacity benefits.

References

Barnes, Colin. 1991. *Disabled People in Britain and Discrimination*. London: Hurst and Company/BCoDP.

Beveridge, Sir William. 1942. *Social Insurance and Allied Services*. Cmnd. 6404. London: HMSO.

Bonner, David. 2008. 'Employment and Support Allowance: Helping the Sick and Disabled to Return to Work?' *Journal of Social Security Law* 15(4): 123–50.

Bonner, David, Ian Hooker, and Robin White, eds. 1991. *Non-means Tested Benefits: The Legislation 1991 Edition*. London: Sweet and Maxwell.

Bonner, David, Ian Hooker, Richard Poynter, Robin White, Nick Wikeley, and Penny Wood. 2013. *Social Security Legislation 2013/14: Non-Means-Tested Benefits and Employment and Support Allowance*. London: Sweet and Maxwell.

Department of Health and Social Security. 1981. *Sickness Benefit Law and Procedure. Code SB 1969, as Amended, 1981*. London: HMSO.

Department of Social Security. 1994. *The Medical Assessment for Incapacity Benefit*. London: HMSO.

Disability Alliance. 1987. *Poverty and Disability: Breaking the Link—The Case for a Comprehensive Disability Income Scheme*. London: Disability Alliance Educational Research Association.

Grue, Jan. 2015. *Disability and Discourse Analysis*. Farnham: Ashgate.

Hampton, Jameel. 2016. *Disability and the Welfare State in Britain: Changes in Perception and Policy 1948–79*. Bristol: Policy Press.
Harrington, Malcolm. 2010. *An Independent Review of the Work Capability Assessment*. London: The Stationery Office.
Hooker, Ian, Richard Poynter, Robin White, Nick Wikeley, John Mesher, and Edward Mitchell. 2017. *Social Security Legislation 2017/18 Non-Means-Tested Benefits and Employment and Support Allowance. Vol. 1*. London: Sweet and Maxwell.
Lawrence, Charles. 1926. *Report of the Royal Commission on National Health Insurance Cmd. 2596 Appendices to Minutes of Evidence Vols 1–4*. Cmd. 2596. London: HMSO.
Litchfield, Paul. 2014. *An Independent Review of the Work Capability Assessment: Year Five*. London: TSO.
Low, Lord, Baroness Meacher, and Baroness Grey-Thompson. 2015. *Halving the Gap? A Review Into the Government's Proposed Reduction to Employment and Support Allowance and Its Impact on Halving the Disability and Employment Gap*. London: Royal Mencap Society. mencap.org.uk/esa-review.
Martin, Jean, Howard Meltzer, and David Elliot. 1988. *The Prevalence of Disability Among Adults OPCS Surveys of Disability in Great Britain Report 1*. London: HMSO.
Ministry of Health. 1923. *Reports of Decisions on Appeals and Applications under Section 67 of the National Insurance Act 1911 and Section 27 of the National Insurance Act 1913, Vol 2—Part I*. London: HMSO.
———. 1933. *Approved Societies Handbook: Being a Revised Handbook for the Guidance of Approved Societies in Their Administration of Benefits Under the National Health Insurance Acts, 1924 to 1932*. London: HMSO.
Ministry of Pensions and National Insurance. 1960. *Instructions to National Insurance Offices on Law and Procedure Relating to Sickness Benefits under the National Insurance Acts Code SB*. London: HMSO.
National Audit Office. 2010. *Support to Incapacity Benefits Claimants Through Pathways to Work*. London: TSO.
National Health Insurance Commission (England). 1919. *Reports of Decisions on Appeals and Applications under Section 67 of the National Insurance Act 1911 and Section 27 of the National Insurance Act 1913 Part V* Cmd. 134. London: HMSO.
National Health Insurance Committee (Joint Committee). 1917. *National Health Insurance. Report on the Administration of National Health Insurance During the Years 1914–17* Cd. 8890. London: HMSO.
National Health Insurance Joint Committee. 1914. *National Health Insurance. Appendix to the Report of the Departmental Committee on Sickness Benefit Claims Under the National Insurance Act. Volume I*. Cd. 7688, 7689, 7690, 7691. London: HMSO.
Rahilly, Simon. 2010. 'Employment and Support Allowance: More Fine Tuning of the Incapacity Tests and the End of Incapacity Benefit'. *Journal of Social Security Law* 17: 137–40.

Shakespeare, Tom, Nicholas Watson, and Ola Abu Alghaib. 2017. 'Blaming the Victim, All Over Again: Waddell and Aylward's Biopsychosocial (BPS) Model of Disability'. *Critical Social Policy* 37 (1): 22–41.

Thomas, Carol. 2007. *Sociologies of Disability and Illness: Contested Ideas in Disability Studies and Medical Sociology*. Basingstoke: Palgrave Macmillan.

Walker, Alan. 2010. 'Disability'. In *The Peter Townsend Reader*, edited by Alan Walker, David Gordon, Ruth Levitas, Peter Phillimore, Chris Phillipson, Margot Salomon, and Nicola Yeates. Bristol: Policy Press.

Wikeley, Nick. 1995. 'The Social Security (Incapacity for Work) Act 1994'. *Modern Law Review* 58 (4): 523.

4

The Necessity of Questioning the Doctor: Medical and Other Evidence

Introduction

> Against the continued advance of a tide of unjustified claims to … benefit there are two main lines of defence. The first is the adoption of measures to secure that a proper standard is applied in the issue of medical certificates for incapacity while the second consists in strengthening the safeguards to be adopted by [decision makers] in connection with the supervision of claims. (Ministry of Health 1931, AS278 National Health Insurance control of Expenditure on Sickness and Disablement Benefits, filed in ACT 1/582, p. 1)

This statement comes from a circular, issued in 1931, by the Ministry of Health to Sickness Benefit decision makers. Echoes of this circular can be seen in discourse about "unjustified claims" today. These anxieties had been expressed since the start of the National Insurance Scheme in 1911 and continued across the twentieth century, as decision makers and policy makers struggled with how best to collect evidence of a claimant's incapacity for work. The statement mentions two main forms of evidence: the medical certificate and safeguards used by decision makers in supervising claims. This chapter looks at the different types of evidence that decision makers have used to assess whether or not someone was incapable of work. The doctor's medical certificate, confirming the claimant's incapacity for work and providing a diagnosis of any relevant medical condition, has been the starting point for all incapacity benefits. Such certificates confirm the privileged status of medical knowledge in assessing incapacity for work, a symbol of the power of the "medical gaze" described by Foucault (1973, cited in Hughes 2015, p. 82). The doctor's medical certificate has often been sufficient for decision makers to allow a claim. However, policy

© The Author(s) 2019
J. Gulland, *Gender, Work and Social Control*, Palgrave Socio-Legal Studies,
https://doi.org/10.1057/978-1-137-60564-1_4

makers have shown a continuing suspicion that the medical certificate alone might not be adequate. At best, the argument goes, doctors misunderstand the nature of incapacity benefits and sign certificates inappropriately. Doctors find it difficult to refuse claimants who demand certificates and so sign the certificates to maintain their professional relationship with their patients. At worst, doctors might deliberately issue certificates in order to benefit financially by keeping patients on their lists. Meanwhile, claimants are always under suspicion of malingering. To counteract this concern, policy makers developed mechanisms to obtain additional evidence in cases where there was some uncertainty as to the validity of the claim, where the claim appeared to have been going on for too long or where there was contradictory evidence from some other source which suggested that a claimant was capable of work. Usually, this additional evidence has taken the form of further medical checks but other sources have also been used. All of this evidence is collected and evaluated with the intention of seeking the "truth" about a claimant's working capacities.

Medical knowledge has its own particular prestige in modern Western societies, in many areas of social life, but particularly in disability benefit assessments. Stone's groundbreaking book from 1984 describes the development of medical evidence as the key determinant of incapacity for work in Western welfare states (Stone 1984). She also points to other mechanisms which could be used to assess the validity of claims, including the "testimony of acquaintances", which, she argues, was common in early modern attempts to alleviate poverty and prevent vagrancy. Here, neighbours, employers and a range of semi-official locals would be asked for their opinions on claimants (p. 100). "Social inquiry" involved more formal mechanisms where officials would be engaged to make inquiries about claimants (p. 101). "Revelatory signs" involved officials creating tests which would show whether or not people were telling the truth. The prime example of this was the English workhouse test, whereby conditions would be made sufficiently unpleasant in order to deter all but the most desperate (p. 102). Stone also discusses the "adversarial test" as a validating device, arguing that the need to take a case to court acts as a deterrence against frivolous claims (p. 103). Finally, Stone argues that the medical professionals' "clinical judgment" came to be the standard validating device on disability claims in the twentieth century (p. 103). Although Stone does not discuss the UK twentieth-century incapacity benefit schemes in her book, her analysis is clearly relevant to the development of medical evidence in benefit decision making in the UK. Medical knowledge has a special status but one that is contested, in particular by disability activists for its focus on impairment as individual failure rather than on social barriers to inclusion. Despite this valorisation of medical knowledge, decision making on incapacity benefits has often included a more understated challenge to this expertise. Medical experts may understand diseases and injuries but they do not necessarily understand the real world of work. Decision makers have therefore used the additional checks and validating devices identified by Stone to test people's claims to incapacity. Much of this depends on common-sense understandings of what work really is and how people with different impairments and health challenges might engage with the world of work. Valverde's insightful exploration of "common sense" administrative knowledge brings another dimension to this discussion (Valverde 2003). Valverde distinguishes between the "common knowledge" held by ordinary people and that held by professionals such as judges and doctors. She argues that professionals' common knowledge is granted higher status because of their professional standing (2003, p. 179). In the case of incapacity benefit decision making, we can see this where medical and legal decision makers make reference to their knowledge of working-class occupations and women's domestic labour, which is not based on their professional training but on their personal knowledge of the everyday world. These professionals might also refer to their own views on whether a particular impairment is likely to have a particular disabling effect on a claimant's chances of working, again, not based on medical or legal professional knowledge but on their own experience of the world. Their everyday knowledge of the world might be no different from a layperson's experience but could be taken more seriously as evidence because they are also lawyers or doctors. I discuss examples of some of these below.

Valverde also identifies a form of "administrative knowledge" which, she argues, is neither scientific nor lay but which lies in the minds of state administrators (p. 20). Valverde's examples concern the common knowledge held by people involved in the regulation of alcohol, who do not have the knowledge recognised by a professional certificate, but whose "common knowledge" of the effects of alcohol is held in greater esteem because of their administrative role (p. 192). She asks questions, similar to Foucault's "who is authorised to interpret acts and representations and situations for legal purposes?" (p. 23). In the case of decision making in incapacity benefits, a variety of actors are expected to have this kind of common knowledge of what it means to be incapable of work. This knowledge is then used to test or validate the initial doctor's certificate.

During the twentieth century, two main forms of additional evidence were developed to test or validate the initial doctor's certificate: highly valued medical knowledge in the form of second medical opinions and a form of social inquiry evidence through the sick visiting scheme. These two types of knowledge are in constant conflict, a conflict which continues today, based on the idea that only medical knowledge can determine a claimant's true state, and the contradictory view that there is a common-sense knowledge of the everyday world of work. Until late in the twentieth century, claimant knowledge was not formally considered in the assessment of claims. That changed in the 1990s with the introduction of lengthy claim forms for Incapacity Benefit and Employment and Support Allowance (ESA). These forms enable claimants to add their own knowledge of their impairments and everyday experience so that decision makers can include claimant knowledge in the formal assessment of claims. This knowledge must always be endorsed by medical professionals in order to have any value.

This chapter considers these three sources of evidence in incapacity benefit decision making: medical evidence, in the form of initial medical certificates and second medical opinions, the evidence of sick visitors and other social inquiry mechanisms and the evidence of claimants themselves. The chapter considers first of all the development of these mechanisms from 1911, with the use of the medical certificate as initial evidence, the creation of a system of second medical opinions through the Regional Medical Service and the use of sick visitors as a form of social inquiry. The chapter considers how these mechanisms were converted to a fully state service under the post-war National Insurance Scheme. Finally, the chapter considers the ways in which evidence has been used in decision making since 1995 with the introduction of Incapacity Benefit and ESA.

The Medical Certificate

The National Insurance Act 1911 did not prescribe the form in which evidence of incapacity for work should take, requiring only that "notice has been given" of the claimant's incapacity (NI Act 1911 S8(c)). This led to some initial debate about what form this notice might take. The question was discussed in a very early court case regarding the operation of the scheme (Heard v Pickthorne and others (1913) KB 3 299). The court found that, while medical evidence of some kind was necessary to establish the initial claim, there was no requirement that this must come from a panel doctor. The 1914 inquiry into Sickness Benefit considered the status of doctors' certificates, including the concern that panel doctors might sign sick certificates in order to keep patients on their lists (NHIJC 1914, p. 35). This suspicion has continued throughout the incapacity benefits schemes and continues today, but had a particular narrative at this early stage. The 1914 report noted that doctors often regarded their responsibility to be to their patients and not to society at large or to the Approved Societies in particular. While recognising that this was an admirable professional position, the authors of the report noted that doctors must recognise their responsibility to the sickness insurance scheme as a whole. Doctors had a role, not only in supporting their own patients, but in policing the scheme against possible malingerers (NHIJC 1914, p. 37). Witnesses to the inquiry had alleged that both claimants and doctors had been trusted not to abuse the voluntary schemes run by Friendly Societies in the past because the relationship between the doctor and the Society was based on reputation and trust, while that between the members and the old Friendly Societies was based on shared responsibility for the scheme. This trust, they argued, had been lost with the new state scheme. The report was sceptical of this tendency to look back to a "golden age" (p. 8). Even if there was any validity to this view of the past, the authors argued that times had changed, claimants now had a right to benefits, giving the sickness certificate a "new sanctity", and that therefore more stringent checks were now necessary (p. 10). The conclusion of the inquiry was that the sickness certificate constituted only one source of evidence and that the decision to award or refuse benefit rested with the Approved Society. Therefore, the Society had the right and duty to consider the quality of the evidence and to consider whether further evidence might be necessary in order to make a decision. Such evidence might come from a second medical opinion or the evidence of sick visitors. Weighing up these different sources required an administrative judgement about the value of evidence.

Medical Referees and the Regional Medical Service

To begin with Approved Societies employed their own medical referees to provide second opinions on claims, using a wide variety of procedures for referring claimants. Societies would often prefer the evidence of these medical referees over the claimants' doctors, on the grounds that referees were independent of the claimant and less likely to be swayed by considerations of loyalty, professional duty, or a financially motivated desire to keep the patient on their lists. The potential conflict between claimants' own doctors and these medical referees is apparent in the early appeal cases. The legal adjudicators in appeal cases, however, did not assume that family doctors must be on the side of claimants, stressing instead that disputed cases were examples of a conflict of medical opinion. They argued that it was the duty of the Societies to collect sufficient evidence to make a balanced decision, rather than to prefer any one source of medical evidence. The adjudicator in Case 36 spelled this out:

It should be remembered also that there is nothing sacred about a referee's report and that societies are under no obligation to treat it as necessarily binding and conclusive. It is rather a piece of additional independent testimony to be weighed with the other facts and circumstances of the case before the society comes to a final conclusion. (Case 36, NHIC England 1916, p. 188)

This did not necessarily mean that appeals would be successful. Sometimes the adjudicators preferred the evidence of the medical referees. However, given that Societies tended to prefer the views of medical referees, claimants who did not appeal against refusals of benefit did not have the advantage of the two sources being treated as equally valid. In some appeal cases, adjudicators preferred the evidence from the claimant's doctor, on the grounds that they would have better knowledge of the claimant's health. One of the very early cases in 1914 is an example of this. Mr P, a foundry worker, and the Society were represented by solicitors at the hearing and both provided evidence from two doctors. Mr P's evidence was from his own panel doctor and a specialist, while the Society provided evidence from two separate medical referees who had examined Mr P. The evidence was conflicting but the adjudicators preferred the evidence provided by the claimant "we were more impressed by the evidence of the panel doctor, who had been in constant attendance on the Appellant for a considerable period and had periodically examined him" (Case 6, NHIC England 1915, p. 16).

Another example from 1915 shows how the adjudicators weighed up the different sources of medical opinion. In this rather unusual case, the appeals of nine female herring workers were held together and reported as a single case. All of these women had intermittent patterns of employment, leaving them under suspicion of malingering, and all had the same doctor (Dr X), who had provided certificates of incapacity. Their cases had come to light as a result of "certain information" received by the Society (presumably from a local informant). The Society referred all nine women to the same medical referee (Dr Y), who had found them fit for work. At the appeal hearing, the adjudicators were very critical of Dr X, the claimants' doctor, for being too ready to issue medical certificates and for being unhelpful in his lack of provision of information to the Society. However, despite the concerns about the claimants' doctor, five out of the nine women were successful on appeal and had their claims of incapacity confirmed. The other four were found to be fit for work. The adjudicators concluded that these cases had arisen because of a failure by Dr X to provide relevant information requested by the Society but also because of a failure of communication between Dr X and, the medical referee, Dr Y:

> No blame ought, we think to be imputed to Dr Y on this account… but We have on many occasions pointed out how desirable it is that in cases of this kind the doctor who is requested to examine patients on behalf of a Society should afford an opportunity to the panel doctor to lay before him any circumstances which in the opinion of the latter ought to be taken into consideration before an opinion is given. (Case 56, NHIC England 1916, p. 153)

This case shows that there were suspicions that doctors were providing certificates of incapacity for work when they should not. It provides another example of the Society preferring the evidence of the medical referee. In this case, where five of the nine women were successful on appeal, the adjudicators relied on balancing up the evidence of opinions of the two doctors, rather than considering one or the other source as being inherently true.

While there was often suspicion that claimant's doctors would be too subjective in their recommendations, there was also a concern that the doctors providing second opinions should be seen as independent of the Societies. The 1914 inquiry concluded that a system of independent medical referees should be established:

> It is essential that there should not be the remotest ground for a suspicion arising in any quarter that the referee holds a brief on behalf of either party interested in his decision. It is of great importance that he should have no motive other than a desire to give a true judgment in all cases brought before him, and his utility necessarily depends on the confidence reposed in his judgment. (NHIJC 1914, p. 61)

This view was confirmed in a further report in 1917 which recommended the institution of a system of state medical referees who could provide more fully independent second opinions (NHIC (JC) 1917, p. 80). The plan was delayed by the war but, from 1920 onwards, a state system of Regional Medical Officers (RMOs) produced a more standardised system of oversight (Ministry of Health 1921, p. 154). The new system extended to Scotland and was described by the Scottish Board of Health in 1923 as an "indispensable part of the machinery of national health insurance" (Scottish Board of Health 1923, p. 66). By the time of the Royal Commission in 1926, the RMOs were clearly embedded in the system. Again, the Ministry of Health was at pains to note that the evidence provided by the RMOs was intended as a second opinion only and not as the provision of a final statement on the claimant's capacity but that "it would be unusual for a society to continue payment after the RMO had reported him capable of work" (Lawrence 1926, appendices to minutes of evidence, para 69 page 20). This observation that it would be unusual for a Society to continue payment after an adverse RMO opinion can be seen in appeals from the 1920s. Adjudicators did not always accept the Societies' view and, again, emphasised that disputed cases were examples of a conflict of medical opinion. An example where the adjudicator preferred the evidence of the claimant's doctor over the RMO is that concerning Mr H, a former miner, described as having "incurable deafness" and in "poor physical condition". Mr H was found fit for work after a medical examination by the RMO. The adjudicator was not impressed by this evidence, preferring that of the claimant's doctor, Dr M:

> The case for the Society rested entirely upon the report and evidence of the Regional Medical Officer who had only an opportunity of examining the respondent once. I am satisfied, however, by Dr M, who has naturally had much greater opportunities of studying the case. (PIN 63/1/406, 1927)

In another similar case from 1929, concerning Miss R, a thirty-nine-year-old milliner, the adjudicator considered detailed evidence from both the panel doctor and the RMO. The evidence showed that Miss R had pain in her hip "probably tubercular in origin" and had difficulty standing or remaining in a seated position for any length of time. Miss R had been claiming Disablement Benefit for eight years and said that she could not work because of the pain. Her own doctor confirmed that the scarring on her hip joint was likely to cause constant pain and that it would be impossible for Miss R to work. The RMO, on the other hand, said that he "could find no condition present which would account for the pain of the frequent character spoken of by the respondent". Deciding in favour of Miss R, the adjudicator noted:

> Without the least disrespect to [RMO]'s undoubted skill and experience I am bound to take into account the advantage which has accrued to [claimant's doctor] over a period of years. (PIN 63/4/528, 1929)

The Society was using the RMO to check up on a woman who had been claiming benefit for several years. The Society then viewed the RMO's opinion as final and so stopped her benefit, despite the panel doctor's ongoing medical certificates. The adjudicator, on the other hand, insisted on considering the two sources of medical evidence as potentially equally valid. His decision in the end was based on preferring the panel doctor's knowledge of his patient rather than the "objective" but limited view of the RMO. This case exemplifies the dilemma which has faced decision makers throughout the course of incapacity benefit policy regarding the status of the deeper, but perhaps biased, knowledge held by claimants' doctors, compared with the apparently more objective, but perhaps more superficial knowledge of the RMOs.

Adjudicators at appeal hearings were assisted in the task of weighing up these contrasting sources of medical evidence by the presence of medical assessors who attended most hearings after 1920. Medical assessors were doctors who would provide advice to the adjudicators where there were questions of medical knowledge. In cases concerning women, the Ministry of Health usually appointed female medical assessors in an attempt to ensure that at least one woman was present at the hearings. Although they usually provided only advice, sometimes medical assessors also carried out medical assessments directly. Adjudicators would often note that the medical assessor helped them to make a difficult decision and used this officially sanctioned form of medical knowledge to support either the RMO or the claimant's doctor's opinion. The adjudicators frequently used terms such as "I was advised by the medical assessor", "the medical assessor suggested" or the stronger "I had the great advantage of having the medical assessor" (PIN 63/1/411), "I am indebted to the medical assessor" (PIN 63/3/488). These references to the invaluable advice of the assessors suggest that the adjudicators used the medical assessor's opinion to give additional medical weight to what they otherwise considered to be a legal decision.

These examples from the appeal hearings show that legal adjudicators were usually careful to treat the evidence from the claimant's doctor and the RMO as potentially equal in value and often emphasised their need to show respect to both professionals, by noting the medical assessor's opinion as central to the final decision. What is more revealing from these cases is that the Societies would tend to accept the RMO evidence as having higher value and refuse benefit as soon as an RMO made a finding of fitness for work. This perspective was often maintained by the internal reviewers. This meant that the claimant would only be able to challenge the RMO view by appealing to the independent Ministry of Health adjudicators.

This debate about the use and value of RMO evidence continued right through the period of the Approved Societies system, evidenced by volumes of correspondence between Societies, the Ministry of Health and representatives of doctors and the Regional Medical service throughout the 1930s. The Ministry of Health reported that the RMO service stopped during the Second World War and although it was "revived for a few months during 1940" was suspended again as a result of continuing wartime demand for doctors and reintroduced in April 1945 (Ministry of Health 1946, p. 66). However, there is evidence that there was some form of Regional Medical Service in 1942 when a debate arose about its role in assessing claims for exemption from fire-watching during the war. The fire-watching scheme was compulsory and there was an appeals procedure for those who sought exemption. A debate arose in 1942 regarding what ought to happen if someone was certified as unfit for work through the Sickness Benefit scheme but was considered fit for fire-watching duties, or vice versa. An MP raised this issue in Parliament, leading to an agreement whereby people seeking exemption on the grounds of health would be referred to the Regional Medical Service. Any relevant information on assessments for fire-watching, for example that a claimant was fit for these duties, would be passed to Societies. The decisions on whether fitness for fire-watching duties constituted capacity for work was left to the Societies but it seems likely that this would lead to benefit being stopped (correspondence in PIN 13/941). This overlap between state decision making on compulsory war service and regulation of the Sickness Benefit scheme shows the Ministry of Health as unwilling to intervene in the day-to-day decision making of Societies while trying to ensure that information gained for another purpose was passed on.

When the new National Insurance Sickness Benefit scheme was introduced in 1948, the RMOs were retained as a source of second opinions and debate on their role continued in a very similar vein to that in the Approved Society system. The key questions were when to refer a claimant to a RMO, how to balance the evidence provided by the RMO with that provided by the claimant's doctor and the continuing principle that administrative staff should make the final decision, based on this range of evidence. The 1933 Approved Societies handbook and memos from the 1920s were cited in advice about how to develop the new RMO service (PIN 35/7). In the early 1950s, the Ministry of Pensions was concerned that local appeal tribunals were relying too heavily on the evidence of claimants' doctors. One archive file concerns the drafting and redrafting of a memo for tribunal members to explain to them the role of medical evidence in decision making about Sickness Benefit. It starts with a memo dated 5 February 1953:

> I am a little worried by the persistent recurrence of cases where Local Tribunals do not give full weight to RMO (H) reports and prefer the certificates of the claimant's doctor as representing more reliable evidence of incapacity.... They [the tribunals] do not like contrary decisions by a Ministry doctor being made without reference to the insured person's own adviser which is apt to lead to unfortunate situations. (from HW Stockman (Ministry of Pensions and National Insurance) addressed to C G Dennys Esq CB, filed in PIN 35/86)

This memo led to a leaflet aimed at tribunal members, outlining how the Ministry understood the status of different forms of medical evidence and explaining how and why claims would be referred to the Regional Medical service. These included cases where "an illness lasts appreciably longer than is to be expected in the light of the certified cause of incapacity or if there is other evidence suggesting that the claimant may be capable of some work" (Ministry of Pensions and National Insurance 1953, pp. 2/3). A revealing memo in the archive file shows that the Ministry of National Insurance was at great pains to respect the role of medical evidence and to suggest that all medical evidence should be regarded as objective:

> I would also suggest very strongly that we should not talk about "the claimant's doctor". This rather gives the impression that the claimant has a doctor and we have a doctor, and that the two are at daggers drawn. What we want to emphasise is that we ask for two opinions but they may well be the same opinion. (Memo from WP Barnes to Mr Uppington, dated 21/4/53, in PIN 35/86)

This position was confirmed in a Commissioners' decision from 1956 which summarised the need to take account of different sources of medical evidence. This case concerned Mrs B, a woman, in her fifties, who worked in a cotton mill and had been claiming Sickness Benefit as a result of general debility and weakness. Mrs B had been examined several times by RMO staff and was found fit for work. She appealed against this decision and her appeal was upheld by the local tribunal. The local office appealed to the National Insurance Commissioners. At the Commissioner's hearing, the Commissioner was not satisfied with any of the medical evidence provided and called for a psychiatric report. The psychiatrist concluded that there were "no physical signs of organic disease" but that Mrs B was incapable of work as result of her "psychological condition" (R(S)4/56). This Commissioner's decision was important at the time because it confirmed that psychological conditions could be relevant to a claimant's capacity for work. It is of interest here because it shows another example of the local office preferring the views of the Regional Medical Service over that of the GP, while a legal adjudicator confirmed the need to look at all evidence and to seek specialist advice if the different medical reports were inconclusive or contradictory.

GPs have often been wary of providing certificates of incapacity for work, arguing that it is not their role to make these assessments. In the 1970s, the British Medical Association argued that GPs were not in a position to state that a claimant was, or was not, incapable, although could advise the claimant as to whether she or he should "refrain from work" (Ogus and Barendt 1978, p. 153). This led to a change of wording in the GP's certificate in the 1970s so that, instead of certifying that the claimant was incapable of work, the GP would instead certify that she or he merely "advised the claimant to refrain from work" (National Insurance Advisory Committee 1976). This distinction was clearly important to the medical profession but the National Insurance

Advisory Committee did not imagine that it would make much difference in practice (NIAC 1976, para 9).

Debates about medical evidence continued into the late twentieth century where Ministry of Pensions and Department of Health and Social Security (DHSS) guidance included detailed advice about when to refer to RMOs, based on the claimant's diagnosis and length of claim, as well as circumstances when immediate control action was considered necessary. This guidance suggests that claimant's doctors' certificates were always subject to scrutiny and to the possibility of testing by obtaining a second medical opinion, if there was any suggestion of malingering or possible capacity for work (DHSS 1981).

Leading up to the major change in medical assessment in 1995, a National Audit Office report sought to discover an explanation for the recent growth in expenditure on Invalidity Benefit. The report concluded that "a potentially effective control system has been established by the Department in a difficult and complex area" and that improved information and training would enable the Department to "ensure that only claimants satisfying the qualifying conditions receive the benefit" (National Audit Office 1989, p. 5). There were critics of the procedure however. A report by the Disability Alliance in 1983 looked at the everyday realities of people claiming Invalidity Benefit. The claimants' evidence cited in this report confirmed the long-standing position that RMO's opinions tended to be viewed as more objective than the views of claimants' doctors and that sometimes claimants' doctors would stop issuing medical certificates after a negative RMO report, believing it to be "an instruction from the DHSS to stop issuing sick notes". The report gives an example of a Mrs K whose doctor told her "I know you were sick the whole time [six months] but I cannot give you a sick note when the RMO has decided that you are fit for work" (Disability Alliance 1983, p. 14). The Report notes that such people would have no right of appeal since the withdrawal of GP support would end the claim.

Case law on evidence of incapacity by the early 1990s confirmed that medical evidence was important but that decision makers were required to take account of all evidence before them and that the evidence of the RMO had no special status over that of the GP (or vice versa) (R(S)4/60 cited in Bonner et al. 1991, p. 26). Despite this case law and the views of civil servants cited above that all medical evidence should be regarded as equally valid, in practice, it seems that the RMOs' opinions were usually preferred in the first instance. The principle of treating all medical evidence equally was only likely to be followed when claimants appealed. Nevertheless, medical evidence, whether from the GP or from another source had privileged status. Meanwhile, sick visitors provided the other main source of evidence on incapacity benefit claims for most of the twentieth century.

Sick Visitors

Sick visitors were used by Approved Societies as a mechanism for checking claims, following on from the practice of Friendly Societies in the nineteenth century. The 1911 National Insurance Act provided for the use of sick visitors and the inquiry into Sickness Benefit in 1914 noted the widespread use of sick visitors as a first stage mechanism for checking up on claims before referral to a medical specialist. This was reinforced in guidance from the Ministry of Health (1920) and was confirmed in the Ministry of Health evidence to the Royal Commission in 1926:

> The function… is in general oversight … that rules of behaviour during sickness are observed and bringing to the notice of the society.. circumstances which would raise doubt about continuance of incapacity. The society would not ordinarily suspend payment.. merely on the strength of the sick visitor's report …. The more usual course would be to refer the member to the Regional Medical Officer. (Lawrence 1926, appendices to minutes of evidence, para 69 page 19)

From the appeal hearing evidence, it is clear that sick visitors were indeed used to supervise claims and to alert Societies to people whose incapacity may have been in doubt. This would usually lead to a referral for a second medical opinion. Societies often quoted sick visitors' reports at length as part of their case at appeal hearings. While it is more difficult to ascertain the extent to which this evidence was used in decisions that did not reach the appeal hearings, it is likely that the Societies relied heavily on the evidence of sick visitors to make decisions about the validity of claims. At the appeal hearings, adjudicators were less likely to be convinced by the evidence of sick visitors. Where the sick visitors' reports had triggered a referral to a medical referee, it was this medical evidence rather than the sick visitor's evidence which would be taken seriously at the appeal hearings. In this sense, the suspicions aroused by the sick visitor's visit contributed to the narrative of the claim, rather than counting as evidence as such.

In a case from 1917, the adjudicators discussed the balance between the sick visitor's observations and medical evidence. In this case, Mrs S had been claiming Sickness and then Disablement Benefit for over a year because of a back problem and suspected cancer. While her medical certificates clearly stated that she was incapable of work, and this had been confirmed by a medical referee, benefit was stopped after a sick visitor observed her "in the streets, shopping". The Society argued that this was evidence of her capacity for light work. The adjudicators disagreed, preferring the evidence from the doctor, confirmed by the medical referee and by evidence from a local hospital (Case 110, NHIC 1919, p. 266).

There are similar cases regarding sick visitors' evidence in appeal cases from the 1920s and evidence of sick visitors' evidence being used to refuse benefit in the records of the Ideal Benefit Society in the 1930s. For further discussion of these, see Chapter 9. Sick visitors continued throughout the interwar period and into the post-war system. Some individual Societies preferred to use sick visitor evidence over the Regional Medical Service. For example, in an inquiry in Scotland into the problem of "lax certification" by doctors, individual Society representatives explained how they used the different mechanisms. The representative from the Amalgamated Society of Woodworkers said that his Society "had sick visitors and have not had occasion to use the Regional Medical Service at all extensively" (papers in HH 3/9, National Records of Scotland 1930). It is worth noting that this Society had no women members and was probably reliant on previous Friendly Society traditions of checking up on their members through community surveillance. A guide to the National Health Insurance Scheme from the 1930s refers to a statutory system for sick visitors in Northern Ireland having been set up in 1930 but I have been unable to find further details of this (Foster and Taylor 1937, p. 251).

Sick Visitors After 1948

Preparation for the post-war National Insurance Scheme led to draft guidance on the use of sick visitors confirming the role of the sick visitor as a mechanism for checking claims which could then be referred to medical referees, rather than as the sole source of evidence on the claim (PIN 8/106). Memos from the late 1940s and early 1950s suggest that the sick visiting scheme continued to follow guidance from the Ministry of Health handbooks from the 1930s (PIN 35/37). However, during the 1950s, the Ministry of National Insurance became concerned at the cost of the sick visiting service and indicated a change in policy to making more use of the Regional Medical service at the expense of sick visiting. This is summarised in a memo from 1952:

> Sick visiting is not entirely satisfactory for several reasons: it is expensive (it is estimated that the average time for a sick visit is 40 minutes), it arouses resentment among doctors unless very carefully carried out, and it cannot immediately be followed by disallowance of benefit since the Ministry of National Insurance must

have medical evidence of capacity for work to set against the general practitioner's certificate of incapacity. In brief, sick visiting, while necessary in some cases and useful for its general deterrent effect on malingering and working while claiming benefit, cannot be effective without a parallel system of RMO reference. (Memo dated December 1952 "memorandum agreed by Ministry of National Insurance, Ministry of Health and Department of Health for Scotland", in PIN 35/125 [underlining in original])

The emphasis on the need for medical evidence confirms the decline in the value of social inquiry evidence provided by sick visitors. The apparent effectiveness of this change in policy is summarised in a memo from 1956 which gives figures for a reduction in sick visits from over a million in 1951 to six hundred thousand in 1954 but concluding that the corresponding increase in referrals to the RMO was more efficient since it usually led to benefit being stopped. (Letter dated 12/1/56 from MJ Hewitt [MoH] to Rr Ashford at the Treasury, regarding expansion of RMO referrals in PIN 35/125.)

However, the sick visiting scheme did continue into the 1980s, with DHSS guidance providing detailed advice about the use of sick visitors to monitor claims (DHSS 1981). The system appears to have dwindled by the 1990s and the transfer to Incapacity Benefit. For example, there is no reference to the sick visiting scheme as a means of controlling claims in the National Audit Office report of 1989, which refers only to the Regional Medical Service as a mechanism for checking up on GP certification (NAO 1989).

The use of sick visitors was inherited from the old friendly society system and continued through most of the twentieth century. Early in the century sick visitors seemed to be an important source of evidence which could be used to stop a claimant's benefit if the claimant appeared to be malingering, breaching the behaviour during sickness rules, or especially if they were women carrying out household duties. Legal decision makers were less impressed by the evidence of sick visitors and preferred medical evidence in deciding a claim. This led to the balance of evidence being tipped in favour of the medical evidence. Sick visitors were considered to be an important stage in the control of claims but their role became that of an initial check and as a lever to refer claimants for second medical opinions.

Claimant and Other Evidence

Medical evidence carries the most weight in deciding claims about incapacity benefits, but other evidence from sources such as sick visitors and the direct observations of decision makers has played an important part in triggering medical reviews. At appeal hearings in the early twentieth century, the direct evidence of claimants themselves could serve to sway a decision. Usually, this would be when the adjudicator had difficulty deciding between the conflicting evidence from the decision maker and the claimant's doctor. The key issue would be either the claimant's reliability as a witness, or adjudicators' observations of the claimant's manner or behaviour at the hearing.

We can see an example of these observations in a case from 1927. This case concerned a thirty-year-old woman, Mrs N, who had a visual impairment. The adjudicator considered the evidence of the RMO who thought that she was "capable of work not involving the use of her vision" and from her panel doctor who considered that "on the contrary that her vision was so impaired that she was from a practical point of view incapable of undertaking work as an employee". But it was the adjudicator's observation of Mrs N herself and her own evidence which influenced his decision that she was incapable of work:

> The letter (written by the claimant) was read through by the claimant at the hearing standing in a good light. .. she had to hold it very close to her face, and even then was not able to make out one or two words…she could still write tolerably well, although she had a greater difficulty reading what she had written… I was impressed with the fairness with which she gave her evidence. (PIN 63/1/409, 1927)

The adjudicator was impressed by Mrs N's presentation of her evidence and willingness to be subjected to the humiliation of trying to read a letter at the hearing. The adjudicators' observation of claimants' appearance and demeanour could also work against their claims to incapacity. For example in a case from 1919, Mrs H was a widow, aged 49 who had been claiming benefit for several years. Her benefit had been stopped after a review by a medical referee. She gave evidence at her appeal, detailing her difficulties with everyday life and her attempts to find work. However, the adjudicators were not convinced by this evidence:

> after duly weighing the panel doctor's evidence, we were satisfied of the soundness of the view held by the Medical Referee which was based on a very wide experience of cases of this kind and was indeed confirmed by the Appellant's own appearance and evidence. (Case 121, NHIC 1919, p. 290)

The adjudicators reached a similar conclusion in 1920, regarding a woman, Miss S, who had been claiming benefit for about two years. In their assessment of the evidence provided by Miss S, the adjudicators noted that "She did not look anaemic". The adjudicators were not convinced by her account, preferring that of the medical referee and saying that "We were unable to accept her own estimate of her incapacity for work (which her appearance rather belied)" (Case 2/15, 1920, Ministry of Health 1923, p. 43).

Although justifying this decision by reference to the medical referee's expertise, the adjudicators' reference to the claimant's appearance "she did not look anaemic" suggests that their own common-sense knowledge was also part of the evidence considered. In another case, a woman with epilepsy, Miss B, had a seizure during the appeal hearing, but her quick recovery was regarded as evidence of her capacity for work (PIN 63/1/411, 1927). The adjudicator's own assessment of the extent of Miss B's epilepsy and her apparent "intelligence" was sufficient for him to conclude that she could surmount the evident discrimination that she was experiencing and turn her hand to any kind of work which would enable her to come off benefit.

These adjudicators' observations of claimant's medical conditions were common. It seems that adjudicators could be swayed by a claimant's evidence, in either direction. An unconvincing claimant, who showed evidence of acting up, of not being genuine, or looking "healthy" would be less likely to be believed. On the other hand, a claimant who appeared genuine, honest and displayed, what the adjudicator considered to be, appropriate, disabled behaviour at the hearing could persuade the adjudicator to favour the panel doctor over the RMO. These examples from appeal hearings show how adjudicators used evidence provided directly by claimants, either in their accounts of their daily lives, or in their appearance, to weigh up the conflicting evidence provided by the medical experts. The records of the appeal hearings cannot show directly how or whether Approved Societies used claimant evidence in their front-line decision making. However, work on street-level bureaucracy in many fields suggests that front-line decision makers are likely to have been affected by this kind of evidence (Lipsky 2010). Lipsky says that "clients evoke sympathy or hostility" (p. 108) and that "general evaluations of social worth that inform society will also inform the decisions of street-level bureaucrats" (p. 109) but also "the culture in which they are embedded" (p. 181). The appeals cases certainly reveal examples of clients who have evoked hostility because of their apparent lifestyles or behaviours. The decision makers' experience of working-class occupations was also likely to be limited and based on their assumed knowledge, knowledge which was sometimes challenged by claimants, or their supporters. Adjudicators (who were all middle-class men) often cited their apparent knowledge of housework to support a view that a woman would be able to carry out domestic tasks, either at home or for an employer. The status of doctors and adjudicators as medical or legal experts enabled them to turn this assumed "common knowledge" of women's domestic lives into apparent facts. One adjudicator, however, challenged a doctor's apparent common knowledge. In a case where the medical referee stated that a woman in her fifties who had broken her arm was capable of "performing, dressmaking, sewing, domestic work, or light charring", the adjudicator questioned the basis of the doctor's knowledge. The doctor "frankly admitted" that he did not have much knowledge of what this kind of domestic work might involve. The adjudicator concluded that the claimant was incapable of work and that he could not

> conceive of any domestic work upon which an employer would be likely to employ her; and it appears to me that light charring is an academic phrase without relation to the realities of life. (Case 2/31, Ministry of Health 1923, p. 97)

In this case, the adjudicator challenged the apparent professional opinion of the doctor but replaced this with his own common knowledge of domestic service. In this example, the adjudicator's claim to common knowledge worked in the claimant's favour but this was not always the case.

As the system became more standardised after 1948, decision making was moved from the street-level bureaucracy of the Societies, where the individual opinions of Society administrators and their knowledge of claimants might sway decisions, to the behind the scenes bureaucracy of the Ministry of Pensions and the DHSS. Decisions at this stage were made on paper by civil servants, following strictly bureaucratised procedures, outlined in code manuals (e.g. Ministry of Pensions and National Insurance 1960; DHSS 1981). Here, the decision makers would be relying almost solely on the medical certificates from GPs and the second opinions provided by the RMO, combined with the guidance on the likely length of time to allow for particular conditions and the triggering evidence provided by sick visitors or other informers. Claimant evidence at this stage would arise only during appeals.

Some examples of post-war appeal cases where claimant evidence was important include many difficult cases regarding self-employed people and whether or not they had continued working while claiming benefit. Several of these concerned farmers or people running small business, where the claimants argued that they could not completely ignore their business while claiming benefits but provided detailed evidence to show that they were not really working. R(S)24/52 concerned a farmer, Mr A, who had been claiming benefit for several months after an accident. A sick visitor had visited the farm and observed him "wearing overalls and dirty boots", suggesting that Mr A was working. Mr A denied this, stressing that he had been "Seen in Wellington Boots by inspector - not overalls" and that he had continued to pay a manager to run the farm while had been unable to work (claimant evidence on form LT3 local tribunal, dated 31/5/52 in CT11/64). It is not clear whether anyone was convinced by the evidence regarding the wellington boots and the overalls but the Commissioner was convinced by the claimant's evidence that he had employed a manager to replace him. Examples like this where the claimant's evidence swayed a decision would only apply if a claimant appealed. At the appeal stage, decision makers would use a combination of medical evidence, other social evidence from witnesses or sick visitors and their own common knowledge assumptions about the world to weigh up conflicting evidence.

Incapacity Benefit and the Move to Points-Based Assessment

The major change in definitions of incapacity for work brought about by the introduction of Incapacity Benefit in the 1990s, followed by ESA in 2008, introduced a new points-based assessment of "functional capacity" against a set of statutory indicators. Part of the reasoning in bringing in the points-based assessment for Incapacity Benefit included a concern at the time that GP assessments were unreliable. The role of GPs had been explored in a Department of Social Security (DSS) sponsored research report (Ritchie et al. 1993). This reported that GPs had concerns about their role in assessing claimants for Invalidity Benefit and would have appreciated more help and training. Many also thought that assessments should be made by GPs since they knew their patients, rather than other official doctors who would not have the full picture. Many GPs agreed that they considered wider social factors in assessing their patients' capacity for work and were sympathetic to the problems of patients who were discriminated against in the job market, and to patients who would find the whole process of looking for work stressful and detrimental to their health (Ritchie et al. 1993). Mirroring many of the concerns from the early twentieth century, the DSS interpreted this to mean that GPs were "reluctant to contradict patients", that they "did not feel qualified to make judgements on a person's capacity for work" and that some were "influenced by local labour market conditions". The points-based assessment for Incapacity Benefit was designed to "refocus provision on people who were genuinely incapable of work" (DSS 1996, p. 2).

The new rules for Incapacity Benefit meant that more people were referred for an independent assessment than had been the case under the old Invalidity Benefit scheme. Most claimants were referred for an "all work test" assessment after twenty-eight weeks, although some were exempt (see Chapter 3) and others would be referred from the start of their claim, if they had not recently been in the labour market. While the GP certificate was still essential in establishing the initial claim and was sufficient for some people with specific impairments to qualify for Incapacity Benefit, these points-based assessments became the main source of evidence of incapacity for work. This change in the definition of incapacity for work meant that the control system and the role of second medical opinions also changed. When Incapacity Benefit was first introduced, the test was carried out by the Benefits Agency Medical Service (BAMS), which employed doctors on a contract basis. These assessments were no longer a second opinion on a claimant's capacity for work but highly regulated and formulaic assessments against the points system. The introduction of the new system required a major recruitment and training exercise, training doctors in the new system, involving 14,000 days of training in the first year (DSS 1996, p. 2).

The BAMS was soon disbanded as part of the government's process of outsourcing many activities in the name of efficiency. Arrangements were in place for contractors to bid for the medical services contract in 1996, and the contract was awarded initially to the SEMA Group in 1998 (NAO 2001). This organisation then employed doctors to carry out the medical assessments on behalf of the DSS. After an initial assessment by DSS staff, claimants would be awarded benefit or referred for a medical assessment, carried out by doctors employed by SEMA. The final decision on the claim was made by Benefits Agency staff, based on all the evidence submitted, including any specialist reports requested or submitted in addition to the SEMA report (NAO 2001, p. 47). The contract with SEMA continued through the early 2000s although the company was bought over several times during this period, with its name changing to Schlumberger, and finally to ATOS in 2004. When the contract was due for renewal in 2005, ATOS was again awarded the contract for another seven years (NAO 2012). Incapacity Benefit also introduced a specific element of claimant evidence into the procedure. The claim form included a questionnaire on "the claimant's views of his/her medical condition" (DSS 1994, p. 12). Although this introduced a formal opportunity for claimants to provide their own evidence, the questionnaire was heavily criticised as difficult for claimants to fill in and, perhaps more significantly, generally ignored in decision making. Disability groups had been supportive of the idea of self-assessment, but there were also reservations about the suitability of the questionnaire when it focused so closely on the medical test (Disability Alliance 1994).

Employment and Support Allowance

When ESA was introduced with its new revised points system in 2008, the net of points-based assessment was widened to include almost all claimants. This was a major change compared to Incapacity Benefit, where many claimants had been exempt from medical testing (see Chapter 3). The new two-part test introduced by ESA which separates successful claimants into those who have "limited capability for work" or "limited capability for work-related activities" means that the ESA assessment has to make this distinction too. Those found capable of work-related activities are subject to stringent work-seeking conditionality and are also eligible for lower rates of benefit. The complex tests introduced for ESA, therefore, matter not only for entitlement to benefit but also for what happens to those found eligible. The contract for medical assessment remained with ATOS, although the mechanisms for assessment were very different. ATOS subsequently withdrew from the contract and was replaced by Maximus in 2015 (NAO 2016).

Shortly after the introduction of ESA, the format of doctors' medical certificates changed from the "sick note" with the advice to "refrain from work" to the "fit note". The concept of the fit note came from a report in 2008 on solutions to the problem of occupational sickness. The report concerned sickness absence for those in work but also looked at people who were further from the labour market. The report recommended the fit note as part of the solution to this identified problem, based on a theory that people should not be told that they are "sick" but should instead be encouraged to focus on what they can do (Black 2008, p. 12). The form of the fit note was defined by regulations in 2010, which apply to medical certificates for both employer-based Statutory Sick Pay and other incapacity benefits such as ESA (Social Security Medical Evidence Regulations 2010).

Despite the change of language in ESA from "incapacity" to "limited capability", the fit note requires the doctor to state that the claimant is either "not fit for work" or "may be fit for work". The note allows for further comments such as advice about how an employer might assist in a return to work by amending duties, a phased return, altering hours or adapting the workplace (Social Security Medical Evidence Regulations 2010). Although the fit note was intended to move away from the binary fit for work/not fit for work distinction, in practice it is used as a "sick note", providing social security claimants with the first stage in the claiming process. Recent research shows that GPs are most unwilling to use the "may be fit for work" tick box, with only around seven per cent of notes using this option (Department for Work and Pensions and

Department of Health 2017, p. 42). This suggests that the wording and form of the fit note did little to change perceptions of its purpose.

Although the introduction of fit notes may not have had much impact on the claiming process, the changed definition of incapacity for work and the expanded use of second-tier assessors has had a much greater effect on people's experience of claiming benefits and the way in which different forms of evidence are assessed. The use of claimant evidence followed a similar pattern to that used for Incapacity Benefit. All claimants must complete a questionnaire with detailed questions about their health, impairments and their ability to carry out a range of tasks. As with Incapacity Benefit, claimants and campaigning organisations have criticised the forms for their length, their difficulty and their inability to capture the day-to-day realities of people's lives (Citizens Advice Scotland 2017; Harrington 2010; Litchfield 2013; Work and Pensions Committee 2009).

Another major change with ESA was the move from using doctors as the main assessors of the points system to the use of "healthcare professionals" (Harrington 2010). The Harrington review found that these healthcare professionals were appropriately recruited and trained for the job. Claimants were less impressed, with frustration often expressed that the healthcare professionals were not doctors or did not have appropriate specialist knowledge of particular health issues. The more recent Litchfield review also noted the lack of public confidence in the assessments by healthcare professionals (Litchfield 2014, p. 69). The principle of a healthcare professional, rather than a doctor, carrying out the medical tests, has been the focus of much of the public frustration with the ESA system, immortalised in the film *I Daniel Blake*, where the protagonist questions the healthcare professional's qualifications by asking "Are you medically qualified? Are you a nurse? Are you a doctor?" (Loach 2016).

The implementation of the Work Capability Assessment (WCA) was subject to annual independent reviews during its first five years (Harrington 2010, 2011, 2012; Litchfield 2013, 2014). The first review confirmed what campaigning organisations had long argued, that benefits decisions makers rarely challenged the medical assessment carried out for the WCA, usually "rubber-stamping" the opinion of the medical assessor (Harrington 2010, p. 10). This appears to follow a long history of the independent medical assessment being preferred over GP or other evidence in initial decision making on incapacity benefit claims. The fifth independent review of the WCA suggested that this had changed with decision makers somewhat less likely to rubber-stamp the medical assessor's assessment in "complex cases", which Litchfield interpreted as cases where the claimant is most likely to complain or appeal (Litchfield 2014, p. 51). Decision makers in these cases will use "medical records" relating to the claimant's diagnosis to support the decision but do not tend to look further to other non-medical sources of evidence. A House of Commons review of the WCA recommended giving decision makers more power to proactively seek out evidence from a range of professionals including occupational therapists and social workers as well as GPs (House of Commons Work and Pensions Committee 2014, p. 5).

There is no doubt that the everyday experience of claimants subjected to the ESA assessments has been unacceptable, with a recent enquiry by the Work and Pensions Committee noting that it had received "thousands of individual accounts of medical assessments that range from frustrating to gruelling and oral testimony from claimants and advocacy groups that strongly reinforced that picture" (Work and Pensions Committee 2017).

Criticism of ESA has often focussed on the day-to-day experiences of people being inappropriately subjected to medical testing, or being treated badly at assessment centres. ATOS themselves noted that it would be unlikely that the "toxicity" associated with ESA would be removed by a change of assessor (House of Commons Work and Pensions Committee 2014, para 76). Increasing public and media exposure of stories of people with severe impairments and degenerative health conditions led to the announcement that some claimants will be exempt from repeated assessments (Grover 2017). However, this will mean that only people diagnosed with particular types of severe and degenerative medical conditions will not have to be called back frequently for reassessment. It does not change the principles of ESA or the mechanisms of assessment for most claimants.

Conclusions

Stone demonstrated in 1984 that medical assessment had come to be the main mechanism for establishing "disability" in the twentieth century (Stone 1984, p. 108). This chapter has shown how the form and status of that medical assessment has changed across the twentieth and early twenty-first centuries. The privileged status of medical evidence has been a constant thread throughout the incapacity benefit regimes. Since the 1990s, it has taken a particular form, the points-based medical test, which has moved from the relying on the expert opinion of individual doctors to a standardised and, some have argued, bureaucratised tickbox approach (Gulland 2011). These standardised tests have come to hold a special status. Their basis in numbers suggests that incapacity for work can be quantified, implying something much more objective than the opinion of a doctor, however well qualified. In an interesting twist, the introduction of the healthcare professional as the main administrator of the test under ESA may have served to undermine the status of these tests. Critics of the ESA assessment process have pointed to the lack of expertise that these professionals hold. The box-ticking introduced by computerised assessment is singled out for its lack of sensitivity and inability to see the real challenges that many claimants face (Litchfield 2014).

This has led to heavy criticism and has led to calls for a more realistic assessment process that takes into account wider factors. There has been a debate, throughout the twentieth century, and continuing today, about the relative value of GP evidence compared with the alleged "objective" medical evidence that can be provided by second-level medical experts and "real world" knowledge that can be provided by a range of sources, including the claimant her/himself and the twentieth-century sick visitor system. The nature of the debate has changed but fundamental questions remain concerning what kind of evidence and what kind of expertise are required to assess capacity for work.

References

Black, Carol. 2008. *Working for a Healthier Tomorrow Dame Carol Black's Review of the Health of Britain's Working Age Population*. London: TSO.

Bonner, David, Ian Hooker, and Robin White, eds. 1991. *Non-means Tested Benefits: The Legislation 1991 Edition*. London: Sweet and Maxwell.

Citizens Advice Scotland. 2017. *Burden of Proof: The Role of Medical Evidence in the Benefits System*. Edinburgh: Citizens Advice Scotland.

Department of Health and Social Security. 1981. *Sickness Benefit Law and Procedure. Code SB 1969, as Amended, 1981*. London: HMSO.

Department for Work and Pensions, and Department of Health. 2017. *Improving Lives: The Future of Work, Health and Disability CM 9526*. London: HMSO.

Department of Social Security. 1994. *The Medical Assessment for Incapacity Benefit*. London: HMSO.

———. 1996. *Social Security Committee Incapacity Benefit Minutes of Evidence*. London: The Stationery Office.

Disability Alliance. 1983. *Invalid Procedures? A Study of the Control System for Invalidity Benefit*. London: Disability Alliance Educational Research Association.

———. 1994. *Response to 'A Consultation on the Medical Assessment for Incapacity Benefit'*. London: Disability Alliance Educational Research Association.

Foster, William Justus, and F. G. Taylor. 1937. *National Health Insurance*. 3rd ed. London: Sir Isaac Pitman and Sons.

Foucault, Michel. 1973. *The Birth of the Clinic: An Archaeology of Medical Perception*. Translated by Alan Sheridan. London: Routledge.

Grover, Chris. 2017. 'Ending Reassessment for Employment and Support Allowance for Some Disabled People in the UK'. *Disability & Society* 32 (8): 1269–74.

Gulland. 2011. 'Ticking Boxes: Understanding Decision Making in Employment and Support Allowance'. *Journal of Social Security Law* 18: 69–86.

Harrington, Malcolm. 2010. *An Independent Review of the Work Capability Assessment.* London: The Stationery Office.

———. 2011. *An Independent Review of the Work Capability Assessment—Year Two.* London: The Stationery Office.

———. 2012. *An Independent Review of the Work Capability Assessment—Year Three.* London: The Stationery Office.

House of Commons Work and Pensions Committee. 2014. *Employment and Support Allowance and Work Capability Assessments First Report of Session 2014–15 HC 302.* London: HMSO.

Hughes, Bill. 2015. 'What Can a Foucauldian Analysis Contribute'. In *Foucault and the Government of Disability*, edited by Shelley Tremain, 2nd ed. Ann Arbor: University of Michigan Press.

Lawrence, Charles. 1926. *Report of the Royal Commission on National Health Insurance Cmd. 2596 Appendices to Minutes of Evidence Vols. 1–4.* Cmd. 2596. London: HMSO.

Lipsky, Michael. 2010. *Street Level Bureaucracy: Dilemmas of the Individual in Public Services.* 30th Anniversary Expanded Edition. New York: Russell Sage Foundation.

Litchfield, Paul. 2013. *An Independent Review of the Work Capability Assessment—Year Four.* London: TSO.

———. 2014. *An Independent Review of the Work Capability Assessment—Year Five.* London: TSO.

Loach, Ken. 2016. *I, Daniel Blake.* Sixteen Films.

Ministry of Health. 1920. *First Annual Report of the Ministry of Health 1919–20. Part IV. Administration of National Health Insurance (1917 to 31st March 1920). Welsh Board of Health.* Cmd. 913. London: HMSO.

———. 1921. *Second Annual Report of the Ministry of Health, 1920–1921.* Cmd. 1446. London: HMSO.

———. 1923. *Reports of Decisions on Appeals and Applications Under Section 67 of the National Insurance Act 1911 and Section 27 of the National Insurance Act 1913, Vol 2—Part I.* London: HMSO.

———. 1946. *Report of the Ministry of Health for the Year Ended 31st March 1946 Including the Report of the Chief Medical Officer on the State of the Public Health for the Year Ended 31st December 1945.* Cmd. 7119. London: HMSO.

Ministry of Pensions and National Insurance. 1953. *National Insurance Act, 1946 National Insurance (Industrial Injuries) Act 1946 Medical Certification: Notes for Chairmen and Members of Local Tribunals L.T. Memo No 4.* London: HMSO.

———. 1960. *Instructions to National Insurance Offices on Law and Procedure Relating to Sickness Benefits under the National Insurance Acts Code SB.* London: HMSO.

National Audit Office. 1989. *Invalidity Benefit: Report by the Comptroller and Auditor General HC 91.* London: HMSO.

———. 2001. *The Medical Assessment of Incapacity and Disability Benefits Report by the Comptroller and Auditor General HC 280.* London: HMSO.

———. 2012. *Contract Management of Medical Services HC 627*. London: The Stationery Office.

———. 2016. *Contracted-Out Health and Disability Assessments HC 609*. London: House of Commons.

National Health Insurance Commission (England). 1915. *Reports of Decisions on Appeals and Applications Under Section 67 of the National Insurance Act 1911 and Section 27 of the National Insurance Act 1913*. Cd. 7810.

———. 1916. *Reports of Decisions on Appeals and Applications Under Section 67 of the National Insurance Act 1911 and Section 27 of the National Insurance Act 1913 Part III*. Cd. 8239. London: HMSO.

———. 1917. *Reports of Decisions on Appeals and Applications Under Section 67 of the National Insurance Act 1911 and Section 27 of the National Insurance Act 1913 Part IV*. Cd. 8474. London: HMSO.

———. 1919. *Reports of Decisions on Appeals and Applications Under Section 67 of the National Insurance Act 1911 and Section 27 of the National Insurance Act 1913 Part V*. Cmd. 134. London: HMSO.

National Health Insurance Committee (Joint Committee). 1917. *National Health Insurance. Report on the Administration of National Health Insurance During the Years 1914–17*. Cd. 8890. London: HMSO.

National Health Insurance Joint Committee. 1914. *National Health Insurance. Report of the Departmental Committee on Sickness Benefit Claims Under the National Insurance Act*. Cd. 7687. London: HMSO.

National Insurance Advisory Committee. 1976. *Social Security Act 1975 Social Security (Medical Evidence) Regulations 1976 (S.I. 1976 No. 615). Report of the National Insurance Advisory Committee HC 349*. London: House of Commons. 1975-065773.

Ogus, Anthony, and Eric Barendt. 1978. *The Law of Social Security*. London: Butterworths.

Ritchie, J., K. Ward, and W. Duldig. 1993. *GPs and Invalidity Benefit: A Qualitative Study of the Role of GPs in the Award of Invalidity Benefit DSS Report No. 18*. London: HMSO.

Scottish Board of Health. 1923. *Fourth Annual Report of the Scottish Board of Health*. Edinburgh: HMSO.

Stone, Deborah. 1984. *The Disabled State*. Philadelphia: Temple University Press.

Valverde, Mariana. 2003. *Law's Dream of a Common Knowledge*. The Cultural Lives of Law. Princeton: Princeton University Press.

Work and Pensions Committee. 2009. *Decision Making and Appeals in the Benefits System Second Report of Session 2009–10 HC 313*. London: HMSO.

———. 2017. 'ATOS, Maximus and Capita Questioned on "Gruelling" Medical Assessments'. http://www.parliament.uk/business/committees/committees-a-z/commons-select/work-and-pensions-committee/news-parliament-2017/atos-maximus-capita-medicals-17-19/.

5

Bridge Toll Attendants and Driving a Quiet Horse: The Labour Market and Structural Barriers to Work

Introduction

In 1919, Miss T claimed Sickness Benefit after her wrist was damaged as a result of tuberculosis and subsequent surgery. She had previously worked as a domestic servant. After six months, when she started claiming Disablement Benefit, her Society referred her to a medical referee who found her "fit for work requiring the use of one hand". The Society continued to pay Miss T Disablement Benefit for four months, to give her time to find another job. They then stopped her benefit on the grounds that she "had made no serious attempt to find suitable work". When Miss T appealed, she disagreed with the Society, arguing that she "had been most diligent in attempting to find work, through the Labour Exchange and otherwise but was unsuccessful". The adjudicator at her appeal decided that she was capable of work and not entitled to benefit, saying that it was her duty to find work, even if that would be more challenging for her, given her impairment:

> It is for the applicant for insurance benefit to prove that he is suffering from a specific disease or bodily or mental disablement of such a nature and to such a degree that he is unable to do any work which it is reasonably open to him to obtain. It is common knowledge that persons with the use of only one hand frequently find and engage in remunerative work. The difficulty of obtaining such work may be greater than that of obtaining ordinary work. (Case 2/9, 1919, Ministry of Health 1923, p. 34)

Miss T's case is an example of how the definition of incapacity for work has usually ignored the question of whether there are any suitable jobs for disabled people. Miss T had been unable to find a job but she was considered to be capable of work nevertheless. Thirty years later, another appeal heard the case of Mr W, a sixty-four-year-old miner who had lost much of the use of his left hand in an industrial accident. He had been claiming Sickness Benefit for four years and his benefit had been stopped after two Regional Medical Officers (RMO) found him "fit for work not entailing full use of his left hand". Mr W was represented at his hearing by an official of the National Union of Mineworkers. The representative stressed the difficulty of finding work in the area, while the local office referred to the recent opening of several factories in the area as possible sources of work for Mr W. The Commissioner found Mr W fit for work, arguing that the existence, or otherwise, of actual job vacancies was irrelevant:

> the question in claims for sickness benefit is not whether this claimant can get work but whether he can do work. (R(S)24/51, case papers, filed in CT11/208)

These examples, from 1919 to 1951, show that it has been central to the operation of incapacity benefits in the UK that people who are incapable of work can be distinguished from people who are unemployed, since these two categories create different expectations of labour market participation. Unemployment benefits are always conditional on engagement with the labour market, often requiring explicit evidence of work seeking, whereas incapacity benefit claimants have usually been assumed to be exempt from this requirement. This has changed recently in the UK with the new work-seeking conditionalities introduced for many claimants of Employment and Support Allowance (ESA). However, the argument in this book is that the distinction between conditional unemployment benefits and unconditional incapacity benefits is much more fluid, since many incapacity benefit claimants have also been expected to show attachment to the labour market. Failure to show sufficient effort to look for work could be used as evidence of malingering and thus evidence of unemployment rather than incapacity. Others have been exempted from this requirement but only if they could be labelled as unlikely to ever join or return to the labour market. The current rules for ESA make this division explicit by allocating people into three groups: people who are fully fit for work and must instead claim Jobseeker's Allowance; those who are expected to return to the labour market and so are required to make themselves work ready, and those who are considered to be unlikely to return to the labour market and so are exempt from labour market participation. Under ESA, assessments of capacity for work are based on an entirely medical model of disability, which takes very little account of social or structural barriers to employment, including the state of the labour market where the claimant lives. Yet, access to work is highly structured by the labour market: in times and places of high unemployment, it is more difficult for disabled people or people with chronic health issues to find work. Conversely at times of high labour demand, for example, during the two world wars of the twentieth century, access to paid work has been somewhat easier for some disabled people.

This chapter explores the division between unemployment and incapacity and the role of the labour market in definitions of incapacity for work, first of all by considering the legal position, then considering the discursive methods used to define some claimants as capable of work because of their perceived lack of engagement with the labour market. Finally, the chapter considers the extent to which the social model of disability can help to clarify the issue.

The Relationship Between Unemployment and Incapacity

Structural unemployment and access to work for disabled people are clearly related. Tomlinson's and Whiteside's work on the relationship between Sickness Benefit and Unemployment Benefit during the depression of the 1930s makes this very clear (Tomlinson 1984; Whiteside 1987, 2014). Macnicol's work, looking at patterns of benefits payments and economic changes over a hundred and fifty years, takes the argument further by showing the relationship between unemployment, incapacity benefit claims and definitions of old age and pension provision. He has described it as a "truism" that claims for incapacity benefits go up in times of high unemployment (Macnicol 2013, p. 37). Work on variations in claims for Incapacity Benefit shows a clear link between benefit claims and structural unemployment (Houston and Lindsay 2010; Webster et al. 2010).

The task of matching up individuals with particular jobs in an open labour market is clearly structured by the social characteristics of potential workers and the social expectations of employers, even when demand for labour is high. Where demand for labour is low and when people have characteristics which may make their chances of finding a job more difficult, the fiction of open competition in the labour market becomes more visible. The UK welfare state deals with this problem by defining the unsuccessful job seekers as unemployed. For people with chronic health issues, or those who are disabled by the employment market, being defined as unemployed moves the responsibility for finding a job to the individual. Unemployment benefits are conditional on claimants making sufficient effort to look for jobs. Those who do not or cannot meet these conditions may find that their benefits are cut or that they are not entitled to benefit at all, the theory being that this will drive them so seek harder, to travel further or to accept lower pay or poorer conditions of employment. This theoretical reasoning does not necessarily work in practice but is essential to the structure of work-seeking conditionality in unemployment benefits (Paz-Fuchs 2008; Wright 2012). Yet, in the discourse and legal reasoning for incapacity benefits, there has, until recently, been an assumption that there is clear water between incapacity and unemployment. Incapacity benefits systems have however been concerned by the possibility of "malingerers" and have attempted to find ways to weed out those who are either faking their health problems or who have genuine health issues but are making insufficient effort to find work within their capabilities. This approach to identifying malingerers takes no account of the social barriers which make it difficult for many disabled people to find work. New explicit work-seeking conditionality in ESA is based on an assumption that malingerers can be identified; using this revelatory sign but that there is little evidence that it has this effect (Dwyer et al. 2018). However, the history of incapacity benefits shows that there was implicit work-seeking conditionality in the ways in which decisions about incapacity have been made at the street level.

Statutes and Case Law

There were no references to the labour market or to work-seeking conditionality in statutory definitions of incapacity for work until the introduction of ESA in 2008. Although not constituting formal case law (see Chapter 1), the early twentieth-century appeals did include some revealing discussion of engagement with labour market which later decision makers might refer to for guidance, for example, in the case from 1919, discussed at the beginning of this chapter. Another example from the early twentieth century showing the relationship between unemployment and incapacity can be found in 1928 where the claimant, Mr H, was a former coal miner, living in an area where most of the work available was connected to the coal industry. It was accepted that Mr H might be able to do "lighter work" within the mining industry. The adjudicator at his appeal recognised that there was a shortage of suitable jobs in the local area but concluded that the economic situation as such should not be taken into account in assessing capacity for work:

> I fear there is little chance of alternative employment being, in the present state of the local coal trade, available. The man will in due course be entitled to unemployment benefit. (Case PIN 63/2/463, 1928)

Here, the adjudicator made an explicit reference to the availability of unemployment benefit, implying that Mr H had fallen on the wrong side of the incapacity/unemployment boundary. The adjudicator also cited Case 82 (discussed below, p. 84) from the published cases in support of the view that unemployment was distinguishable from incapacity. These examples show how the issue was addressed by some adjudicators in the early twentieth century. Reported National Insurance Commissioners' Decisions after 1948 did create case law and began to address the issue, with R(S)11/51 confirming that the state of the local labour market should not be a consideration in assessing capacity for work. The Commissioners referred to an earlier unreported case CS 316/50 where it was argued that the state of the local labour market was not relevant to the assessment of incapacity. In R(S)11/51, they agreed that "This statement of general principle appears to us to be correct" (R(S)11/51, para 5). The decision in R(S)24/51, discussed above, p. 80, is another example from this time.

Thirty years later, the next key case on the question of the labour market was R(S)2/82, at a time of high unemployment. Again this concerned a disabled miner, aged fifty-one. The claimant had been claiming benefit for five years, since injuring his back. He was found fit for work and appealed to a local tribunal which upheld his case. The local office appealed to the Commissioners. The key legal point was whether or not the labour market was relevant in making decisions about incapacity for work. The claimant's representative from the National Union of Mineworkers argued that there was no realistic prospect of employment for the claimant in his local area. The local office produced a report from the local Disablement Resettlement Office that there were around a thousand vacancies in the area which would be suitable for the claimant. The claimant's representative noted that the local level of unemployment was twenty-four thousand, suggesting that there was no realistic prospect of the claimant actually getting any of these jobs. The Commissioners considered these points but decided that the decision must be made on the basis of assessed capacity, not job availability (R(S)2/82). Although this excluded the situation where the only job the claimant could do was an "imaginary job" (Bonner et al. 1991, p. 25, citing CS19/1987), the abstract concept of separating out whether someone could do a job if it was available continued to be kept separate from whether in reality, they were likely to get such a job.

The introduction of the points-based medical tests in the mid-1990s removed the need for these abstract debates, although Incapacity Benefits systems continued to require that people were categorised as either incapable of work or unemployed and patterns of claim continued to reflect structural unemployment. ESA brought in new categories of people who should be making an effort to look for work but also continues to define successful claimants as distinguishable from those who are unemployed.

Attachment to the Labour Market

Although the statutes do not discuss the role of the labour market in assessing incapacity for work, the later twentieth-century case law was fairly clear and, to some extent, reflected practice from early years. The earlier twentieth century-appeals cases, however, demonstrate another way of looking at how the problem was understood. Discourse in the early appeal cases and policy documents shows that there was an attempt to distinguish between people who were unemployed and people who are incapable of work by making judgements about whether claimants were making sufficient effort to make themselves available for work. The example of Miss T from 1919, cited at the start of this chapter, is an example of this. Miss T's case was typical of many cases from the early years of the 1911 Sickness Benefit scheme. Another example comes from 1916, concerning Mr O, a fifty-six-year-old former miner. Mr O had lumbago and rheumatism and could no longer work in the mines. He was one of the first people to claim the new Sickness Benefit. After six months, he became entitled to Disablement Benefit and his Approved Society referred him for a second medical opinion. This second doctor agreed that he was clearly unable to work in the mines but believed that he was capable of "light work". When he appealed the adjudicators found him to be incapable of work and entitled to benefit, but they felt the need to stress at the end of the decision that Mr O had a continuing responsibility to make himself available for work:

> With regard to the future we think that the Society might properly consider the suggestion that we have made above [to pay benefit in the mean time] and afford the Appellant a reasonable period in which he may endeavour to fit himself to obtain other work, his case being subject to reconsideration when that period has elapsed. (Case 82, NHIC 1917, p. 213)

Some cases in the earliest appeals against refusals of benefits provide examples of past unemployment or recent periods of sickness being used as evidence that claimants were likely to be malingering. For example, in a case from 1915, Mr S, a sixty-nine-year-old tailor, claimed Sickness Benefit and his Approved Society refused to pay, commenting that "From the look of his card and book it is a clear case of out-of-work, not sickness benefit". The reference to his card was an allusion to his record of work and recent claims, suggesting that he had only been intermittently in the labour market. The adjudicators in this case disagreed and found that there was clear medical evidence that Mr S was incapable of work and noted

> It was abundantly clear from the evidence from the Appellant himself and from that of his daughter with whom he lived, that he was wholly incapacitated through rheumatism and unable to follow his own or any other occupation. (Case 17, NHIC 1915, p. 49)

Here, the Approved Society made a judgement about a claimant's authenticity based on his recent record of variable employment. Although the adjudicators rejected this approach, expecting a stronger reliance on medical evidence, the case suggests that Approved Societies might well be using this kind of knowledge of past unemployment to make judgements about which side of the unemployment/incapacity line claimants fell. There is another example in a case from 1918. Mr F claimed Sickness Benefit and his Society stopped benefit after four days because they believed that he had been "malingering on a previous occasion" (Case 137, NHIC 1919, p. 321). When Mr F appealed, the adjudicators disagreed with the Society's view, arguing that the previous claims were irrelevant and that the Society should make its decision based on current medical evidence, not on past experience and hearsay about the claimant's alleged malingering. These examples suggest that Societies were using judgements about past sickness and unemployment records as well as local knowledge about perceived attachment to the labour market to make decisions about new claims. On the other hand, in some appeal hearings, claimants were applauded for their efforts in trying to get back to work and these efforts were regarded as evidence of their incapacity for work. A case from 1919 concerned Mr L, a "discharged soldier", who had been a weaver before the First World War. He was in receipt of a war pension in compensation for his war injuries and so this provided verification of his level of impairment. Since he could no longer work as a weaver, Mr L's appeal concerned whether there was any work which he could be expected to do. In an attempt to get back to work, Mr L had tried working in a grocer's shop and had started and stopped a training course in clerical work. His Approved Society interpreted these efforts as evidence of capacity for work. The adjudicators, however, took a contrasting view:

> We regard his unsuccessful attempts extending over three weeks to do the work of a "general man" in the grocer's shop his improvement under treatment and his inability to do the work of the clerical training course as corroboration of our view [that he was incapable of work]. (Case 140, NHIC 1919, 330)

An example, from the 1920s, shows the adjudicator praising the claimant, Mr C, for making an effort to look for work and saying that it was the claimant's effort in looking for work which convinced the adjudicator of his honesty and authenticity and therefore helped to conclude the case that he was currently incapable of work:

> He has been constantly applying by letter for such advertised jobs as he thinks he could undertake such as the job of a caretaker canvasser or collector. .. he has only heard … of one suitable job.. for which he applied unsuccessfully.[…] If the Appellant were found to be neglecting real opportunities of obtaining work within his capacity or even of training himself in such a manner as might be reasonably expected to obtain work within his capacity, it might well I think be reasonable to infer that in the circumstances his failure to obtain work was due rather to lack of inclination and effort than of capacity and that he was no longer to be regarded as incapable of work. (PIN 63/2/452, 1928)

This view that the claimant's failure to look for work might be evidence of "lack of inclination rather than lack of capacity" is a clear statement that adjudicators considered people's perceived effort in looking for work as part of the assessment of their capacity for work. In other cases, the opposite occurred as the existence of jobs in the local labour market was used as evidence that the claimant *was* capable of work. In Cases 93 and 100, both of which concerned men who had leg amputations, adjudicators were unsympathetic to the claimants for their apparent unwillingness to look for work. Mr P was a former shipyard worker who had been claiming Sickness and Disablement Benefit for around eighteen months after an amputation. His benefit had been stopped when a sick visitor and a medical referee considered him fit for light work. In their decision that Mr P was fit for work, the adjudicators spelled out their view that he should be looking for work:

> It is his duty to make every endeavour to fit himself to earn his livelihood in some other way and during the past twelve months he appears to have made no attempt to do this. The commissioners have had other cases before them where insured persons have suffered even graver misfortunes and have yet fitted themselves again to become wage earners and they cannot believe that in the present case the Appellant has exhausted all the means upon him to do the same.

They went on to say

> [we] desire it to be clearly understood that a Society are justified in refusing to pay benefit where they are satisfied that a member has not made every effort that

is in his power to overcome a disability but is content to let matters drift and to remain a pensioner on the Society's funds. (Case 93, NHIC 1917, p. 232)

The adjudicators considered that a failure to make an effort to get back to work was, in itself, evidence of capacity for work. Case 100 also concerned a man who had a leg amputation. Mr W was a thirty-nine-year-old factory worker who had returned to work after the amputation but had stopped working in the factory, as a result of "neurasthenia". Mr W claimed benefit successfully for two years but benefit was stopped after a referral to a medical referee. At his appeal hearing, there was a discussion about whether the medical evidence supported his claim of incapacity. However, the Society's main argument, as supported by the adjudicators, was that he was not making sufficient effort to look for work within his capacities.

> Mr H (secretary of society) suggested to the Appellant that he should try to get work and even gave him the name and address of a person who had promised that he would find him work. (Case 100, NHIC 1917, p. 243)

The adjudicators appeared to set great store by this kind of evidence, referring to there being "no difficulty at all in present circumstances in getting employment in the trade with which he is familiar". This reference to the state of the labour market shows that, although later cases argued that high unemployment was not a consideration in assessing incapacity for work, a buoyant labour market could be evidence of a failure to make an effort, and thus evidence of capacity. There is a contradiction in thinking here, where on the one hand, the labour market is considered to be not relevant if there is a shortage of jobs, while, on the other hand, plentiful jobs can count as evidence of a claimant's lack of effort in seeking work.

Case 2/20 included a similar discussion of the claimant's failure to look for work as evidence of his capacity for it. The claimant, Mr M, had worked as a signalman on the railways for thirty-seven years but was unable to continue "because he was too deaf". Mr M claimed that his hearing impairment, a visual impairment, headaches and difficulty sleeping made it difficult for him to work. On the other hand, the medical report from the Society said "I cannot think that he is unable and unfit to perform any kind of work whatever. If the will to work were there he would soon be at it". The adjudicator concluded that Mr M was capable of work. Tellingly, the adjudicator noted in his report:

> The partial disablement of the appellant compels sympathy but that sympathy would have been greater and the appellant's case much stronger had he complied

with the respondents' suggestion and tried to obtain some work suitable to his condition. (Case 2/20, Ministry of Health 1923, p. 57)

This suggests that any, unsuccessful, attempts to look for work might have helped Mr M's case but the fact that he had not even tried went against him. In a later case, from the 1920s an adjudicator found that a young woman, Miss S, aged twenty-three, was eligible for benefit. Miss S had contracted tuberculosis five years earlier and, although it was not still active, her doctor believed that any exertion would be detrimental to her health. The adjudicator could not think of any work that Miss S could do which would offer "true remuneration" and upheld her appeal. However, the adjudicator felt it necessary to note at the end of the decision his "guidance for the appellant", where he said that "a review of the circumstances in the near future would not be unreasonable", indicating to the Society that they should keep an eye on this claimant and make sure that she was making an effort to get back to work:

> She would be well advised not to treat this award as any ground for refraining from a genuine effort to improve her state of health and so to attain to a capacity for some form of employment. At the hearing the appellant seemed to suffer from an inertia of mind and outlook which, if persisted in, is likely to result in the mistake of regarding the receipt of benefit as a pension. (PIN 63/2/459, 1928)

There is a clear warning in this statement that Miss S was expected to start looking for work again before long or risk losing her benefit. Another woman in 1928 was Miss M, an unmarried woman in her fifties who had worked as a dressmaker but had been unable to work since a road accident, which had led to mental health issues. The adjudicator accepted medical evidence that Miss M had no physical impairments and that she was not "malingering". However, he felt that it would be good for her to get back to work and dismissed her appeal. In making this decision, the adjudicator went on to consider whether she ought to be reconsidered for benefit sometime in the future:

> I feel bound to state that this is a case in which in the near future such a review may well be desirable in that the effect of a further period without receipt of benefit may throw some light on the question whether or not mental incapacity may reasonably in the future be held to exist. (PIN 63/2/437, 1928)

In other words "let's see what happens if we take the money away from her", an example here of what Stone describes as a "revelatory sign", a test that will check whether or not the claimant is genuine in their claim to incapacity (Stone 1984,

p. 101). These cases from the early years of the National Insurance Scheme show a clear argument that people with impairments who could no longer continue in their original trades were expected to make every effort to look for alternative work. In some of these cases, it was the apparent lack of willingness to seek work which was used as evidence of the claimants' capacity, rather than a medical assessment as such, which led to their benefit being stopped.

Alternative Work

Another way in which decision makers might argue that a claimant was capable of work was by suggesting alternative work that they might be able to do. These cases are particularly illuminating in showing the structural barriers to work for many claimants. Suggestions of alternative work were not required in the legislation although case law in the later twentieth century led to the listing of alternative jobs as common practice. In the earlier part of the twentieth century, consideration of alternative jobs was often used as a discursive device to show that a claimant was capable of work. An early example of the custom of suggesting alternative work as a way of demonstrating capacity for work comes from 1928 concerning Mr C (discussed above, p. 86) who was a former furnace-man who had not worked since a stroke some 8 years previously. He had lost his ability to speak for three months and had been using a "bath chair", although was now able to walk a little. It was suggested that Mr C could "drive a quiet horse and do goods delivery work of a light character". Quite how he was supposed to find work in which the main requirement was a "quiet horse" did not seem to concern the Society. Fortunately for Mr C, the adjudicator agreed that the suggestion of driving a quiet horse was not sufficient evidence of capacity for work and awarded him benefit, arguing that the test was whether "he would [...] be regarded as an eligible candidate for most kinds of work by the ordinary employer" (PIN 63/2/452, 1928).

This view that the test of incapacity was whether or not Mr C would be an "eligible candidate" was in contrast to the usual assessment of capacity to do work rather than to get work. Over the twentieth century, decision makers varied in their emphasis on specifying what alternative work a claimant could do. An analysis of cases from the early twentieth century shows an interesting, if unsurprising, pattern. Almost all the occupations suggested to claimants as alternatives to their usual work were heavily gendered. Men were frequently told that they could work as caretakers or watchmen, while it was almost always suggested to women that they could do domestic work. Women were very frequently told that they could work as housekeepers, cleaners or domestic servants, or that they could take in work at home, doing knitting, sewing, laundry or mending. One of the differences between the alternative occupations suggested for men and those for women was that the suggested occupations for women often entailed homeworking, while suggestions for men were more likely to be as employed earners outside the home. Examples from the 1920s where homeworking was suggested include Miss C, who was no longer able to work as a shorthand secretary as a result of a stroke. In an effort to regain her ability to work, she had acquired a typewriter and was relearning how to type with her affected hand. The adjudicator decided that because she was capable of using a typewriter, and had been taking the trouble to relearn how to type after the stroke, she could work from home as a typist. However, echoing some of the stories that have appeared in the press in the UK in relation to recent assessments for incapacity benefits where people have later been hospitalised or have died, the decision carried a footnote which noted that since the date of the decision:

> The appellant lost the sight of her right eye … which would seem to indicate that her incapacity is progressive and I understand that she is shortly to return to hospital. In that event I understand from her Society they naturally are prepared to admit that she is again incapable of work and recommence the payment of benefit. (PIN 63/3/475, 1928)

Miss C's case concerned her ability to carry out clerical work related to the job that she had previously held. However, there are many cases where the discussion of women's capacity to work from home seems more closely linked to their gendered role in the home. Miss B, who had epilepsy and had held several jobs in the past, as a bookkeeper, typist and domestic servant, but had frequently lost these jobs because employers did not like her having seizures in the workplace. The adjudicator in this case accepted in full that Miss B had the health issues she claimed and that this would prevent her from getting work in the open labour market but believed that her ability to work from home meant that she was not incapable of work:

> I have come to the conclusion that the Appellant is … able to do clerical work including typewriting and bookkeeping, domestic work and a certain amount of sewing and knitting but that she is unlikely ever to get employment in any of this work outside her home because of her fits. The Appellant however is an intelligent and capable girl and with her abilities ought, with endeavour, to be able to earn more than her disablement by work at home either by sewing and knitting or by typewriting or bookkeeping. (PIN 63/1/411, 1927)

It is clear that Miss B's difficulty in finding work outside the home was caused by discrimination by employers who "did not like" her seizures. The issue of discrimination in Miss B's case is discussed in more detail below, p. 97. Miss B, like Miss C, above, had worked as a clerical worker in the past and so it seems reasonable that the adjudicator thought she might be able to continue doing this kind of work from home. However, the adjudicator also referred to the possibility that Miss B might be able to do "domestic work", from home including sewing or knitting. These activities are clearly gendered and there are many references in the appeal cases to the possibility that women could do this kind of work from home. Working from home did not appear to be considered for men or if it was, it was not considered seriously.

In the example of Mr O from 1916, discussed above, p. 84, the doctor for the Society had recognised that he could not work in damp conditions or do heavy manual work but suggested that he could work from home. When the adjudicators upheld his appeal, considering that he was unfit for work, they did not discuss the proposal that homeworking would be an option for Mr O. Similarly, in a case from 1919, it was suggested that a Mr L could do work "addressing envelopes". Mr L was a "skilled workman" who was no longer able to carry out his usual trade after a stroke. Although there was extensive discussion of the possible work that he might do, the possibility of addressing envelopes, presumably from home, was not taken seriously (Case 130, NHIC 1919, p. 306). (For further discussion of Mr L's case, see below, p. 100.)

This suggests that the option of homeworking was usually only considered seriously for women, reflecting gendered assumptions about what kind of work could be done in the home and who should do such work. Gendered expectations of what kinds of occupations were suitable for men and women are not at all surprising but they illustrate that the argument that the definition of incapacity for work was dependent on different assumptions about what men and women could do. It was never suggested to men that they could work as domestic servants, and it was never suggested to women that they could do the range of jobs usually expected of men. There were a few occupations which were suggested for both men and women. These included lift attendants, shop work and clerical work.

The idea that people claiming incapacity benefits could work as lift attendants or similar seemed to become embedded in decision makers' thinking about suitable work for disabled people. These became "reserved occupations" after the Second World War where disabled people would often be referred for this kind of work by Disablement Resettlement Officers (Shah and Priestly 2011, p. 122). However, the idea that this kind of work was suitable for disabled people predates this. The first suggestion that a claimant could work as a lift operator that I have seen was in 1927 when Miss N claimed benefit because she was unable to carry out her previous job as a shorthand typist as a result of a severe visual impairment and hearing impairment. It was accepted that she could not work as a typist but the RMO thought that she could "work a lift or act as a cloakroom attendant". Her own doctor, however, disagreed and said that he "did not consider that she would be able to act as a lift attendant as she would not be able to see sufficiently well to bring the lift regularly to the right level". In Miss N's case, the adjudicator agreed with her own doctor and upheld her appeal, confirming her entitlement to benefit (PIN 63/1/409).

Work as a lift attendant was also suggested in 1929 for Mr S, a sixty-year-old-former labourer who had a heart condition and had been assessed by his own doctor as "physically a man of 70 years of age and his condition is chronic and incurable". The adjudicator in this case also found Mr S to be incapable of work and upheld his appeal, noting that "I cannot regard either of these jobs [the work of a watchman or lift attendant] as a job which would be reasonably available to him" (PIN 63/4/525). Mr S lived in a rural area in Lancashire and perhaps the adjudicator's reference to the reasonable availability of this kind of work referred to the lack of premises for which watchmen or lift attendants would be needed, rather than the labour market as such. The reference to work as a lift attendant or watchman suggests that the RMO had a mental list of likely suitable work for older disabled men. On the other hand, women were almost always considered to be able to find work either in factories or in domestic labour of some kind. The fact that such work might bring very low levels of pay was not considered relevant.

It is useful to compare the unwritten work-seeking requirements in the interwar incapacity benefit scheme with the more explicit work-seeking requirements of the unemployment benefit scheme at the time. The "genuinely seeking work" test of the interwar unemployment benefit scheme is well known to social historians and historians of social policy as a particularly harsh mechanism for weeding out "scroungers" from access to benefits. But the genuinely seeking work test did allow unemployment benefit claimants to exclude jobs which were not paid at a reasonable rate for the job (Deacon 1976, p. 23). Unemployment Benefit claimants were also only expected to look for work which they were "reasonable capable of performing", although there were gendered and class assumptions about what might be. Women, for example, were almost always assumed to be capable of domestic service work (Deacon 1976, pp. 23–25). These gendered assumptions were also used in incapacity benefits decision making. However, the question of adequacy of pay was not. For more discussion of the issue of pay, see Chapter 7. In the male world of workmen's compensation in the mining industry, there were similar battles over whether disabled men were able to carry out "light work", what that work might consist of and the realities of such work being available (Turner and McIvor 2017).

Attachment to the Labour Market After 1948

Although the case law in the post-war era was, in some respects, clear about the irrelevance of the local labour market, individual decisions did sometimes appear to take account of a claimant's unsuccessful attempts to find work as evidence of incapacity. In a case from 1954, a Commissioner's decision concerned a fifty-seven-year-old coal miner in Wales, Mr H, who had been injured in an industrial accident and was no longer able to work in the mines. The examining medical officer considered that he was fit for some kind of light work. Mr H and his own doctor disagreed. In their evidence to the Commissioner, Mr H and his representative included information about jobs that he had applied for and failed to get. Copies of letters from possible employers are included in the archive file, including statements such as:

> "The above named person has applied for employment here. Unfortunately we have nothing to offer him". "I have nothing to offer him" "There is no suitable work for him".

The Commissioner accepted these letters as evidence of his incapacity for work rather than as evidence of a lack of jobs:

> The claimant has submitted notes from five different employers stating that he is unsuitable or that they have no work to offer him. I regard those applications for employment not as evidence that the claimant considers himself to be capable of doing some kind of work, which he is seeking, but rather as tending to show that there is no work which he is capable of performing. (R(S)10/54, correspondence in TNA CT11/212)

This decision was also referred to by the Commissioners in R(S)2/82, who argued that that the evidence in these letters provided evidence of the "claimant's personal limitations" rather than "any consideration stemming from the needs of the particular employer or the state of the labour market in the area" (R(S)2/82, para 7).

This confirms the interpretation of incapacity for work, through an individual model of disability, with the focus on claimants' "personal limitations" rather than the wider social and economic circumstances in which they might be trying to find work. With the development of case law in the second half of the twentieth century, Commissioners began to ask for alternative jobs to be specified by decision makers. This seems to have led to a standardised set of "disabled" jobs being listed as alternatives for most claimants and a counter-movement by welfare rights advisers to provide a range of reasons why these jobs were not suitable in many cases. The examples of lift operators and car park attendants, stemming from the reserved occupations of the early post-war years, were common. In my own time as a welfare rights adviser in central Scotland in the 1980s, claimants would often be advised that they could work as bridge toll attendants, reflecting the existence of the tolls on the Forth Road Bridge. Usually, tribunals would accept that claimants could not do this kind of work because claimants often had back injuries, for which sitting in a fixed position for hours at a time was wholly unsuitable. The fact that there were unlikely to be any vacancies on the Bridge at any particular time was not relevant. These, however, are questions of strategy; on the one hand, by decision makers to try and show why people were capable of work and on the other by representatives to show that they were not.

The idea that local offices should specify the work which claimants should be able to do was developed in R(S)6/85, a case which Mesher describes as one which "contrasts strongly with the overgeneralised and crude approach" usually used in decision making (Mesher 1986, p. 53). This case concerned a man in his late twenties, who had been claiming benefit for a year or so, since a back injury had prevented him from working in a factory. He had been referred for several possible retraining opportunities, most of which had proven to be unsuitable in relation to his impairment, or in one case in relation to his past education. The Commissioner suggested there should be clearer specification of the jobs that he could do:

> I do not find it acceptable to decide against a claimant without forming an affirmative conclusion, within reasonably precise and practical parameters, as to *what* work, within the overall sphere of employments for which an employer would pay, it is of which he is properly to be considered to have been capable (as distinct from holding the claimant capable of work upon mere abstract assumption that there "must be something" by way of work which he could reasonably have been expected to do and for which an employer would have paid. (para 5)

The Commissioner argued that job descriptions for suitable alternative employment should be suggested by local offices:

> I am much assisted if provided with evidence introduced by the adjudication officer of specific job descriptions – not job vacancies - which are submitted and

relied upon by him as description of work of which the particular claimant was capable at the material time. (para 6)

The Commissioner commended "the professional social security press" for their recent publication of job descriptions for the kinds of jobs that the Department of Health and social Security (DHSS) often suggested. He referred here to an article by the Child Poverty Action Group (CPAG) in the Welfare Rights Bulletin (CPAG 1984), which reported a case heard by the same Commissioner. In this article, the writer described a case for which they had provided representation, the case of Mr T. Mr T's experience of claiming benefit and appealing was similar to many of the alternative work cases which can be seen across the twentieth century. His own doctor and the RMO confirmed that he was unable to do his usual job, in this case as a milkman. The RMO described him as "a pleasant and well-motivated man" with a range of physical impairments and thought that he was fit for "light van driving" or "light clerical work" or could "help his wife with a small business". The first tier tribunal agreed and Mr T appealed to the Commissioners with the support of an adviser (presumably from the CPAG). The adviser assisted in Mr T's appeal by securing evidence that he could not manage light van driving or clerical work and arguing that the suggestion that he "could help his wife" was irrelevant since Mr T's wife did not have a small business. The DHSS then offered a list of possible jobs that Mr T might be able to do, including selling newspapers, working as a car park attendant, attendant at a sports hall or museum or working in a garage forecourt. His adviser made further inquiries with "people doing these jobs" and trade unions as to what these jobs might involve. The findings from these inquiries are listed in the article and detail the extent of bending, lifting, sitting for long periods in cramped positions, acting as a security guard or dealing with potentially violent people, that these jobs would involve. This evidence was sufficient to enable the Commissioner to allow Mr T's appeal.

The experiences described in R(S)2/82, R(S)6/85 and the case in the Welfare Rights Bulletin seem to reflect standard practice at this period which was for the DHSS to suggest a range of jobs that people found "fit for light work" might be able to do but which often included the roles of car park attendant or similar, particularly for men. The response of the adviser in the case reported in the Welfare Rights Bulletin and similar advice in CPAG handbooks in this period was to show why this kind of work was often not suitable for many claimants. The CPAG handbook from 1986 advised that claimants should consider the range of tasks involved in work of this kind and, if they felt they would be unable to do that kind of job, to collect evidence about what the job actually involved, advising that "A letter from a supervisor at work may be worth more than a doctor's letter" (Smith and Rowland 1986, p. 38). Wikeley

(1995) describes the era as one where tribunal members "have come to be experts in the skills required for photocopier assistants, light electrical goods assemblers, lift attendants, bingo callers and the like" (p. 525). These skills required to assess claimants against plausible real jobs became redundant with the introduction of the points-based medical test for Incapacity Benefit in the 1990s.

Using the Social Model of Disability to Understand Incapacity for Work

The evidence discussed above, in case law and in examples from appeals, shows that the principles behind incapacity benefits have always assumed that capacity for work has no relationship with the existence of a particular job. Using the social model of disability to analyse the development of incapacity benefits can help to show how focussing on individual limitations is an impossible task. French and Swain's (2012) version of the social model summarises three different ways in which society disables people. They list "structural barriers, environmental barriers and attitudinal barriers". The importance of the social model of disability is that it focusses on these barriers rather than the supposed lack of capacity or ability of individual people with impairments. These barriers have usually been ignored in defining incapacity for work.

Attitudinal barriers to work for people with health issues and impairments have been common across the twentieth century. Legal protection from discrimination in employment on the grounds of disability has been available in the UK since 1995 with the introduction of the Disability Discrimination Act 1995 and, subsequently, the Equality Act 2010. It is clear that discrimination on the grounds of disability was both legal and widespread before this (Barnes 1991; Shah and Priestley 2011). There is plenty of evidence of continuing discrimination with disabled people struggling to find and retain work, calling into question the effectiveness of disability discrimination legislation (Barnes 2012; Barnes and Mercer 2005; Roulstone 2012, 2015). During most of the twentieth century, there was no such protection against discrimination. Some of the appeal cases show what happened when people were generally able to work but were finding considerable difficulty finding work because of discrimination in the form of employer attitudes.

In most of the early appeal cases where discrimination was the key issue, the adjudicators found that the claimants were fit for work and therefore not eligible for benefit. The clearest cases of this type of discrimination can be found in cases concerning people who had epilepsy. The first of these cases, and one that was subsequently cited in later appeals, concerned Miss D in 1917. Miss D had worked as a domestic servant. She had epilepsy and had lost her job as a result of recent seizures at work. She claimed Sickness Benefit and was paid for about ten months before benefit was stopped when a medical referee declared her capable of work. When her benefit stopped, she found another job in domestic service but, again lost it after a seizure at work. This time she received benefit for six weeks before benefit was stopped and had been unable to find another job. At the appeal hearing, there was a difference of opinion in the medical views of her position: her own doctor felt that working would make her condition worse, while the doctor providing evidence on behalf of the Society believed that working would "help her condition". The adjudicators in this case considered whether difficulty in finding work constituted "incapacity" and whether Miss D's case was similar to one where "for example an illiterate manual labourer disabled by illness from continuing his ordinary employment cannot reasonably be held to be capable of work merely because he be physically able to sit in an office and hold a pen". They concluded that it was not and that she was capable of work, although they recognised that it would be difficult for her to find work (Case 102, NHIC 1917, p. 249). The case of Miss D is clearly one where her main barrier to employment was employers' attitudes rather than her own impairment.

The adjudicator in a later case, from 1927, came to a similar conclusion with the case of Miss B who also had epilepsy and had lost several jobs as a result of discrimination. The adjudicator concluded that, although "unlikely ever to gain any employment outside the home", she was fit for work (PIN 63/1/411, 1927). These cases show that the existence of discrimination in the labour market was usually not considered relevant to the assessment of capacity for work. As with the general labour market issues discussed in the first part of this chapter, this also had a gendered element to it. Disabled women who had difficulty finding work in the open labour market as a result of discrimination were often expected to find work which they could do in their homes, however, low paid this might be.

There are clear effects of discrimination in the labour market where claimants had previously worked for employers who were considered sympathetic. The claimants had lost their jobs, either because they had been effectively made redundant or because another health problem had arisen which made it difficult to do this previous job. In a case from 1927, Mr D had worked as a labourer since the age of sixteen in a metal factory in a post which had been created for him because of his family connections with the company. Mr D had epilepsy and had to take frequent rests. His father had also worked in the factory and his mother provided domestic services to the company, the whole family living in a house nearby. Mr D had been paid at a reduced rate because of his impairment and arrangements had been made that he could go back to the house to rest if necessary if he had a seizure at work. This arrangement had broken down after the company closed down, and Mr D had been unable to find any further employment. At the hearing, he was represented by a former works manager at the factory who argued that "he was only fit for work found for him by way of compassionate charity" and was therefore unfit for any other work. The adjudicator did not agree, emphasising instead that Mr D's medical condition had not changed and therefore, if he had been able to work before, he could still work. The adjudicator did express his concern by noting that he was "sorry to think that the appellant's prospects of actual employment are not favourable" but found him capable of work and so refused him benefit. In his legal argument, the adjudicator outlined the problem:

> The appellant belongs to a class of persons as to whom the test of incapacity under the Act might be thought artificial in that in his case one has to put forward the hypothesis of a generous employer finding a type of work in which the appellant's disadvantages can be ignored. (PIN 63/1/415)

It was irrelevant that Mr D would be unlikely to ever find work. Similar decisions were made in other cases concerning people with epilepsy, including a woman who had worked for fifteen years as a domestic servant for "considerate employers". The employment had come to an end and she was now unable to find another job. Despite her argument that she had only been able to work for her recent employers because they had been sympathetic, the adjudicator followed the argument from Case 102, discussed above, p. 97 (cited by the Society in the hearing) and found her fit for work (63/3/486, 1928).

Other examples of claimants who had been able to work where employment was suitable concerned employers who were family members. The claimants had often been working as part of a family business, where the social circumstances enabled them to and earn a living. When the work in that business ceased, the claimants struggled to find work that would suit them. An example of this can be found in 1928. In this case, the claimant was a man in his forties who had a diagnosis of neurasthenia and a war pension paid in relation to his experiences in the First World War. Since then he had worked from time to time in a family bakery business, where his contribution to the business was recognised by his brother. This work was no longer available to him. The doctors who gave evidence in his case suggested that he was "unemployable" but the adjudicator decided that he was capable of work because:

The application of the test to cases of mental neurasthenia of this type must always remain a matter of difficult, particularly as a period of probation and training for work would clearly in fact be an advantage as affording some guide as to the degree of mental disability. In the absence of any scheme for the provision of such training the test becomes more than usually hypothetical. (PIN 63/3/488)

In 1928 another man, Mr F, aged twenty-six, who had previously worked as a farm labourer, had been injured in an accident, leaving him blind. After the accident, Mr F returned to live on his parents' farm and then followed some training in brush making at an "institute for the blind". After his father died, Mr F returned to the family farm, claimed Sickness and then Disablement Benefit and, at the time of his appeal, was also doing some work around the farm to help his mother. In his appeal, the adjudicator found Mr F for fit for work, although recognising that the work Mr F was doing on the farm was wholly dependent on the fact that he knew the farm well and could find his way about. The adjudicator noted that

> That condition [work on the farm] is however precarious and if he has to leave that farm he would have difficulty in getting another suitable place - any work he might get then would be almost "a charity job" although when he got accustomed to the new farm he would be able to do a considerable amount of work. The appellant's best chance of meeting the possibilities of this precarious outlook is to train at an institution.. and to learn one or more crafts which would give him a fair chance of earning a living. (PIN 63/2/469)

The adjudicator in this case recognised that Mr F could only do his current work because of the very particular circumstances of the family farm and that it would be difficult for him to find work on another farm. The adjudicator did not believe that this exempted Mr F from the expectation that he should retrain for a different kind of work.

A case from 1929 provides another example of a man who had been able to work, so long as he was working within a family business but who would have difficulty finding work in the open labour market. The man, Mr B, was fifty-two and worked in his father's scrap iron business. After his father died, Mr B's brother took over the business and Mr B continued to work until the business folded. Mr B had been unable to find work in the open labour market and had not worked since. The adjudicator considered that Mr B was fit for work and that discrimination was not relevant:

> The appellant's difficulty is that he is known to be subject to fits and it is this reputation which prevents him getting work. I have considered this evidence very carefully along with my medical assessor and have come to the conclusion that

the fits are not of themselves such as to have rendered him incapable of work … although I agree that the fact that it is known that he is subject to fits will hamper him very seriously in getting work. (PIN 63/4/536)

The adjudicator did not consider what work Mr B might be able to do. All of these people were found fit for work and were refused incapacity benefits. Disability, for these people, while linked to impairment, was caused primarily by the attitudes of employers. The effect was a lack of access to work but the interpretation of incapacity in most cases did not enable people to access benefits either. There were some cases, however, where the adjudicators recognised these social barriers to work and, defining incapacity for work more generously, found that the claimants were eligible for incapacity benefits. An early example of this can be found in 1919 in a case concerning a Mr L (discussed above, p. 91) who was described as "a skilled workman" who had become "paralysed on his right side" possibly as a result of a stroke. He had reduced mobility and a visual impairment and was, as far as everyone was concerned, unable to return to his previous occupation as a wheelwright. The Society, however, believed that Mr L could carry out light work and that the main reason he was unable to find such work was that employers would not want to employ him:

> It was the urged by the Society that the real reason why the appellant failed to obtain work was not that he was incapable of work but that he was unemployable partly because his appearance and physical condition would prejudice employers against him and partly because no employer would engage a man whose health was such as to expose him to the possibility of an accident with consequent claims under the Workmen's Compensation Act. (Case 130, NHIC 1919, p. 306)

This argument suggested that Mr L was likely to be discriminated against, both because of "his physical condition" and by possible concerns that he might constitute a future risk. The adjudicators in this case discussed the argument that Mr L was "unemployable" rather than incapable of work but decided that he was in fact incapable of work because there was no reasonable work that he could do and that therefore the argument about employability was not necessary. It is useful to note that the discussion in this case also stressed Mr L's eagerness to return to work if at all possible:

> We are satisfied of his honesty and his desire to earn money in order to support himself. He is a man of some education and in no sense a wastrel or a shirker and if he were capable of work we are convinced he would be working. (p. 306)

In Mr L's case, being "unemployable" was not a negative label but one which confirmed his moral legitimacy in claiming benefit. For other claimants, a label of "unemployable" carried more negative connotations and did not necessarily lead to a finding of incapacity for work. For example, Miss N had been claiming benefit for about ten years as a result of "nervous debility". While weighing up the conflicting evidence very carefully, the adjudicator decided

> I rather agree with the closing submission of [claimant's solicitor] that the respondent is in all probability unemployable using that word in relation to her prospects of employment in the present condition of the labour market. But as has often been pointed out in these cases that test is not by any means conclusive. Subject to the limitations suggested by [RMO] I agree with his view as to her ability for work in the legal sense [that she is capable of work]. (PIN 63/3/500, 1928)

In guidance to RMO from 1930, the Ministry of Health made it clear that discrimination was not grounds for considering someone incapable of work, describing instead their circumstances as "Unemployment through conditions that do not incapacitate". Giving examples of people with infectious diseases, disfigurements, or epilepsy, the guidance described these circumstances as "suffering from unemployment as a result of their sickness" and advised Societies to consider these claimants to be "capable of work" (draft guidance to RMO in MH62/201).

The cases discussed above concern overt discrimination against disabled people, where the clearest barriers to work were the attitudes of potential employers. Disabling barriers, however, take many forms. Another set of clear cases are those where people's access to work was limited by environmental barriers, for example, lack of adequate transport, equipment or adaptations. An appeal decision addressed this question in 1916, where a claimny a man who was unable to use a prosthesis because it was being repaired, was accepted as a temporary period of incapacity for work. Mr R had been a miner and had lost both of his legs in an accident in the mine in the late 1890s. He used prosthetic legs and was, usually, quite able to work. He claimed Sickness Benefit when one of his prosthetic legs was damaged, leaving him unable to walk and therefore to do his usual job. His Approved Society refused benefit on the grounds that damage to the artificial leg was not a "bodily disablement", and that therefore, he was not entitled. The adjudicators in this case disagreed, arguing that Mr R's relevant bodily disablement was the loss of the legs in the original accident and the fact that he did not have the appropriate adaptations to compensate for that did not take away the bodily disablement and therefore that he was incapable of work. However, they qualified this decision by saying that they:

did not wish it to be understood that a member of an Approved Society who has the opportunity of fitting himself for work by procuring an artificial leg is entitled to refrain from doing so and to claim sickness and disablement benefit for the rest of his life. He must be allowed a reasonable time to obtain the necessary appliance and is entitled to benefit during that time. If he is guilty of any unreasonable delay in taking the necessary steps to procure a leg, it appears to the Commissioners that his incapacity for work ought then to be regarded as due to causes for which he is himself responsible. (Case 90, NHIC 1917, p. 229)

The use of the word "guilty", if only in anticipation of what might go wrong in the future, underlines the claimant's responsibility rather than the structural barriers making it difficult for him to work. A similar approach was taken in 1929, where a claimant, Mr S, had a leg amputation and argued that he could not afford a suitable prosthesis. The adjudicator considered this to be irrelevant since Mr S could manage other work, even without the prosthesis, preferring the evidence of the RMO who said that Mr S was

fit for any light occupation such as a one-legged man could perform. Sedentary or clerical work, such as a time keeper, or man about a warehouse where there was no heavy lifting to do. (PIN 63/4/537, 1929)

Continuing into the post-war period, a couple of cases in the early 1950s confirmed that the assessment of capacity for work was an individual medical assessment and should not take into account barriers which were inherently part of the structure of employment rather than the individual. For example, in R(S)24/54, Mrs E was a school teacher and was pregnant. She was advised by her doctor to stay away from her work because of an outbreak of rubella at her local school. It was known that contracting rubella in pregnancy could lead to damage to an unborn child and Mrs E did not want to take the risk of harming her unborn child. Since, in her view, she was unable to work, she claimed Sickness Benefit with supporting evidence from her doctor. When she was refused, she appealed to a local tribunal. The local tribunal upheld the decision to refuse benefit and so Mrs E appealed to the National Insurance Commissioners. With the advice of her trade union, she sent supporting evidence from the head teacher of her school, confirming that there had been ninety-six cases of rubella at the school. She also submitted a letter from a specialist doctor, who confirmed the risk that rubella might carry for Mrs E's unborn child. The Commissioner considered whether her circumstances could fit within the regulations for Sickness Benefit but concluded that they could not because her lack of access to work was caused, not by her state of health but by "an attribute of the places in the employment" in her area

There was nothing in her state of health to affect her working capacity at the time in question and it was an attribute of the places of employment in her district, not an attribute of the claimant, that rendered her place of employment unsuitable for the claimant to attend. (R(S)24/54, para 6, case papers in TNA CT11/128)

This case was unusual and subsequent Commissioner's Decisions considered that preventative measures of this kind were appropriate reasons for a person to be considered incapable of work (Ogus and Barendt 1978, p. 156, referring to R(S)8/61 and R(S)1/72). Despite the subsequent interpretations of the legislation which allowed people to be considered incapable of work when there was a threat to their health or the health of others, the decision regarding Mrs E provided a clear distinction between "attributes of the claimant" and "attributes of places of employment", suggesting that the definition of incapacity for work should be solely focussed on the former. Another similar case from the early 1950s concerned Mr M, who had a prosthetic leg and who was unable to travel to work during a period of severe winter weather. His argument was that he was unable to work during that period because of the risk to his health if he attempted to walk on ice and snow. Again the Commissioner disagreed, arguing that, although he had a "bodily disablement"

> he was however not incapable of work by reason of his bodily disablement; he was perfectly capable of work but was incapable of getting to work. If his work could have been brought to his home, or if he could have been transported to his place of work, he could have done it. The claimant was not incapable of work but was prevented by circumstances beyond his control from reaching his place of employment. A disabled man, who was capable of work but was obliged to use a conveyance to reach his place of work, could not be said to be incapable of work if his conveyance were to break down and so prevent him from reaching his place of employment. (R(S)8/53 para 3, case file in CT11/211)

In each of these cases, the claimants had jobs and so there was strong evidence that they were capable of working. Mrs E did not have a "bodily disablement" because, although she was recognised to be "under medical care", pregnancy did not constitute disablement. Mr M, however, did have a "bodily disablement" but it was recognised that the barrier to work in his case lay with the lack of access to transport and not in his own bodily impairment. Their claims were short term, in Mrs E's case, covering around a month when her usual work was not available to her because of a risk to her unborn child's health and, for Mr M, a period of about week when there was no available transport because of poor weather. Although each of these cases concerned a short-term period when the claimants' jobs were unavailable to them, the decisions of the Commissioners focussed on the fact that their incapacity lay not in their individual bodily or physical impairment but on structural barriers to them accessing work. So, despite the case law at the time acknowledging the social factors, such as education, past employment or sometimes discrimination, which affect people's ability to access work in the real world, it stopped short of enabling incapacity benefits to be paid to people whose incapacity for work was identified as being caused by structural barriers preventing them from accessing a particular workplace. These decisions are quite unusual in the context of the general principle, applied at the time, that people claiming benefit for short-term incapacity should be assessed in relation to their capacity to do their usual jobs, a principle confirmed by case law in the late 1970s and 1980s (see Chapter 3). However, the usual job rule applied only to claimants who had jobs to return to or who had recently been in the labour market. Claimants who did not have this recent attachment to the labour market would be expected to retrain or to find work, despite the structural barriers in place.

An example can be found in the case of Miss F, a single woman, aged thirty-three, who lived with her mother and brother. Miss F had agoraphobia, which meant that she could not leave her home alone. She argued that this prevented her from being able to work. She had received benefit for about a year when her benefit was stopped, after a RMO found her fit for work. She appealed against this decision to a local tribunal and then to the National Insurance Commissioners. Although accepting her diagnosis of agoraphobia, the local office and the first-tier tribunal thought that she could work from home, doing "sewing or similar work". The Commissioner agreed:

> If she cannot go out alone and cannot make arrangements to be accompanied to and from work by a friend or relative, she must adapt herself to her limitations and choose for herself some form of work at home in which persons are employed. Her agoraphobia has been persistent and it is reasonable to expect her to take into account work in her own home as a means of earning remuneration. (R(S)20/52. Case papers in CT11/73)

The Commissioner clearly viewed it as the claimant's responsibility to "make arrangements" and to "adapt herself to her limitations" in order to fulfil her duty to engage with the labour market.

The changes to an almost wholly medical assessment for Incapacity Benefit in the 1990s and ESA today mean that social issues such as discrimination and structural barriers are mostly irrelevant to benefit decision making. Recent case law has addressed this issue. A decision of the Upper Tribunal in 2013 found that a woman with epilepsy and other long-term health conditions was fit for work because any employer would have a duty under the Equality Act 2010 to make reasonable accommodations to make it possible for her to work (and would not be permitted to discriminate against her) (CE/811/2013 (2013) UKUT 518 (AAC)). In this case, it looks as if the Equality Act undermined her possibility of entitlement to benefits, without necessarily helping her to access work.

Conclusions

The interpretation of incapacity for work is strongly led by a medical model of disability, with the evidence of medical professions considered the most valuable in decision making. Where the wider social context of work is considered, the existence of discrimination in the labour market is usually not considered relevant and there is a strong expectation that it is the duty of claimants to find remunerative work at all costs. Legal adjudicators have not always made consistent decisions regarding these questions but it is clear that there is an underlying concern with promoting the work ethic and the moral necessity of engaging with the labour market. It is clear that an attempt has been made across the twentieth century to keep the issue of unemployment separate from the issue of incapacity for work. This is clear from policy documents, from case law and from popular discourse. Insights from the social model of disability show that it is not possible to separate out a person's individual capacity for work from the labour market, structural barriers to work and discrimination. So long as benefits systems maintain this fiction, there will be no way to square this circle. The two are inextricably linked. The reforms introduced by ESA attempted to create a new category of claimants who may be capable of work in the near future and who should be making an attempt to return to work. It could be argued that this new intermediate category resolves the problem. It does not, because the assessment continues to rely on an individual medical model of disability which forces the responsibility for finding and keeping work onto the claimant.

References

Barnes, Colin. 1991. *Disabled People in Britain and Discrimination.* London: Hurst and Company/BCoDP.
———. 2012. 'Re-thinking Disability, Work and Welfare'. *Sociology Compass* 6 (6): 472–84.
Barnes, Colin, and Geof Mercer. 2005. 'Disability, Work and Welfare: Challenging the Social Exclusion of Disabled People'. *Work, Employment & Society* 19 (3): 527–45.

Bonner, David, Ian Hooker, and Robin White, eds. 1991. *Non-Means Tested Benefits: The Legislation 1991 Edition*. London: Sweet and Maxwell.
Child Poverty Action Group. 1984. 'Work Within Limits'. *Welfare Rights Bulletin* (61) (August): 10–11.
Deacon, Alan. 1976. *In Search of the Scrounger*. Leeds: University of Leeds.
Dwyer, Peter, Katy Jones, Jenny McNeill, Lisa Scullion, and Alisdair Stewart. 2018. 'Welfare Conditionality: Sanctions, Support and Behaviour Change. Final Findings: Disabled People'. www.welfareconditionality.ac.uk.
French, Sally, and John Swain. 2012. *Working with Disabled People in Policy and Practice*. Basingstoke: Palgrave Macmillan.
Houston, Donald, and Colin Lindsay. 2010. 'Fit for Work? Health, Employability and Challenges for the UK Welfare Reform Agenda'. *Policy Studies* 31: 133–42.
Macnicol, John. 2013. 'The History of Work Disability'. In *Disability Benefits, Welfare Reform and Employment Policy*, edited by Colin Lindsay and Donald Houston. London: Palgrave.
Mesher, John. 1986. 'Recent Social Security Commissioners' Decisions'. *The Journal of Social Welfare Law* 8 (1): 52–64.
Ministry of Health. 1923. *Reports of Decisions on Appeals and Applications Under Section 67 of the National Insurance Act 1911 and Section 27 of the National Insurance Act 1913, Vol 2—Part I*. London: HMSO.
National Health Insurance Commission (England). 1915. *Reports of Decisions on Appeals and Applications Under Section 67 of the National Insurance Act 1911 and Section 27 of the National Insurance Act 1913*. Cd. 7810. London: HMSO.
———. 1917. *National Health Insurance. Report on the Administration of National Health Insurance during the Years 1914-17*. Cd. 8890. London: HMSO.
———. 1919. *Reports of Decisions on Appeals and Applications Under Section 67 of the National Insurance Act 1911 and Section 27 of the National Insurance Act 1913 Part V*. Cmd. 134. London: HMSO.
Ogus, Anthony, and Eric Barendt. 1978. *The Law of Social Security*. London: Butterworths.
Paz-Fuchs, Amir. 2008. *Welfare to Work Conditional Rights in Social Policy*. Oxford: Oxford University Press.
Roulstone, Alan. 2012. 'Disabled People, Work and Employment'. In *Routledge Handbook of Disability Studies*, edited by Nick Watson, Alan Roulstone, and Carol Thomas. Abingdon: Routledge.
———. 2015. 'Disability, Work and Welfare'. In *Disabled People, Work and Welfare Is Employment Really the Answer?*, edited by Chris Grover and Linda Piggott. Bristol: Policy Press.
Shah, Sonali, and Mark Priestley. 2011. *Disability and Social Change: Private Lives and Public Policies*. Bristol: Policy Press.
Smith, Roger, and Mark Rowland. 1986. *Rights Guide to Non-means-tested Social Security Benefits*. 9th ed. London: Child Poverty Action Group.
Stone, Deborah. 1984. *The Disabled State*. Philadelphia: Temple University Press.

Tomlinson, J. 1984. 'Women as "Anomolies": The Anomolies Regulations of 1931, Their Background and Administration'. *Public Administration* 62: 423–37.

Turner, Angela, and Arthur McIvor. 2017. '"Bottom Dog Men": Disability, Social Welfare and Advocacy in the Scottish Coalfields in the Interwar Years, 1918–1939'. *The Scottish Historical Review* 96 (2): 187–213.

Webster, David, James Arnott, Judith Brown, Ivan Turok, Richard Mitchell, and Ewan Macdonald. 2010. 'Falling Incapacity Benefit Claims in a Former Industrial City: Policy Impacts or Labour Market Improvement'. *Policy Studies* 31: 163–85.

Whiteside, Noel. 1987. 'Counting the Cost: Sickness and Disability Among Working People in an Era of Industrial Recession, 1920–1939'. *Economic History Review* XL: 228–46.

———. 2014. 'Constructing Unemployment: Britain and France in Historical Perspective'. *Social Policy & Administration* 48 (1): 67–85.

Wikeley, Nick. 1995. 'The Social Security (Incapacity for Work) Act 1994'. *Modern Law Review* 58 (4): 523.

Wright, Sharon. 2012. 'Welfare to Work, Agency and Personal Responsibility'. *Journal of Social Policy* 41 (2): 309–28.

6

Fit for the Ordinary Work of the Home: Women and Domestic Work

Introduction

Mrs W was a married woman with two small children. She had worked as a weaver in the 1920s but had stopped this work after developing epilepsy while pregnant. She had been claiming Sickness and Disablement Benefit since then. Her Society stopped her benefit after a referral to a Regional Medical Officer who claimed that there was "no reason why she should not perform suitable household duties". Mrs W appealed. At her hearing in 1929, evidence was presented to show that her epilepsy was severe and that she had experienced several accidents in the home in recent weeks. It had become too difficult for Mrs W to look after her children and she had moved back in with her mother. The lawyer representing the Society emphasised that Mrs W had not worked outside the home since the birth of her children and that she had made no attempt to learn new skills in the weaving trade which might enable her to work safely. At the appeal hearing, the adjudicator concluded that Mrs W was not capable of work and so was entitled to benefit (PIN 63/4/522, 1929).

Mrs W's case illustrates two issues with married women's claims: the question of their attachment to the labour market and the assessment of their capacity for housework within the home. The Society's lawyer at Mrs W's hearing stressed that she had not returned to the labour market since the birth of her children, indicating that this was key evidence of her status as a "housewife" rather than a "worker". The Regional Medical Officer's evidence that she was capable of "suitable household duties" also indicated that the test of her entitlement to benefit was about her role in the home rather than her capacity for paid employment. Mrs W's appeal was successful but only because she was able to present evidence of her difficulties in being able to work outside the home

© The Author(s) 2019
J. Gulland, *Gender, Work and Social Control*, Palgrave Socio-Legal Studies, https://doi.org/10.1057/978-1-137-60564-1_6

and that she was unable to carry out her expected duties as a wife and mother. The legislation on Disablement Benefit did not distinguish between men and women in its definition of incapacity for work, did not require evidence of attachment to the labour market beyond the requisite national insurance contributions and did not require women to pass any additional household duties tests. However, it was common through most of the twentieth century for married women to encounter this double test. Work in the paid labour market in the early twentieth century was (and continues to be) heavily gendered, so, when considering what kind of jobs a claimant might be able to do, decision makers understandably looked through a gendered lens. This led to decision makers treating men and women differently when considering whether or a claimant was capable of work. Paid domestic work was often considered as an option for women and almost never for men, as shown in Chapter 5. Decision makers often suggested that women could find paid work as cleaners or domestic servants or could take in laundry or sewing in their own homes, however unlikely the existence of such work or unrewarding the payment. More importantly, however, while these suggestions of alternative paid work show clear gendered differences, it was women's potential capacity for unpaid domestic work in their own homes which showed the greatest gender difference in incapacity benefit decision making. Women could be refused benefit because of these unpaid activities, even when there was no explicit suggestion that they could carry out similar domestic duties in the paid labour market. This chapter traces the history of this gendered approach to women's claims across the twentieth century.

Legislation and Case Law

The legislation governing the incapacity benefits schemes did not distinguish between men and women when it came to defining incapacity for work (except in the case of HNCIP see below). However, the benefits schemes did make important distinctions between men, unmarried women and married women in the eligibility rules for national insurance and in levels of payment. Under the 1911 scheme, women paid lower contributions and were eligible for lower rates of benefit than men. Particularly, harsh rules regulated whether or not married women were eligible to join the scheme in the first place, making it much less likely that married women could become eligible for benefits (Lewis 1983; Pedersen 1993; Whiteside 1987). Despite these complex regulations, many married women did work in the paid labour market, did pay contributions and were potentially eligible for benefit if they became ill or disabled.

6 Fit for the Ordinary Work of the Home: Women and Domestic Work

After 1948, single women and all men were treated in the same way in relation to contribution and payment rules, while married women were assumed not to be fully part of the scheme and could elect to pay a lower contribution which then disqualified them for benefits in their own right. Some married women however paid the full contribution and so were entitled to benefits or had a continuing entitlement because of transitional arrangements from the earlier scheme. After equalities legislation and a series of high profile legal cases in the 1970s, the incapacity benefits schemes became gender neutral in their contribution and eligibility rules. The earlier differences in contributions and eligibility were an attempt by policy makers to reflect the difference (or perceived difference) in men's and women's working lives and an assumption that married women would usually be financially dependent on their husbands. To an extent, this reflected reality but also created and reinforced gender inequalities both in terms of contributions and of payments. This book, and this chapter in particular, however is concerned with the ways in which gender played a role in the *definition* of incapacity for work for those men and women who met the eligibility requirements. The legislation on this was mainly silent with regard to gender. Case law developed in ways which reflected gendered assumptions about work and the labour market, but there was a marked difference in the treatment of men and women in the discourse and everyday decision making of policy makers and decision makers across the twentieth century. In particular, they worried about housework.

Housework in the Interwar Sickness Benefits Scheme

From its introduction, decision making on the benefits introduced by the National Insurance Act 1911 was heavily gendered. In the early twentieth century, policy makers and decision makers continually struggled with how to treat women's unpaid work in the home. It had been understood from the beginning of the Sickness Benefit scheme that women had, what feminists today call a "second shift" (Hochschild 1989). Mary Macarthur described women's additional responsibilities in 1914 as a "treble strain", including childbearing along with the burdens of paid work and domestic chores (NHIJC 1914b, p. 79). The questions that decision makers had to consider were whether this domestic work was or was not work, and if it was work, then whether women could be entitled to incapacity benefits if they continued to carry out these tasks. The apparent contradiction between incapacity for work and capacity for domestic tasks was highlighted by a Mr Sanderson in evidence to the inquiry into excessive claims in 1914. In relation to four hundred women who had been refused benefit by his Society because they were doing housework, Mr Sanderson said:

> I think that we ought to have a special certificate for women stating that they are unable to follow their usual occupation or that they are unable to do their household duties. It is very different from men. Women can work at home and they work perhaps harder at home than they would work in the mill. (Evidence of Mr Sanderson Managing Secretary of the Amalgamated Association of Card, Blowing and Ring Room Operatives in NHIJC 1914a, Appendices, p. 10)

Mr Sanderson understood that domestic work was work but he thought that evidence of capacity to do this work ought to prohibit women from receiving Sickness Benefit. Mr Sanderson's views were extreme but they illustrate the policy and decision makers' dilemma regarding women who could do housework. Other Societies giving evidence to the 1914 inquiry also described taking a hard line on women doing housework while claiming benefit. For example, the Co-operative Wholesale Society stopped benefit from women who were found to be washing or dressing their babies while claiming Sickness Benefit, although the Society conceded that breastfeeding was acceptable (Evidence of Mr R Smith of the Co-operative Wholesale Society in NHIJC 1914a, Appendices, p. 380).

The main inquiry concluded that it was up to individual Societies to decide how to deal with women found carrying out housework while claiming benefit but that they should also "educate their women members to appreciate the necessity of abstaining from prohibited housework" partly in the interests of women's health but also "to have a deterrent effect [on claiming benefit]" (NHIJC 1914b, p. 56).

This reference to a dual purpose of protecting health while deterring claims shows that there was a concern that women doing housework might not really be eligible for benefit and should therefore be discouraged from claiming. Mary Macarthur had a different perspective on the issue, recognising that if women claimants did not do their own housework there would be no one to do it for them. Even she did not expect men to do housework in the early twentieth century. Her view was that women should be credited for doing the housework while ill and that their benefits should only be withdrawn if they were carrying out household tasks in direct contradiction to their doctors' advice (Mary Macarthur, in NHIJC 1914a, Appendices, p. 330).

The appeal cases in the early years of the Sickness Benefit scheme and into the 1920s provide examples of Societies stopping or suspending women's benefits if they were considered capable of housework. Examples from the archives of

6 Fit for the Ordinary Work of the Home: Women and Domestic Work 113

particular Societies show women being refused benefit for "washing", "doing" "homework" and "plucking a duck" (Leek Textile Federation: health insurance minute book, 1913, in WCML TU/SILK/7/3).

Despite this, women were sometimes successful on appeal if they were able to show that the housework evidence was inadequate as evidence of their capacity for paid work. An example of this is Mrs P, a widow in her sixties, who had been claiming Disablement Benefit for seven years. Her benefit was stopped after she was alleged to have been "cooking, cleaning and even a little bit of dusting". At her appeal, the adjudicator dismissed this evidence, relying instead on medical evidence which supported Mrs P's case that she was incapable of work (Case 2/26, Ministry of Health 1923, p. 72).

In some cases, it was clear that the Society was arguing that the alleged housework was evidence that the woman's impairment was less severe than she alleged. In many other cases, however, there was much less clarity about why household duties were relevant to the question of capacity for work. An example of this was a woman, Mrs B, who had been caught doing her own laundry by a sick visitor who had been sent to check up on Mrs B's alleged incapacity. Mrs B had previously worked in the weaving industry and had continued to work in the industry after the birth of her two older children, who were now eight and five, but had not had paid work since the birth of her youngest child who was one and a half. Mrs B had been ill around the time of her child's birth and had subsequently claimed Sickness Benefit. The sick visitor reported that she had seen Mrs B hanging out washing, giving a detailed account of what she had seen (PIN 63/1/416, 1927). (See also Chapter 9 for details of the sick visitor's report). The adjudicator accepted this as evidence of Mrs B's capacity for work but did not specify what work she might be expected to do, other than her own housework. The test in Mrs B's case seemed to be about something other than her capacity for work. The reference to her lack of paid work since the birth of her youngest child and her proficiency in doing the laundry suggested that the Society regarded Mrs B primarily as a housewife and that she was not really in the labour market. This is despite the fact that Mrs B had continued to work in the weaving industry after the birth of her older children. Mrs B's case was representative of an attitude to married women's claims which was widespread.

In the 1920s, expenditure on payments of Sickness and Disablement Benefit to married women had been steadily increasing (Watson 1929). There was a suspicion that married women were claiming Sickness Benefit rather than Unemployment Benefit because it was relatively easy for married women to qualify (Whiteside 1987). Harsh amendments to the procedures for claiming Unemployment Benefit were introduced to deter married women from claiming and to encourage women to take up work in domestic service (Deacon 1976, p. 25). Much of the debate about how to assess married women's claims concerned whether these women were really available for work, or whether they were in fact housewives who had left the labour market. If so, they were not entitled to claim Unemployment Benefits. The same reasoning was applied to incapacity benefits, but, because incapacity benefits did not have a formal work-seeking conditionality attached, the tests of women's attachment to the labour market was carried out through the definition of incapacity for work.

Married women who had been in employment before marriage and who continued in employment afterwards were fully entitled to join the National Health Insurance Scheme and to claim benefits when they were unable to work. However, they were continually under suspicion of not really being in the labour market, and their claims were subjected to greater scrutiny than claims by men. Single women were less likely to be scrutinised so heavily, but they were also at risk of being considered to not really be in the labour market. Legislation in 1928 introduced the concept of Class K contributors. This clause provided for women who were considered to have left the labour market after marriage to continue paying contributions and to claim Sickness Benefit for up to six weeks, a maternity payment on childbirth and the right to the services of a panel doctor, but only for a limited period (National Health Insurance Act 1928). The legislation was introduced to establish a difference between people who were considered to be still in the labour market but lacking a job (unemployed men and single women) and married women, who were considered to have left the labour market. This distinction was important in understanding the perception of married women at this time, but the perception of married women's othered status was also extended to women who were full contributors to the scheme.

In 1931, the Government Actuary, Alfred Watson, recommended addressing the problem of married women's claims by either increasing the level of contributions or reducing the level of benefits (Watson 1931, p. 37). Amending legislation introduced in 1931 made it more difficult for married women to qualify for unemployment benefits (Tomlinson 1984), This, it was alleged, encouraged married women to claim Sickness Benefit instead and further legislation in 1932 reduced the rate of Sickness and Disablement Benefit payable to married women, in attempt to reduce the cost of payments and to discourage claims (National Health Insurance and contributory Pensions Act 1932). During a debate in the House of Commons on the 1932 Act, regarding an amendment which would have restricted women's entitlement even further, a couple of female MPs objected to the assumptions being made about working married women. Florence Horsbrugh (Conservative MP for Dundee) noted

6 Fit for the Ordinary Work of the Home: Women and Domestic Work 115

that many married women were fully in the labour market and that (perhaps not out of choice) were the main breadwinners in their families:

> I am told over and over again that married women are in a different class, because their money is not going to support a family as is the money of the man. I wish it were so and I am certain that many of the married women wish it were so. We have to look at the facts in the case. In many industrial districts … the majority of the people in the mill are women, and not men. Unfortunately it is very often upon the woman that the whole burden of supporting the household falls. (Florence Horsbrugh, Hansard 21/6/32 col 944)

Perhaps her experience of working patterns in Dundee was particular to the industrial patterns in that city at the time but another female MP, Mavis Tate (Conservative MP for Willesden West), representing a constituency from a quite different part of the country, was also concerned about the unequal treatment of married women:

> The whole system of English law has been built up on the assumption that a person is innocent of any crime whatsoever until proved guilty; but if this Clause were ever to be accepted it means that in future all married women are to be considered malingerers and cheats until they have definitely proved that they are not. There is no reason why a genuinely employed married woman should be put into a position where she has to prove herself neither a liar nor a cheat. (Mavis Tate, Hansard 21/6/32 col 945)

In the same debate, the Minister for Heath explained how he saw the position of married women:

> Some 225,000 insured women marry in the course of the year, and, of those, 150,000 genuinely and directly [come] out of insurance because they do not intend to remain in the employment market and some 50,000 women remain genuinely and directly in insurance because they are genuinely still remaining in the employment market. There is a balance, the exact size of which may be controversial but which is around 20,000 persons about whom there is – how shall I put it? – a well founded suspicion that they are not genuinely entering into the employment market; yet they are continuing to draw benefit and to continue in insurance as if employed. (Sir Hilton Young Minster of Health, Hansard col 948 21 June 1931)

In this statement, the Minister of Health defined precisely what the issue was. Married women claiming Sickness Benefit were suspected of not being "genuinely in the labour market", and so mechanisms had to be found to stop them from claiming benefit. Apart from reducing the rates of benefit, the main mechanism was to consider household duties in the definition of incapacity for work. A file in the National Archives includes correspondence between the Ministry of Health and various Approved Societies, giving an insight into the development of this crackdown on supervision of claims by married women. The file contains the thoughts of civil servants at the Ministry of Health in response to a letter from the Prudential Approved Society concerning whether a married woman's incapacity should be judged against her previous factory work or her "duties as a housewife", reflecting the views of Mr Saunders in 1914:

> it would appear that the criterion to be applied is whether she is capable of performing her duties as a housewife (letter from Prudential Approved Society to Ministry of Health, 4/9/1930, filed in MH62/201)

The Ministry of Health published revised guidance in 1932, noting that:

> It has accordingly been decided that if, in referring to the Regional Medical Officer in the case of a woman in this position, the Society desire to know, not only whether the woman is unfit for her ordinary occupation, but also whether she is incapable of carrying out unaided the daily work of the house, it would be open to them to include that question on the Form RM1 under the "Reasons for referring the case," and in that event the Regional Medical Officer in his report to the Society will give his opinion on that point. It will of course rest with the Society to decide, subject to the member's right of appeal, whether in view of the Regional Medical Officer's report the woman is or is not to be regarded as incapable of work. (Circular A.S 284, 1932, filed in MH62/301)

Although this guidance may have appeared clear, the correspondence on the development of the guidance provides an insight into some of the difficulties, including how anyone could interpret the meaning of the "ordinary work of the house", whether this only applied to married women and whether it applied to men who were carrying out housework:

> One further point is raised by the D.M.Os. References are received from which it appears very improbable that the insured person can be the "domestic head of the household" e.g. in the case of a single girl of 17 whose ordinary occupation is domestic service. Thinking it undesirable that the Medical Staff should be involved in the task of discriminating on a matter of non-medical facts, I have advised the DMOs to leave the responsibility in this respect with the Society, and to proceed with the reference on a housework basis – unless such a course seems

obviously ridiculous, e.g. where the insured person is a man. (Minute sheet from Whitaker to Hackforth 29/11/31, filed in MH62/201)

The comment that it might be relevant to include unmarried women and that it would be "obviously ridiculous" to include men in this crackdown on claims shows how clearly the issue was about gender andnot just about married women. In this same memo, Mr Whitaker explained why some Societies considered that housework might be considered to be remunerative even when it was not paid:

> It is indirectly remunerative since they are able to save the money they would otherwise pay to a woman to do the housework for them, and if fit to do this work they do not need any compensation by way of sickness benefit for loss of remunerative employment

Mr Whitaker went on to disagree with this view, describing it as a "fallacy":

> One knows of course that the whole doctrine is really based on knowledge of the general economic position of these people. The married woman whom the officials of these Societies have in mind is not, so to speak, an economic unit. She is a member of a family which constitutes the real unit, the earnings of the family being pooled, and if she does the housework herself instead of employing another woman, she is being supported by the earnings of the rest of the family. (Minute sheet from Whitaker to Hackforth 29/11/31, filed in MH62/201)

This discussion shows that the whole question of whether a married woman's domestic duties should be taken into account was not just about her capacity for work but her role within the household economy, dependent on a man's wages. This underlines the argument that, for some Societies, the test of incapacity for work in the case of women was very different from the one used for men, based not on any assessment of their impairments or capacities for work in the labour market, nor on their past contributions through the insurance system, but on their perceived attachment to the labour market in the first place. While men could also have their claims investigated if they were thought to be carrying out activities which could be evidence of capacity for work, these investigations did not include domestic work such as cleaning and cooking. Men who did carry out these domestic duties in a couple of case were treated very differently from women. Mr J was a forty-two-year-old former boiler worker who had been diagnosed with "neurasthenia". He had been claiming benefit for a couple of years and spent his time "gardening and helping his wife about the house". Although this act of "helping his wife" may have been considered as evidence of his capacity for work, the issue of domestic work was not raised directly and the adjudicator decided that Mr J was capable of "ordinary labouring" (63/2/450, 1928). Another case from 1928 concerned Mr C, a man in his forties, who had worked as a furnace-man until a stroke eight years previously. It was noted in his appeal that he had a wife and five children and that his wife had a job. Mr C meanwhile "looks after the house a good part of the time and does part of the cooking and other housework". This domestic work appeared to have no impact on his claim for benefit and may, on the contrary, have acted as evidence of his good character. The adjudicator found that he was incapable of work (PIN 63/2/452, 1928).

The problem of how to advise Societies rumbled on through the 1930s, with a memo dated 1935 discussing the problems and arguing that heavy-handed use of the housework rules had "become a source of embarrassment to the Regional Medical Staff" (Note of discussion on 14 November 1935 between the Controller, Mr Hackforth, Dr Paterson and Mr Wackrill, filed in MH62/201). By 1935, the Ministry of Health was concerned about the overuse of close scrutiny of women's claims, recognising that this was being used to refuse benefit to single women as well as married women and that there was potential for accusations of discrimination. The file includes a copy of an appeal case from 1936. This concerned a woman who had been caught doing housework, where the adjudicator was adamant that the housework test was inappropriate. In this case, the claimant was a young married woman, Mrs S, in fact, a Class K contributor who had given up work on marriage but who was still eligible for benefits. A doctor had assessed Mrs S as "unfit for work as a domestic servant but fit for the ordinary work of the home". The Society believed that for Class K contributors, the test of incapacity for work should be assessed against women's ability to do housework. The adjudicator emphatically disagreed:

> the Act, [which] lays down the test as incapacity for work by reason of some specific disease or some bodily or mental disablement. In setting a standard of their own, namely that of capacity or otherwise for carrying out the ordinary daily work of her home, the Respondents are in my judgement mistaken. This is not the test laid down by parliament and it is not the test which I am prepared to follow (copy of Case in MH62/201/1099, 1936)

This case is an important reminder that the statutory definition of incapacity for work was no different for married women, including Class K women, than for anybody else. Unfortunately, although there are tantalising references to specific decisions from the 1930s in the civil service files, I have been unable to find further copies of appeal decisions from this period. There are however some examples of lower level appeals from the 1930s in the archives of particular societies. These suggest that Societies routinely used capacity for housework as a reason for stopping benefit.

The minute books of the Ideal Benefit Approved Society include a series of internal appeals against refusal of benefit to women who had been caught doing housework in the period 1936–1940. Almost all of these women, of whom there were three or four every month, had been refused benefit, had appealed using the internal appeals procedure and were confirmed as disentitled to benefit by the internal appeal board. Only a couple of the women in these papers were successful on appeal and only because they were able to establish that they did not do the housework. Mrs B appealed successfully claiming that she was not the domestic head of household because she "resides with her mother who does the housework" (Appeal on 3/10/40 recorded in PIN 24/80). Mrs D was successful because she "brought with her a Mrs R who stated that she had always done the member's house work and washing" (3/10/40 recorded in PIN 24/80).

These women's appeals were successful, not only because of the nature of their impairments but because they were able to show that they were not normally housewives. These women were exceptions to the general rule that women would be refused benefit if found able to do housework. Although some adjudicators, particularly in the case cited above (filed in MH62/201/1099), were clear that the legal test for married women's incapacity for work was not different than the test for men or for single women, individual Societies, and some other adjudicators, took a different view, which was to consider whether ability to do housework was evidence of disengagement from the labour market and therefore a reason to refuse benefit.

Married Women and Housework After 1948

William Beveridge famously stated that married women would not normally be fully part of his National Insurance Scheme because they had "other duties" (Beveridge 1942, para 114). This concept became known as the male breadwinner model of social security provision. Married women would be dependent on their husband's contributions for their retirement pension, while not having any entitlement to unemployment or sickness benefits. Beveridge assumed that married women would not be in paid employment or at least would expect not to be after the end of the Second World War which had brought many women into the labour force. While Beveridge's plan for social security was based on his vision of how the world of work and marriage looked in 1942, the concept of the male breadwinner model has been widely critiqued, both for its failure to recognise the complexity of family life at the time and for its failure to adapt to fundamental changes in the family and the workplace over the late twentieth century (Baldwin and Falkingham 1994; Daly and Rake 2003; Sainsbury 1996).

Although Beveridge's plan assumed that married women would, generally, not be working outside the home or contributing to the National Insurance Scheme, in December 1949 over two and a half million married women were working and were full contributors to the scheme, constituting a million women more than was estimated by the drafters of the legislation (Jay 1951, p. 7). These women were entitled to claim Sickness Benefit if they became ill. Other married women were entitled to benefits because they had been members of the interwar National Insurance Scheme and had transitional protection at the changeover in 1948. Single women paid National Insurance at the full rate and were entitled to Sickness Benefits in their own right. There were around four and a half million single women contributing to national insurance in 1949 (Jay 1951, p. 7). The problem with housework did not go away and decision makers continued to treat married women, and some single women, differently from men in their assessments of incapacity for work.

An early draft of rules for the new Sickness Benefit scheme showed continuity from the 1911 scheme and the obsession with housework. These rules were based almost verbatim on the pre-war model rules, including the rule that claimants "shall not do any kind of work, *domestic or other*" (Ministry of Health draft rules under the Beveridge proposals, 1943, in PIN 8/106, my emphasis). In the final version of the post-war regulations, the term "domestic or other" was removed from the prohibition on working while claiming (National Insurance Act, 1946. National Insurance [Unemployment and Sickness Benefit] Regulations 1948, Regulation 10(d)(iii)). Despite this change, decision makers continued to consider housework as work in making decisions about married women's benefits.

In the first year of the scheme, eighty-six thousand women were referred to Regional Medical Officers for second opinions on their claims, of whom around forty per cent were found to be incapable of work, compared with only forty-seven thousand men, of whom around fifty per cent were found to be incapable of work (Ministry of National Insurance 1950, p. 102). Some women challenged these decisions and early Commissioners Decisions illustrate the debate, with the case of Mrs E in R(S)11/51 providing the case law which would establish the principle that domestic work should not be counted as work in assessing claims. It is worth looking in some detail at Mrs E's case and also that of a Mrs B, (R(S)17/51), and to consider the arguments made by the

6 Fit for the Ordinary Work of the Home: Women and Domestic Work 121

Ministry of Pensions. Mrs E's Sickness Benefit was stopped after a sick visitor spotted her doing housework. The papers for her Commissioner's hearing includes the evidence presented by the local insurance officer, which included the Regional Medical Officer's report that she was "fit for light work". The insurance officer's submission considered that the interpretation of incapacity for work should take account of circumstances of claimants who had "no incentive to declare off [stop claiming benefit] and resume work". By having "no incentive" he meant married women who were otherwise supported by their husbands. Explaining this, he went on to say:

> I submit that the position of a woman who is as capable of doing the normal domestic duties of her household as she was before she started to claim benefit comes in this category; while the work she could do might not commend itself to an employer because she may only be able to perform it in her own time and in any way to suit herself, it is probable that if she were not there to do it, someone else might have to be employed for the purpose and what is actually happening is that she is relying on another person for her maintenance (Local insurance officer's submission to Commissioners, in R(S)11/51, May 1951 in PIN 62/1354)

The clue to his understanding of the problem lies in the final line of this statement, where he refers to "relying on another person", that is, her husband, as being the key to whether a married woman is really available for work in the open labour market. The National Insurance Commissioners did not agree with this interpretation of the legislation and underlined instead that the key test was whether the claimant was capable of paid work:

> In considering the case of a woman who occupies herself in domestic work in her own home, it is necessary to take into account the amount of work of which she appears to be capable as part of the relevant evidence in determining whether she is incapable of work ... Thus for example if a woman is capable of doing the domestic work of a normal household that would be evidence to support the view that she was capable of remunerative work because by doing for an employer what she does for her family she could reasonably be expected to obtain remuneration. (R(S)11/51, para 6)

Here the Commissioners were clearly stating that the relevance of a woman's ability to do domestic work was whether it was evidence of ability to do *paid* work in the open labour market, contradicting the view of the local office which was arguing that ability to do domestic work constituted evidence of a claimant being a housewife and therefore not in the market for paid work. However, the Commissioners did indicate that capacity to do "normal housework" would usually suggest capacity for work in the labour market. Unfortunately, for Mrs E, the Commissioners found that the evidence presented in her case was sufficient to find her fit for work and so her benefit was stopped. The principle of the relevance of the domestic duties test however was firmly established.

A second Commissioner's decision (R(S)17/51) confirmed this interpretation, and this time showing how evidence of capacity to do domestic duties would *not* always be evidence of ability to work in the open labour market. Mrs B was fifty-four and had worked as a cleaner until a stroke in 1947 led her to claim Sickness Benefit (under the Approved Societies scheme). She had continued in receipt of benefit under the post-war scheme until her benefit was reviewed by a Regional Medical Officer and she was found fit for work. She appealed to a tribunal, which upheld this decision, and she appealed again to the National Insurance Commissioners. Unusually, the Commissioners decided that further evidence was needed to decide the case and, bearing in mind the decision in R(S)11/51, asked for further evidence of her capacity for work outside the home:

> Could it be ascertained how much housework the claimant is able to do in her own home and (2) Would the manager of the local employment exchange suggest the type of employment, involving only light duties, that the claimant could be expected to perform. (3) Would he say how long the claimant has been registering for employment and whether the exchange has been able to submit her for any vacancy. (Memo from National Insurance Commissioner to Commissioner's office, July 1951 in PIN 62/1358)

In response to this request, the local employment exchange provided detailed evidence of the kind of work that might be available and explained that that they thought that Mrs B would be unable to get a job doing this kind of work:

> In reply to your enquiry concerning a claimant whose capacity for employment is in doubt, the following information setting out the position from the local employment angle may be of use. Factory work, even in a part-time capacity is competitive and involves a considerable degree of physical fitness. Alternatively, domestic employment demands full use of both hands and as a great degree of general fitness as in in the case of factory workers. In the light of information concerning the applicant in question and having regard to the general set up of industry in the local area, it is not considered that she could usefully fill any position either in a factory or in a domestic household. (letter from local Ministry of Labour and National Service Employment Exchange, to [local insurance office] August 1951 in PIN 62/1358)

6 Fit for the Ordinary Work of the Home: Women and Domestic Work

Following this evidence, the National Insurance Commissioner considered that Mrs B was not fit for work and therefore allowed her appeal. Mrs B's case can be contrasted with that of Mrs E, partly on the grounds of degree of impairment, but the other difference in their cases lies in the evidence, actively sought by the Commissioner in Mrs B's case, about the reality of paid work in the open labour market. Instead of operating on the assumption that capacity for domestic work in her own home would automatically lead to capacity for work in the labour market, the decision was made on evidence about the real world. The evidence from the employment exchange that domestic employment "demands […] a great degree of general fitness" served to counteract the view that paid domestic work was available to any woman who could do some of her own housework. The letter from the Employment Exchange also refers to the state of the local labour market "having regard to the general set up of industry in the local area" but the Commissioner did not suggest that Mrs B ought to seek work elsewhere.

This decision shows how the Commissioner took seriously the meaning of the interpretation in R(S)11/51 that the assessment of capacity for work had to take account of real jobs in the real world. These cases set off a flurry of activity in the Ministry of Pensions and National Insurance, starting with a memo from one civil servant to another, within a week of the decision on R(S)11/51 (PIN 35/41). This resulted in long discussions between the civil servants as to how go about ensuring that all possible "housewives" were being appropriately checked regarding their incapacity for work, and suggesting that more of them should be referred to the Regional Medical Officers for double checking (Memo from Mr Menner to Mr Stockman, September 1951 in PIN 35/41). Mr Stockman agreed, but was wary that it might be seen as "witch-hunt". He also referred to the possibility that there might be single women or even men who could be caught up in this increased scrutiny:

> I think it would be as well to space the review of cases carefully and limit it strictly to the type of case where the woman concerned appears to be capable of and is doing a reasonable amount of housework (not necessarily "charring") such as would, on the basis of the Commissioner's Decision, be equivalent of remunerative employment. I agree that the spinster or widow running a home for her sisters (or brothers) should be covered as well as the married woman but I think we should not be _too_ avid in our search for the mere male who is doing his best with the housework while his wife goes out to maintain the home. (Handwritten note from Mr Stockman to Mr Menner, October 1951, in PIN 35/41, underlining in original)

In his reference to the need to chase up single women and the light-hearted reference to "the mere male who is doing his best", Mr Stockman reflected the views from the 1930s that the basic argument here was about gender and not about evidence of capacity for work. This exchange of memos led eventually to revised guidance to local offices, asking them to intensify the number of sick visits to married women and to consider referring more of them to Regional Medical Officers to double-check their capacity for work. In this guidance, the Ministry of Pensions and National Insurance, referred to R(S)11/51, selectively quoting the section where it said "if a woman is capable of doing the domestic work of a normal household, that would be evidence to support the view that she was capable of remunerative work" (Draft circular regarding Sickness Benefit claimants who do their own housework, December 1951 in TNA PIN 35/41).

This draft circular omitted to mention that the decision stressed the importance of such evidence being evidence of ability to work in the open labour market. The circular went on to say that long-standing cases of married women should be reviewed unless they were "clearly disabled, suffering from a serious disease or bedridden". It also said that cases of single women "acting as housekeepers e.g. to their relatives" should be looked at. This addition of single women, who would have been required to be full members of the National Insurance scheme, indicates that the suspicion regarding women's domestic duties did not apply only to married women but to women in general.

An example of an attempt by a local office to enforce attachment to the labour market for a single woman can be found in a National Insurance Commissioner's case from 1955. Miss H was an unmarried woman in her fifties who lived with her frail elderly father, two sisters and her eight-year-old daughter. Miss H had a visual impairment and had been claiming benefits since the 1930s. There was no dispute as to her incapacity for work and she continued to receive medical certificates from her own doctor and to be found incapable of work by Regional Medical Officers. However, she was visited by a sick visitor who noted that Miss H was looking after her father and her daughter and was able to do some household tasks. The sick visitor suggested that Miss H should take part in a training course run by the local society for blind people which would help her to retrain for the labour market. Miss H said that she could not do this as her domestic responsibilities would not fit in with the hours of the training course and that she would need to be at home during the school holidays. The sick visitor's report led to a referral to the Regional Medical Officer who confirmed her continuing incapacity for work. The local office was clearly incensed by this, noting that

> So long as she continues to receive 45/- a week from public funds she has a strong inducement to remain at home with nothing to do but keep house for her father and infant child. (letter from National Insurance Officer to Regional Finance Office, 12 March 1955, R(S) 3/57, case papers in CT/11/161)

Miss H was referred again to the Regional Medical Officer with a note that this was a "domestic work reference", clearly showing that these references were also being used for single women who were considered to be housewives rather than attached to the labour market. However, the Regional Medical Officer found that:

> she is quite unfit for gainful employment in the ordinary sense of the word. Such incapacity is, in my opinion, permanent. (letter from Regional Medical Officer 30 August 1956)

The attempt by the local office to find Miss H fit for work because of her apparent lack of attachment to the labour market had failed. In a further attempt to prevent her from continuing to receive benefit from "public funds", the local office disqualified her from benefit on the grounds that she had refused to take part in the training course and that this constituted a breach of rules prohibiting "conduct calculated to retard recovery". Miss H appealed against this decision and her case was heard by a local tribunal. In his submission to the tribunal, the local insurance officer argued that "the purpose of sickness benefit was to provide a weekly cash payment, during a period of interruption of employment through incapacity, for persons who, but for that incapacity would be in employment" and that "It was clear that the reasons for her refusal [to take part in the training course] were her domestic circumstances and not her physical condition". The tribunal agreed with this interpretation, confirming the initial disqualification from benefit. Miss H appealed to the National Insurance Commissioners who disagreed with the interpretation of the conduct rules, finding that she was eligible for benefit (R(S) 3/57, case papers in CT/11/161).

While this decision was important in establishing case law on the meaning of the conduct rule (see also Chapter 8), it is equally important as an example of an attempt by a local office to use a rather obscure aspect of the benefits regulations to enforce the unwritten expectation of attachment to the labour market for women who were considered to be full time housekeepers. Guidance in the 1960s continued to advise decision makers to check up on married women's domestic duties and to check on their claims more frequently than other single women or men (Ministry of Pensions and National Insurance 1960). A memo from 1969, explained the reason for this:

> Tighter control has always been exercised for these groups [married women and self-employed people]. For married women, for instance it has always been recognised that the incentive (i.e. the economic pressure) for them to return to work is ordinarily not as great as it is for other working people. (DHSS Memo, dated 1969, "Long Term Sick RMO References summary of arrangements" in PIN35/405)

This gross generalisation that married women were not like "other working people" is symptomatic of the view across the twentieth century that women were not to be trusted in their claims to incapacity. Land records in an article in 1978 that that there was a plan to amend the guidance on household duties to include men, as a result of a Commissioner's decision. Land reports that this Commissioner's decision stated that "If the evidence showed that he undertook household chores, as many men now do, or worked in the garden, that evidence would be admissible on the question whether he is capable of remunerative work" (Cited in Land 1978, p. 264). This amendment does not appear to have been made, since the guidance from 1981 still contained advice to sick visitors to check on women's activities in the home, without any reference to men:

> When visiting a married woman or a woman who is the domestic head of household, the visiting officer should .. also ascertain the extent if any to which she is doing housework and/or looking after her husband, children or other members of the household (DHSS 1981, para 5135)

Note that this did not only concern married women but also included single women who were "domestic heads of household". Guidance continued to advise that where women were thought to be carrying out these household duties, then a special referral would be made to the Regional Medical Officer to consider whether or not the claimant could be able to "perform domestic work for which an employer would be prepared to pay" (DHSS 1981, para 5047). I have been unable to find the Commissioner's decision from 1977 to which Land refers, but there is a difference between using evidence of household duties to support an allegation that a man is capable of work and deliberately constructing guidance to seek out that evidence, as was the case with women. Although the Commissioners' decisions from 1951 had clarified the legal relevance of housework to the interpretation of incapacity for work, the continuing interest in the private activities of married women and other single women who "acted as housekeepers", but not men, suggests that policy makers' concern was not just with capacity for work. What they were really concerned about was attachment to the labour market. Equalities legislation in the 1970s began to bring about changes to these assumptions, at least in theory, but not before the arrival of the discriminatory Housewives Non-Contributory Invalidity Pension and its notorious household duties test.

The Pinnacle of Household Duties—The Case of HNCIP

In the 1970s, benefits for disabled people were extended to include people who had been out of the labour market and who did not have sufficient national insurance contributions to qualify for Sickness Benefit. These new non-contributory benefits were first proposed in a White Paper (House of Commons 1974) The White Paper stressed that potential beneficiaries of the scheme would "normally be breadwinners":

> The negative aspect [of the contributory scheme] is that those who have not paid contributions, even through no fault of their own, have no entitlement to contributory national insurance benefit. This applies with particular force to some 220,000 people under pension age who have been incapable of work for more than six months and who, were it not for their incapacity, would be breadwinners. (para 40)

This conception of disabled "breadwinners" who had missed out through "no fault of their own" did not include married women, who were singled out as an exceptional category of "disabled housewives":

> "Housewives" in this context are essentially married women who do not have paid work, and whose normal job is in the home. Some housewives are so disabled that not only would they be incapable of doing a paid job, but they are unable to cope with the household work which is their working contribution to the family [estimated to be 40,000 women]. (para 43)

This view of disabled men and single women as potential breadwinners and disabled married women as housewives is a clear statement of the thinking behind all of the incapacity benefits schemes: they were intended for breadwinners. The new benefit for men and single women took legislative form in the Social Security Act 1975, which introduced Non-Contributory Invalidity Pension (NCIP) for those claimants who had been considered "incapable of work" for 28 weeks. Married and cohabiting women were excluded but would be entitled if they could establish that they were "incapable of performing normal household duties" (Social Security Act 1975, 36(2)). Regulations provided the details of what this would mean (Social Security Act 1975, Social Security

[NCIP] Amendment Regulations 1977). The test for married or cohabiting women claiming HNCIP required women to be *both* incapable of work in the usual sense *and* incapable of "performing normal household duties" Reg 12 (1)(a), thus introducing an explicit gendered reference to household duties into the legislation. The fact that it was extended to cohabiting women reflected changes in household composition in the 1970s, including these unmarried women in the net of patriarchal dependency.

The thinking behind HNCIP was clear. It was intended to provide for married or cohabiting women who were ordinarily out of the paid labour market and who were dependent on their partners financially but who were unable to fulfil their expected domestic role of carrying out unpaid housework. This was clearly stated in the 1974 White Paper and re-emphasised in a report on the amending regulations:

> invalidity benefit is a substitute for maintenance from earnings and the rationale for its extension to non-earning married women, is that those married women who have chosen not to work in paid employment, but have instead concerned themselves with a wide range of perhaps equally arduous, and certainly equally valuable, but non-paid household duties, should nevertheless be entitled to some benefit if they are prevented from following that activity because of ill health or disablement (NIAC 1977, para 8).

Despite this apparent clarity of purpose, the statutory form of the benefit did not require women to prove that their normal work was household duties. This was assumed to be the case because of their gender and marital status. The NIAC report did consider what might happen if a married couple had swapped roles, but believed that this was unproblematic because a woman who normally worked would have the option to pay full national insurance contributions and thus qualify for Invalidity Benefit if she became ill (para 20). The report did not seem to consider it to be incongruous that her husband would qualify for NCIP without the household duties test if he became ill or disabled.

From the start, HNCIP was controversial and difficult to implement and was not without its critics. Loach and Lister (1978) outline the details of the opposition from women's groups and disability organisations, arguing that it was a sexist scheme based on an outdated model of gendered relationships. To make a claim, women required a certificate of incapacity for work from their doctor and also needed to fill out a lengthy claim form which included questions about ability to dust, iron, stand in a queue, keep the home clean and tidy and other such household activities (Form BF450, copy in PIN 35/657). The form also asked whether the claimant needed to use any "special appliances" to carry out such work. Critics of the scheme pointed out that it was not clear at all what a "special appliance" meant and whether or not it included such things as vacuum cleaners and automatic washing machines (Glendinning and Disability Alliance 1980). In an example from 1979, a woman was refused benefit because, among other things, she conceded "that she has the capacity to do household tasks, such as using a Hoover". On appeal to the National Insurance Commissioners, she was found to be incapable of normal household duties and therefore eligible for benefit (R(S) 6/79). Another woman was refused benefit after the Commissioner concluded that she was capable of household duties, although admitting that she could only do the housework slowly. The decision noted, among other things that she lived "in a two-bedroomed terraced house adequately equipped with domestic appliances" (R(S)4/78, para 4). These, and other similar cases, show the depth of intrusion into married women's daily lives which the household duties test entailed. A couple of National Insurance Commissioners' decisions provided the initial catalyst for the abolition of HNCIP. The story began in early 1978 when a Mrs M, aged 42, who had been disabled since birth, won an appeal against refusal of benefit at a local tribunal. The case was considered to be important and the Chief Insurance Officer appealed to the National Insurance Commissioners (R(S) 5/78). According to papers in the National Archives, Mrs M's hearing was attended by reporters from *The Guardian, The Times* and the *Manchester Evening News*, as well as an observer from the Disablement Income Group (DIG) and two official DHSS observers. The DIG reporters noted in detail the progress of the hearing including that Mrs M was asked about her ability to operate a washing machine, to peel vegetables, to use a hoover and to change the batteries in her radio. She had a dog and had to explain that it was a miniature poodle which did not require much exercising. She was required to explain the daily routine of making coffee, opening tins, occasionally getting fish and chips. The reporter from DIG noted the upsetting effect of this intrusive questioning. The Commissioner found that Mrs M was incapable of household duties and so eligible for benefit (papers in PIN 35/491). This case was followed quickly by a similar decision in R(S)7/78. These two decisions were seen by officials as a widening of the interpretation of the legislation and amending regulations were quickly introduced to tighten up the definition of capacity for household duties. This was reported in the *Guardian* as "Minister blocks loophole in disabled pensions" (Phillips 1978). The outcry in Parliament led to an investigation into HNCIP by the National Insurance Advisory Committee (NIAC 1980) and to inquiries by campaigning organisations (Glendinning and Disability Alliance 1980).

HNCIP was finally dispensed with after campaigning by disability and women's groups, several key legal cases and, ultimately, the introduction of European equal treatment rules (Luckhaus 1986; Sohrab 1994). NCIP and HNCIP were replaced with Severe Disablement Allowance, a theoretically gender-neutral non-contributory benefit, aimed at people without a history of labour market participation. Further details of the history of HNCIP can be found in Loach and Lister (1978), Glendinning and Disability Alliance (1980) and Gulland (2019). The principles behind HNCIP regarding the role of married women as inherently outside the labour market and of their "duties" to do housework reflected previous debates about women, work and housework. The ineffective and intrusive household duties test looked very like the proposals made by Mr Sanderson in 1914. It proved to be impossible to implement.

Domestic Work in the 1990s and Today

Legislation on incapacity benefits since the 1980s has been theoretically gender neutral but access to benefits is still heavily gendered as a result of men's and women's different labour market participation. Since 1995, "domestic work" has been explicitly listed as "work" which a claimant is allowed to do while claiming benefit, but a relatively recent case from 2001 shows that there are still grey areas. In this case, a woman had been claiming Incapacity Benefit, and there was no challenge to her status as incapable of work under the Incapacity Benefit rules. However, her benefit had been stopped after her local office discovered that she had been providing bed, breakfast and evening meals to overseas students for a few weeks each summer. The claimant appealed on the grounds that this was "domestic work" and did not amount to very much more than she was already doing for her own children. The first-tier tribunal agreed and the Secretary of State appealed to the Commissioner. The Commissioner's view was that the provision of bed and breakfast to visiting students was not "domestic work" within the meaning of the Incapacity Benefit regulations:

> I cannot accept that the undertaking of services, including the provision of meals and the changing of sheets in the context of provision of accommodation for money, could properly be regarded as domestic tasks. To do so would be to stretch the phrase "domestic tasks" into tasks which are intrinsically commercial. (R(IB)1/03, 2001)

The key issue here was payment. Carrying out domestic tasks in return for payment constitutes work and means that claimants cannot continue to receive benefit while doing this work. Employment and Support Allowance continues to exclude "domestic work" from its definition of work but carrying out work such as this for pay would constitute work, excluding a claimant from benefit unless they came under the permitted work rules (see Chapter 7).

Conclusions: Housework as a Form of Conditionality or as Evidence of Capacity for Work

There was a constant battle, through most of the twentieth century, to assess married women's claims against both their capacity for work and their attachment to the labour market. In some of the legal cases in the Approved Societies scheme, such as the case filed in MH62/201/1999, and the early post-war Commissioners' decisions, such as R(S)11/51 and R(S)17/51, there was an attempt by the legal decision makers to link the housework tests clearly to assessments of capacity for work. The reaction of the civil servants responsible for the scheme however suggests that there was an attempt to continue to use the housework evidence as a mechanism for ensuring attachment to the labour market for married women well into the late twentieth century. Using evidence of capacity for housework in this way constituted a form of labour market conditionality which is entirely absent from the legislation on incapacity benefits. The explicitly discriminatory HNCIP was an exception where the regulations did subject married women to a different test from that required of single women or of men. This household duties test was described as a test of capacity for dusting and cleaning but it too was a mechanism for testing attachment to the labour market. The fact that decision making on the question of assessment of incapacity for work was so clearly gendered supports the argument that the assessment of incapacity for work is socially constructed and is dependent on a whole range of assumptions about what women (and men) ought to be able to do in terms of work. One of these assumptions is that claimants should show an attachment to the labour market in order to be eligible for benefit. Ironically, early twentieth-century policy makers did recognise domestic labour as work but used this as evidence to exclude married women from benefits, on the assumption that women had male partners to support them financially and were not really in the labour market.

References

Baldwin, Sally, and Jane Falkingham. 1994. *Social Security and Social Change: New Challenges to the Beveridge Model.* Hemel Hempstead: Harvester Wheatsheaf.

Beveridge, Sir William. 1942. *Social Insurance and Allied Services.* Cmd. 6404. London: HMSO.

Daly, Mary, and Katherine Rake. 2003. *Gender and the Welfare State.* Oxford: Polity.

Deacon, Alan. 1976. *In Search of the Scrounger.* Leeds: University of Leeds.

Department of Health and Social Security. 1981. *Sickness Benefit Law and Procedure. Code SB 1969, as Amended, 1981.* London: HMSO.

Glendinning, Caroline, and Disability Alliance. 1980. *'After Working All These Years': A Response to the Report of the National Insurance Advisory Committee on the 'Household Duties' Test for Non-contributory Invalidity Pension for Married Women.* London: Disability Alliance.

Gulland, Jackie. 2019. 'Conditionality and Social Security: Lessons from the Household Duties Test'. *Journal of Social Security Law* 26 (2): 60–76.

Hochschild, Arlie. 1989. *The Second Shift: Working Parents and the Revolution at Home.* London: Piatkus.

House of Commons. 1974. 'Social Security Act 1973. Social Security Provision for Chronically Sick and Disabled People'. HC 274. London: HMSO.

Jay, Douglas. 1951. 'National Insurance Act, 1946. First Interim Report by the Government Actuary for the Period 5th July, 1948 to 31st March, 1950'. London: HMSO.

Land, Hilary. 1978. 'Who Cares for the Family?' *Journal of Social Policy* 7 (3): 257–84.

Lewis, Jane. 1983. 'Dealing with Dependency: State Practices and Social Realities 1870–1945'. In *Women's Welfare Women's Rights*, edited by Jane Lewis. London: Croom Helm.

Loach, Irene, and Ruth Lister. 1978. *Second Class Disabled—A Report on the Non-contributory Invalidity Pension for Married Women.* London: Equal Rights for Disabled Women Campaign.

Luckhaus, Linda. 1986. 'Severe Disablement Allowance: The Old Dressed up as New?' *Journal of Social Welfare and Family Law* 8 (3): 153–69.

Ministry of Health. 1923. *Reports of Decisions on Appeals and Applications under Section 67 of the National Insurance Act 1911 and Section 27 of the National Insurance Act 1913, Vol 2—Part I.* London: HMSO.

Ministry of National Insurance. 1950. *Report of the Ministry of National Insurance for the Period 17th November, 1944, to 4th July, 1949.* Cd. 7955. London: HMSO.

Ministry of Pensions and National Insurance. 1960. *Instructions to National Insurance Offices on Law and Procedure Relating to Sickness Benefits under the National Insurance Acts Code SB.* London: HMSO.

National Health Insurance Joint Committee. 1914a. *National Health Insurance. Appendix to the Report of the Departmental Committee on Sickness Benefit Claims under the National Insurance Act. Volume I*. Cd. 7688, 7689, 7690, 7691. London: HMSO.

———. 1914b. *National Health Insurance. Report of the Departmental Committee on Sickness Benefit Claims under the National Insurance Act*. Cd. 7687. London: HMSO.

National Insurance Advisory Committee. 1977. *Social Security Act 1975, Social Security (Non-contributory Invalidity Pension) Amendment Regulations 1977 (S.I. 1977 No. 1312). Report of the National Insurance Advisory Committee*. Cmnd. 6900. London: HMSO.

———. 1980. *Report of the National Insurance Advisory Committee on a Question Relating to the Household Duties Test for Non-contributory Invalidity Pension for Married Women*. Cmnd. 7955. London: HMSO.

Pedersen, Susan. 1993. *Family, Dependence, and the Origins of the Welfare State: Britain and France, 1914–1945*. Cambridge: Cambridge University Press.

Phillips, Melanie. 1978. 'Minister Blocks "loophole" in Disabled Pensions'. *The Guardian*, 1978, 14 September edition.

Sainsbury, Diane. 1996. *Gender, Equality and Welfare States*. Cambridge: Cambridge University Press.

Sohrab, Julia. 1994. 'An Overview of the Equality Directive on Social Security and Its Implications for Four Social Security Systems'. *European Journal of Social Policy* 4: 263–76.

Tomlinson, J. 1984. 'Women as "Anomolies": The Anomolies Regulations of 1931, Their Background and Administration'. *Public Administration* 62: 423–37.

Watson, Alfred W. 1929. *National Health Insurance. Report by the Government Actuary on an Examination of the Sickness and Disablement Experience of a Group of Approved Societies in the Period 1921–1927*. Cmd. 3548. London: HMSO.

———. 1931. 'National Health Insurance Report by the Government Actuary on the Third Valuation of the Assets and Liabilities of Approved Societies'. Cmd. 3978. London: HMSO.

Whiteside, Noel. 1987. 'Counting the Cost: Sickness and Disability among Working People in an Era of Industrial Recession, 1920–1939'. *Economic History Review* XL: 228–46.

7

Not Incapable of Playing Bingo: Ideas About "Work" in Incapacity Benefits

Introduction

In 1965, a lorry driver injured his back and claimed Sickness Benefit. While he was off work, he spent his time playing bingo and struck lucky, winning £900 over four months. The *Daily Mail* reported his story in a light-hearted fashion "It was eyes down again last night for Mr Bingo" (*Daily Mail*, 2/3/65, copy in PIN 35/72). Mr Bingo was lucky by anyone's standards but what made his story interesting was the effect that his lucky winnings had on his Sickness Benefit. The *Daily Mail* went on to explain that the "eyes" on Mr Bingo were those of the National Assistance Board, which had interviewed him for two hours about his winnings. Mr Bingo was claiming £7 a week in Sickness Benefit but he was also claiming the National Assistance of around £3 a week. Since National Assistance was means-tested, these winnings might take him over the means-test limit. However, the Ministry of Pensions and National Insurance was also interested in Mr Bingo's case because playing bingo might constitute work. If playing bingo was work, then he was not eligible for Sickness Benefit. The Ministry kept copies of the press cuttings in a file which also contains a handwritten note about the case:

> Does this put him in class II [in other words, is he self-employed]? If so he would not be entitled to sickness benefit – not incapable of playing bingo - and we could reclaim the sickness benefit paid for days of bingo. (memo dated 2/3/65, in PIN 35/72)

It is not clear if the civil servants at the Ministry of Pensions were being entirely serious about Mr Bingo being a self-employed professional bingo player. They

© The Author(s) 2019
J. Gulland, *Gender, Work and Social Control*, Palgrave Socio-Legal Studies,
https://doi.org/10.1057/978-1-137-60564-1_7

concluded that the best course of action was to refer him to the Regional Medical Officer to check that he was still incapable of work. By playing bingo, Mr Bingo crossed two imaginary lines in the world of incapacity benefit decision making: he was taking part in a regular activity that may have looked like work and he was making money from doing so. It was the income-generating aspect of playing bingo that attracted the attention of the authorities and the press. In Mr Bingo's case, there was a possibility that his benefit could be stopped because of this work-like activity. This chapter looks at how incapacity benefit decision makers have interpreted and developed the concept of work across the twentieth century.

Legislation and Case Law

Legislation on incapacity benefits did not define work until the 1970s. Both the 1911 Act and the 1946 National Insurance Act stated only that claimants should be "incapable of work" (National Insurance Act 1911, 8(c), National Insurance Act 1946, S11(2)(a)(ii)). This was refined in 1975 when the definition included "work which the person can reasonably be expected to do" (Social Security Act 1975, S17(1)(a)) but none of these statutes defined work as such. Case law since 1948 has been more helpful, with the key case, the case of Mrs E from 1951, cited at the beginning of this book, defining work as

> remunerative work, that is to say, work whether part-time or whole time for which an employer would be willing to pay, or work as a self-employed person in some gainful occupation. (R(S)11/51, para 5)

This case was important in emphasising that work meant paid work and clarifying that such work could be part-time or self-employed. Although the Commissioners confirmed that work that a claimant was capable of needed to be remunerative, they were very careful to note that the level of remuneration was not relevant and that there was to be no assessment of the claimant's ability to support themselves on the wages they could earn from such work. The Commissioners in R(S)11/51 were careful to exclude questions of sufficiency of earnings or the availability of work in the local labour market from their definition. Further clarification of some of these points appeared in later case law, for example, R(S)2/82, which provided a lengthy discussion on the relationship between incapacity for work and the labour market, R(S)6/85 (see Chapter 5), and many cases on the complicated position of self-employed people. A detailed discussion of the case law as it stood shortly before the introduction of Incapacity Benefit can be found in Bonner et al. (1991, pp. 23–29). Although the case law in the late twentieth century was clear on the principle of remunerative work as the key test, the day-to-day meaning of the term work was left to the interpretation of individual doctors, medical referees and tribunal decision makers.

Evidence from the early twentieth century can illustrate some of the ways in which different interpretations of the idea of work operated in practice before 1951. These conceptions of work reflected and reinforced social structures and assumptions about class, gender and disability. The idea of incapacity benefits depended on a vision of a full-time, life-long employed person within a conventional employment relationship. Difficulties of interpretation arose over the principle of pay, the question of self-employment, whether people should be allowed to do some work while claiming benefits and the perennial problem of what to do about housework, discussed in detail in Chapter 6.

Paid Work

The decision in R(S)11/51 was consistent with previous decisions in confirming that incapacity for work usually meant incapacity for paid work and also in evading the issue of whetherremuneration for work should be sufficient. In some senses, this is surprising, since it is of little use to a person to be able to work but to be unable to feed and clothe themselves. On the other hand, expanding the definition of capacity for work to include financial sufficiency would open up a Pandora's Box of questions about inequality, wage adequacy and human need, which is well beyond the technical remit of doctors and frontline decision makers. The possibility of including the concept of ability to earn enough to live on was considered at the time of the introduction of National Health Insurance in 1911. Such considerations were rejected, according to William Braithwaite, a senior civil servant at the time as "astonishingly bad and ambiguous, worthy of amateur politicians" (Braithwaite 1957, p. 190). The 1911 legislative definition of incapacity for work therefore focussed on the work capacity and not the earning capacity of claimants, leading to a constant need to dance around the idea of how much a claimant would need to be able to earn from their hypothetical labour power in order for this activity to be considered to be work.

Early appeal cases confirmed that the definition required the concept of remunerative work. Mr O was fifty-six and a former miner, claiming benefits in 1916. Although his own doctor certified him as incapable of work, the doctor appointed by his Approved Society for a second opinion believed that Mr O was capable of some kind of work:

he has two good hands and arms and one good leg. The special senses in good working order and the organs of speech especially active. He would be an excellent public speaker or preacher.

On the basis of this assessment, the Approved Society stopped paying Sickness Benefit and Mr O appealed. The adjudicators upheld his appeal. In their decision, they dismissed the idea that he could work as a public speaker and argued that "the question of capacity for work cannot be regarded in the abstract without reference to the particular circumstances of the insured person concerned". In discussing the work that he might be able to do the adjudicators referred to his "wage earning capacity", citing the 1911 Act:

> The Statute is entitled "An Act to provide for Insurance against Loss of Health" and both sickness and disablement benefit are payable under it while the insured person is "incapable of work", and in our opinion the mischief at which it aims is the loss of wage earning capacity through illness. (Case 82, NHIC 1917, p. 213)

The emphasis here on wage earning capacity demonstrates the adjudicators' view that incapacity for work in the 1911 Act meant incapacity for paid work. However, in other cases adjudicators were careful to differentiate between the abstract concept of incapacity for work and the amount of money that a claimant might be able to earn. The idea that the test was the claimant's ability to do *any* work, regardless of the level of remuneration, was applied particularly harshly to female claimants.

Mrs H, a woman in her mid-fifties, had previously worked as a cleaner but was unable to continue do so since injuring her arm. When she claimed and was refused benefit in 1918, she appealed. The adjudicators considered that her injury did not prevent her working in some form:

> Doubtless the net effect of her injury will be to prevent her from ever regaining her full earning capacity but this is not the same thing as total incapacity for work. (Case 122, NHIC 1919, p. 292)

The adjudicators recognised that refusing her benefit would cause hardship to her family, noting that Mrs H's household consisted of herself, her "invalid husband" and two adult daughters. In noting the "invalid husband", the adjudicators were highlighting Mrs H's role as the breadwinner in the family, which might have led them to consider more carefully what her earning power might be. However, they also noted that Mrs H's adult daughters "earn their living and support their parents", implying that it would not matter too much if Mrs H was unable to earn very much from her limited capacity for work. The focus was on a hypothetical capacity for work rather than her earning capacity as such.

In another case in 1918, Miss S, a sixty-eight-year-old former nurse with rheumatoid arthritis, had been claiming benefit since the early days of the scheme. She was found to be fit for work by a medical referee who thought that she could do "light housework" or find work as a needlewoman. Miss S agreed that she was able to do some needlework but that she "could only do this work very slowly which made the remuneration thus earned very small". The adjudicators rejected her appeal and found her fit for work. In their decision, they noted that this would lead to hardship but that this was not a relevant consideration. The question was whether Miss S was capable of earning at all and her earning power was irrelevant (Case 129, NHIC 1919, p. 304). References to the fact that a claimant could earn only small amounts of money were common in decisions in cases concerning women. However, an appeal case from 1919, concerning a man, provided a different perspective on the issue. This case concerned Mr D, a former butcher who had a spinal condition which affected his ability to walk, as well as causing pain and discomfort. At his appeal hearing, the adjudicators accepted that he was unable to work as a butcher and deliberated whether there was other work that he might be able to do. In their discussion of Mr D's capacities, the adjudicators concluded that he might be able to do some work, but also

> whether any "light work" of which the [claimant] was capable would have been of sufficient economic value to induce an employer to provide him with it. (Case 2/11, Ministry of Health 1923, p. 36)

This is illuminating for the emphasis on whether work would be of "sufficient economic value" to a potential employer, rather than whether it would be sufficient for the claimant to live on. Such an understanding of the meaning of work is key to understanding the principles of incapacity benefits. It shows that the purpose of benefits is not based on the needs of the claimant but on the needs of the labour market. The question of whether a person can contribute work of "sufficient economic value" is very clearly not something which can be measured by medical assessments.

These cases from the early twentieth century did not act as a case law as such but it is clear that they were used in guiding some Societies and policy makers in their approach to decision making. Commissioners' decisions in the post-1948 period did however create case law and the decision makers in the classic R(S)11/51 confirmed that it was *not* relevant whether "the work which she is capable of doing will not be sufficiently remunerative to enable her to support herself" (para 7). Despite this clear statement that sufficiency was not a relevant consideration, the question of earning power continued to be significant in cases concerning self-employed people. There were two issues with self-employment: whether an already self-employed person could continue with their work and whether a previously employed person could adapt to self-employment as an alternative to their previous occupation. Appeal cases in the 1950s were mostly concerned with how to treat people who were already self-employed but had become ill or disabled and were no longer (or temporarily unable) to continue with their self-employed work. Many of these cases involved people running very small businesses or small farms. The questions concerned whether the small amount of activity that they did keeping the business going constituted work. Claimants often argued that they were not working because their businesses were not as productive or profitable as usual and that therefore their own earning power had diminished. Usually, this was not considered relevant. In R(S)22/51, the claimant was a fifty-seven-year-old man who managed a small box factory. He had emphysema, bronchitis and epilepsy and had found it difficult to find work as an employee. His business was not making very much money and he argued that he was unfit for work. The Commissioners found, however, that the work he was doing in managing the factory counted as work for the purposes of Sickness Benefit and that therefore he was fit for work. The profits from the factory were considered to be irrelevant, although, they said that if the claimant had been clearly paying someone else as a manager, this might have counted as evidence of his incapacity.

A particularly illuminating example comes from 1953 where the claimant had been off sick from her usual work as a doctor's receptionist for about six months as a result of abscesses possibly related to a smallpox vaccination. During this time, she did some part-time work as a "retail corsetiere" which involved seeing clients and fitting them for corsets. She regarded this work as "recreational" rather than "work" since it was something that she had done in her spare time while in her normal job. These periods of work came to light when she later claimed Unemployment Benefit and had to submit details of self-employed earnings. The local office claimed that she was not entitled to benefit on the days that she had worked and that this was evidence of capacity for work throughout the period. The Commissioner's decision was that the days on which she worked disentitled her from Sickness Benefit but accepted that she was generally unfit for work throughout the period. One of the interesting things about this case is the claimant's perspective. In her appeal she said:

> I definitely did not know that evenings or week end part time work debarred me from sickness benefit...... I had no idea what is really a small part-time hobby

of mine and not regular work would stop me from receiving benefit. I am sorry and surprised at any trouble caused

The claimant did not regard this activity as work. She described it as a "hobby" and because she did it while she was working at her usual job she ought to be able to continue doing it while she was off sick (R(S)9/53, case papers in PIN 62/1404).

In another case from this period, a farmer claimed Sickness Benefit when he was no longer able to carry out the manual work on his small farm, after an injury to his shoulder. He was supported in his appeal by a representative from the National Union of Farmers, who argued that the reduction of profits was relevant:

> It has been agreed that the claimant can do some light work and he can supervise farm work. It has however been proved by statistics prepared by the Ministry of Agriculture, that a small dairy farm of 50 acres will only support the farmer if he does the majority of the manual farm work himself. If the farmer employed sufficient labour on the farm so that he was only to do the supervision and light work, he would soon be bankrupt. (evidence from National Farmers Union, dated 13/7/59, in support of claimant's appeal in R(S)2/61, copy in National Archives file PIN 62/1502)

The Commissioners in this case were not convinced and argued that the question was not whether or not the farm was profitable, but whether the claimant could do any work. They concluded that the work done by the claimant was more than trivial, was work within the meaning of the Sickness Benefit scheme and therefore he was not entitled to benefit. During the 1950s and 1960s, there was some correspondence between the National Farmers' Union and the Department of Health and Social Security regarding how farmers' claims for benefit should be regarded. The NFU asked:

> In order that we can give some guidance to our members on this matter I would be grateful if you could give me some details of what work would in fact qualify as so negligible that it can be disregarded, as it is difficult to conceive of anything much more negligible than the signing of a few cheques.

The DHSS replied, saying:

> Sickness benefit is paid not because a man is suffering from a certain condition but because that condition makes him incapable of work. A broken leg can make, say, a bus conductor incapable of work but it does not necessarily make an office worker incapable. Moreover if say, an "executive" has work sent home

to him because he is too unwell to travel to the office, he is not incapable of work. Everything depends on the circumstances and the decision is taken by the independent determining authorities in the light of all the circumstances of the case. (correspondence in PIN 35/392, June 1967)

This correspondence shows how the failure to consider the sufficiency of income was particularly disadvantageous to self-employed people if they could not find a way of showing that the restrictions on their activities constituted total incapacity. These post-war cases throw up some examples of people in relatively well-paid middle-class professions, where the question of sufficient remuneration took on a different gloss. For example, in R(S)33/52 a chartered accountant fractured his wrist and was unable to write. He claimed Sickness Benefit, arguing that he normally spent ninety-five percent of his time writing and that he had to pay his staff overtime to cover the work that he would normally do. The Commissioners did not agree that this constituted incapacity for work as the claimant was still able to supervise the staff in his office. In another case, however, concerning a man who had a short-term impairment as a result of a fractured right hand, the effect on the claimant's business was considered relevant. Mr H was a self-employed salesman who relied on the Christmas trade for the bulk of his annual profits. Mr H argued that he should be considered incapable of work because he was unable to drive and to carry heavy parcels during this important period of his business cycle. The local insurance office argued that he was not incapable of work because he was able to continue to do some of the work of maintaining the business. Mr H appealed to a local tribunal, which upheld the original decision. He then appealed to the National Insurance Commissioners. The National Insurance Commissioner upheld his appeal, agreeing that any work that Mr H was able to do must have been "quite negligible" and therefore he was incapable of work for the period of the claim (CS499/50 KL, further papers in CT11/25). In this case, the particular seasonal effect on the claimant's earnings of his short-term incapacity seems to have been significant. One of the differences between the case of Mr H and many of the cases concerning farmers and other self-employed people was that his incapacity was short term. If Mr H's impairment had been more prolonged, he would have been expected to look for alternative work or to adapt his business such that he would be able to continue running it in the light of his impairment. That would have cost his business money, for example by paying staff to carry out the manual labour required. Had his business been large enough to employ extra staff, Mr H would have found himself more in the circumstances of the farmers or the owner of the box factory in case R(S)22/51 and would no doubt have been found fit for work.

These cases show that the specific issue of sufficiency of earnings or profitability of small businesses was not usually considered relevant to the question of capacity for work. However, these assessments could only be made in relation to businesses or self-employed work which the claimants were already doing at the point of claim. It would be difficult to imagine that people could be told to start hypothetical businesses in order to find work that would be adaptable to their impairments.

Unpaid Work

R(S)11/51 established that the post-war interpretation of capacity for work should be concerned with capacity for *paid* work, although deliberately passing over the question of sufficiency of such pay. However, the decision did continue to stress that consideration should be given to whether unpaid work *should* be paid. There had been some discussions of this issue in the Approved Society period although there was some overlap here with the question of domestic work. An early example concerned Mrs T, a widow in her sixties, who had been working as a housekeeper until her glaucoma caused a severe visual impairment. She continued to live with her former employer although was no longer being paid. Mrs T paid her former employer a weekly amount towards her keep, which the employer paid partly back to her. The Society claimed that this amounted to wages and that therefore she was working. Mrs T's landlady gave evidence at her appeal hearing, saying "[Mrs T] has shown willing. I am sorry she is not able to be of much use" (Case 138, NHIC 1919, p. 324). The description of Mrs T's contribution as "not much use" shows that claimants and those supporting their claims defined work in terms of the contribution that they might make, rather than some abstract notion of capacity. At her appeal hearing, the adjudicators agreed:

> This in our opinion clearly showed that this payment was not made in consideration of the Appellant's services but was merely a piece of generosity on the part of Mrs C [the landlady] towards a disabled servant who had the praiseworthy desire though not the ability to be of some use to her benefactor in return for the kindness she was receiving. (Case 138, NHIC 1919, p. 325)

The adjudicators in this case were interested in whether the small amount of money transferred between Mrs T and her landlady constituted pay but also in whether the work that she did was effective. The decision in Mrs T's case was clearly influenced by her age and the extent of her impairment. A younger woman in a similar position might well have been considered to be able to carry out minimal domestic duties. An example from 1927 concerned a woman, Miss E, who lived with her brother, acting as a housekeeper for him until her illness reduced the amount of work that she could do. Her doctor argued that the limited work that she carried out in her brother's home was quite different from paid domestic work because she was able to rest when necessary and there was "no compulsion as is inherent in a contractual occupation" (PIN 63/1/428, 1927). The adjudicator did not agree with this assessment and decided instead that Miss E's household work constituted evidence of capacity for work.

A much earlier case concerned a woman from Lurgan who claimed benefit under the Sickness Benefit scheme in 1916. Miss L had lived with her mother and brother for several years, acting as a housekeeper and carer for her invalid mother. After her mother died, Miss L's brother wanted her to continue acting as a housekeeper but she refused to do this unless he paid her. They came to an agreement that he would pay her and provide her board and lodging. Shortly, after this Miss L developed rheumatoid arthritis and claimed Sickness Benefit. Miss L had then moved out of her brother's house and another sister had taken over the housekeeping role. The Society attempted to refuse benefit, not on the grounds of capacity for work but on the grounds that she had never been "genuinely employed" and so was not eligible to be part of the insurance scheme. Miss L appealed with the help of a local solicitor's office which was able to help her put together the evidence necessary to justify her argument that she had indeed worked for her brother for pay during the relevant period and was therefore eligible for benefit. Her appeal was upheld (correspondence in D1929/3/1/2, 1916, PRONI).

Miss L's case illustrates an assumption by decision makers that even unmarried women could be considered to be housekeepers rather than workers. Working for a family member in this way was not work. Miss L's situation was complex, since she had been happy to carry out the domestic and caring work unpaid while her invalid mother was still alive but was not prepared to do so for her brother. The Society assumed that Miss L was not a "worker", that she was not attached to the labour market and that therefore she was not entitled to benefit. With the help of a solicitor, Miss L was able to persuade the Society that the relationship with her brother was an employment contract and that she was therefore entitled to benefit.

An early post-war decision by a tribunal of Commissioners (CWS 25/50KL) considered the question of whether work, which had not been paid, but perhaps should have been, counted as work. In this case, Miss F had been claiming Sickness Benefit but was seen helping out her brother on his market stall. Her benefit was stopped on the grounds that she had been working. When she appealed to a local tribunal, she claimed that she was not paid and that she only helped out from time to time. She said that she was getting fresh air on the advice of her doctor. The local tribunal accepted her evidence and decided that her contribution to the market stall did not constitute work:

> [The Tribunal members] are not satisfied that the Applicant was engaged in work on the two occasions referred to by [under manager] for which she would ordinarily receive payment. Her evidence was that she was never paid for doing odd jobs for her brother. They further consider that the evidence given against the Applicant hardly amounts to evidence of "work" within the meaning of the regulations. (CWS 25/50 KL, form LT3, dated 6/12/49, in CT11/204)

The National Insurance office appealed to the National Insurance Commissioners. The evidence presented to the Commissioners also included a letter from Miss F's brother, who agreed that she helped out from time to time but that this did not constitute work because he did not pay her and she did not contribute anything of value to the business:

> I would like to point out Sir, that the only purpose of her being on the stall at the market was to keep "an eye" for petty thieves who trouble us a great deal. She has never received any payment from me as it was never considered as being anything worthy of reward. As regards her serving customers, I'm afraid that's entirely out of the question, unfortunately my sister is a poor scholar and would be anything but an asset where money matters are concerned. (CWS 25/50 KL, Letter from MF, Miss F's brother, to the National Insurance Commissioner, dated 13/3/50 in CT11/204)

The Commissioners considered this evidence, along with further evidence from the local office, which argued that Miss F's contribution to the market stall constituted work because she should have been paid for it. The Commissioners found that Miss F had breached the rules requiring that claimants did not work while claiming benefit, disqualifying her from benefit for six weeks. This decision, therefore, clarified the principle that activities could count as work if they would ordinarily be payable by an employer and so the fact that work was unpaid was not sufficient to qualify a claimant for benefit.

A much later case, in the 1980s, considered whether work counted if the claimant had not been paid directly. In this example, the claimant, a farmer, had been caught working on the farm by fraud investigators and had been convicted of making false representations by working and claiming Supplementary Benefit. His appeal case concerned whether or not this also disqualified him from Sickness Benefit. The Commissioners found that it did

> The claimant contended that "work" meant work for which payment is made and that he personally received no payments. In section 17(1)(a) of the SSAct 1975 "work" in that paragraph is defined as meaning "work which the person can reasonably be expected to do". Work does not necessarily mean manual work or work for which a person is paid: organising, directing and supervising other work constitutes work. (R(S)2/80)

This definition of work to include "organising, directing and supervising" opened up the possibility that almost anybody would be capable of some kind of work, if there was a possibility that they might be paid to do it.

Permitted Work

The question of claimants carrying out work that would "ordinarily" be paid has some overlap with the permitted work rules, whereby incapacity benefits could be paid to people who *were* working, despite being considered incapable. The detailed history of the concept of permitted work is discussed in more depth in Gulland (2017). For the purposes of this chapter, it is useful to see what the concept conveys about the meaning of work. The permitted work rules were developed after the First World War to encourage rehabilitation of ex-service personnel. Complex regulations were established to distinguish between work which was "trivial", work which was "therapeutic" and work which was in some sense "real work". If a claimant could establish that the work that they were doing was either trivial or therapeutic, they could be allowed to continue these activities while still claiming benefit. Policy and case law interpretation of the legislation attempted to define these distinctions in more and more detail over the course of the twentieth century, as ideas about therapy, rehabilitation and work-readiness changed. The two world wars prompted efforts to enable war-disabled people to carry out therapeutic work. After the Second World War, the rise of sheltered workshops and schemes for homeworking for disabled people led to debates about whether or not these activities constituted work, with complex rules about the nature of therapy and the introduction of earnings limits for people claiming benefits. This changed again from the 1990s when work preparation became the focus of the permitted work rules. The permitted work rules are illuminating as they attempted to distinguish between real work, which most people were expected to do, and therapeutic work which was intended for disabled people who were expected not to be in the labour market. This distinction was heavily based on assumptions about class, gender and expectations of disabled behaviour. One interesting development in the idea of permitted work was the introduction of exemptions for certain kinds of civic duties, such as acting as a local councillor or sitting on social security tribunals. These exemptions were created in the 1990s with the introduction of Incapacity Benefit and a small move towards recognising the importance of disabled people's participation in civic life. The specific case of acting as a local councillor came from a piece of case law from the 1980s when a local councillor was considered to be eligible for Invalidity Benefit (for a fuller discussion, see Gulland 2017). However, these kinds of civic activities could always carry a risk that a claimant's benefit would be reviewed and that they would be found fit for work. The permitted work rules have attempted to square this circle by distinguishing between people who would be unlikely ever to return to the labour market and therefore allowing them to do small amount of paid work, those who should be preparing themselves to return to work, and therefore allowing them to do small amounts of paid work, and those for whom the very act of doing paid work is taken as a sign that they are attempting to cheat. The different ways in which work has been defined in these rules reflect changing ideas about disabled people's contribution to the labour market. Under current welfare regimes, almost everybody is expected to be a worker, whether or not sufficient paid work is available to them.

Work as an Individual Activity

One of the many assumptions behind the incapacity benefit schemes is that work is an individual activity. The archetypal benefit claimant would be someone with a contract of employment with a specific employer which they would be unable to fulfil because of a health issue or impairment. There are many people and types of work which do not fit this model. An issue which arose in the early twentieth century, and occasionally in the late twentieth century, concerned people who shared their work with a family member. An early example of this concerned Mr B, a fifty-eight-year-old former iron ore miner, who had been claiming Sickness and then Disablement Benefit for around six months. He had secured a small part-time job as a caretaker, which he shared with his son. His benefit was stopped on the grounds that he was working. Mr B himself did not regard what he did as work, since most of the requirements of the post were carried out by his son. He described what he did:

> In no sense can this be regarded as effective work … The duties are principally carried out by my son, myself being physically unfit even for duties of such a light character. (Case 59, NHIC 1916, p. 160)

Mr B's assertion that what he did was not "effective work" and that his son carried out most of the duties was not sufficient to convince the adjudicator who confirmed that his contract of employment was evidence that what he was doing was work. These kinds of caretaking posts, where the tasks of the job were shared, often between husbands and wives, may have been more common in the early twentieth century and created particular problems for an individualised approach to the definition of work.

A particular issue in the definition of work concerned whether women letting out rooms to lodgers constituted work. These cases had clear overlaps with the gendered issue of whether housework was work but also the question of who was doing the work. If a household had spare room capacity which could be let out to lodgers, the question was whether any income was merely rent from the room or whether the act of letting the room and the associated domestic duties constituted work. There are examples of these debates from the 1920s.

Mrs W had a visual impairment which made working outside the home difficult. Within the home, she did some of the housework but was unable to go near the fire as this was dangerous. Evidence in her case included the fact that she lived with her husband, her ten-year-old son, her sister and the sister's husband. The sister paid rent for the room she and her husband occupied and the sister did the cleaning. Mrs W did some housework herself, helped by her husband and son. They had also employed a cleaner for a period but could no longer afford to so, since Mrs W's benefit was stopped. The adjudicator accepted the medical evidence regarding the extent of her impairment but believed that she could work by taking in lodgers:

> I have come to the conclusion that the Appellant whilst being unfit to work near machinery has a considerable capacity for housework and that she could, if necessity arose, earn her livelihood by taking in lodgers and looking after them. (PIN 63/1/414, 1927)

It is clear that Mrs W's status as a married woman, who would be expected to be doing housework anyway as part of her role as a wife and mother, was relevant to this assumption that adding to that housework burden would constitute work, so long as some extra income was coming in by way of rent from the lodgers. The adjudicator clearly regarded the rent already paid by the sister and her husband as pay for Mrs W's work.

This approach was not always followed by adjudicators however. An earlier case from 1921 illustrates an alternative interpretation. This case concerned, Mrs C, a widow in her 60s who had damaged her ankle and was no longer able to work in domestic service. Mrs C lived in a cottage with her elderly mother

A further example of this can be found in correspondence between the Chartered Accountants Benevolent Association and the Supplementary Benefits Commission in the 1960s concerning the role of the permitted earnings rules. In their letter, the Chartered Accountants Benevolent Association argued that a self-employed disabled accountant would need:

> sufficient income to run a small car so that he can visit clients (his wife would drive) and collect work, return work and discuss matters with his clients. It is of great importance from a morale point of view that someone in this position should feel that he is doing useful work, and from a national point of view it is also important that the ability of such a person should be used as fully as possible.

The Supplementary Benefits Commission disagreed:

> However it was never intended that people capable of working part-time in the usual sense of the word should be able to take advantage of the [permitted earnings] arrangement. (Correspondence, dated May 1968 in PIN 35/392)

In the statement "his wife would drive", the Accountants Association envisaged that accountants' wives would contribute to what was effectively a family business. This model of employment, where women are assumed to support their husbands' employment by contributing their labour unpaid is invisible in a system which assumes that work is an individual activity.

The Opposite of Work

One way of thinking about a conceptual problem is to think about its opposite meanings (Becker 1998). Recent policy rhetoric has made much use of the term "worklessness" (Wiggan 2012). Here, there is a contrast between "'work" as a good thing and "worklessness" as a bad thing, while activation is proposed as the mechanism to move the workless to the world of work. Other terms presented as the opposite of "work" today include such terms as "skivers", "laziness", "dependency" (Patrick 2016). Discourse about "not work" in the early twentieth century contrasted work with "a life of idleness", "loafing about", invalids, malingering, being "pensioned off" and being "unemployable". Some of these terms have distinct negative moral connotations, for example "idleness", "loafing", malingering, while others carry notions of pity, for example "invalid", "pensioner". These terms suggest that not being in work was considered to be a negative state and morally derelict. The contrasting state of being "in work" on the other hand was almost always considered to be morally better and to be a positively health-enhancing activity. The contrast between "not work" and "work" is constructed in moral terms, reflecting the dominance of the work ethic as a means of defining the terms of the debate. So claimants could be criticised for lying about in bed all day and doing nothing but they could also find that attempting to do something could count against their claim to incapacity. Women's unpaid work in the home has been treated in different ways over the twentieth century. In the early years of incapacity benefits, this unpaid work was recognised as "work" but this counted against women's claims to benefit entitlement. If they were able to work in the home then they were not entitled to benefit. Later, these ideas changed, so that unpaid domestic work became invisible to decision makers. The comment from a National Insurance Officer in the 1950s on a woman who cared for her elderly father and looked after her young daughter that she "had nothing to do but keep house" is an example of unpaid women's work being dismissed as having no value (R(S)3/57, case papers in CT/11/161, discussed in more detail in Chapter 6). Domestic work today is almost completely invisible, with parents of young children expected to make themselves available in the labour market as soon as their youngest child is a year old in order to qualify for means-tested benefits. The work of caring for children over that age is invisible in benefits policy. Meanwhile people who act as unpaid carers for disabled children and adults are also under increasing pressure to find "work" which would enable them to stop claiming benefits. These mechanism for making unpaid domestic work invisible are examples of the difficulties which post-work theorisers such as Frayne (2015) and Weeks (2011) have identified as challenges to "work-first" models of social security. The permitted work rules are another example of difficulties with defining "work" for people who might never be able to enter the formal labour market. The complexity of the rules attempted to distinguish between those who were sufficiently disabled to be exempted from the morally laden status of worklessness from those who might be attempting to cheat.

Conclusions

Common-sense understandings of work usually assume that work means paid work under some contract of employment or expectation of payment from self-employment. While statutes have avoided defining work, case law began to define work as paid or work in expectation of payment. Adequacy of pay has never been key in this definition. Feminist and disability studies writers explain that these are gendered and ableist understandings of what work means. Feminists have long noted that work is conceptualised in gendered terms as something that men do in the public domain, while women's work is usually hidden in the private domain as something that does not have the same value, in either economic or moral terms. The concept of work in incapacity decision making is morally loaded as an activity that is superior to perceived worklessness. The moral incentive to find paid work and come off benefit has been intensified in the recent work-focussed conditionality in Employment and Support Allowance but has always been part of the underlying structure of incapacity benefits.

References

Becker, Howard. 1998. *Tricks of the Trade: How to Think About Your Research While You're Doing It*. Chicago and London: University of Chicago Press.

Bonner, David, Ian Hooker, and Robin White, eds. 1991. *Non-means Tested Benefits: The Legislation 1991 Edition*. London: Sweet and Maxwell.

Braithwaite, William. 1957. *Lloyd George's Ambulance Wagon: Being the Memoirs of William J. Braithwaite 1911–1912*. London: Methuen.

Department of Health and Social Security. 1981. *Sickness Benefit Law and Procedure. Code SB 1969, as Amended, 1981*. London: HMSO.

Frayne, David. 2015. *The Refusal of Work: The Theory and Practice of Resistance to Work*. London: Zed Books.

Gulland, Jackie. 2017. 'Working While Incapable to Work? Changing Concepts of Permitted Work in the UK Disability Benefit System'. *Disability Studies Quarterly* 37 (4). http://dsq-sds.org/article/view/6088.

Ministry of Health. 1923. *Reports of Decisions on Appeals and Applications Under Section 67 of the National Insurance Act 1911 and Section 27 of the National Insurance Act 1913, Vol 2—Part I*. London: HMSO.

National Health Insurance Commission (England). 1919. *Reports of Decisions on Appeals and Applications Under Section 67 of the National Insurance Act 1911 and Section 27 of the National Insurance Act 1913 Part V*. Cmd. 134. London: HMSO.

National Health Insurance Commission (Ireland). 1916. *Reports of Decisions on Appeals and Applications Under Section 67 of the National Insurance Act, 1911 and Section 27 of the National Insurance Act, 1913*. Dublin: A Thom.

National Health Insurance Committee (Joint Committee). 1917. *National Health Insurance. Report on the Administration of National Health Insurance During the Years 1914–1917*. Cd. 8890. London: HMSO.

Patrick, Ruth. 2016. 'Living with and Responding to the "Scrounger" Narrative in the UK: Exploring Everyday Strategies of Acceptance, Resistance and Deflection'. *Journal of Poverty and Social Justice* 24 (3): 245–59.

Weeks, Kathi. 2011. *The Problem with Work: Feminism, Marxism, Antiwork Politics, and Postwork Imaginaries.* Durham: Duke University Press.

Wiggan, Jay. 2012. 'Telling Stories of 21st Century Welfare: The UK Coalition Government and the Neo-liberal Discourse of Worklessness and Dependency'. *Critical Social Policy* 32 (3): 383–405.

8

Immoral Conduct: Moral Regulation in Incapacity Benefits

Introduction

In 1922, Edith Sutton made a claim for Sickness Benefit to the New Tabernacle (Old Street Congregational) Approved Society. She had been a member of the Society since the start of the scheme in 1912, had paid contributions since then and had never claimed benefits. When she claimed Sickness Benefit, her Society sent one of their sick visitors to her home to check up on her claim. During the visit, it became clear to the sick visitor that Miss Sutton was pregnant. Being unmarried and pregnant constituted a breach of the Society's rules concerning "immoral conduct" and so the Society expelled her from membership. The fact that Edith Sutton had engaged in sexual activity "under the promise of marriage" was not sufficient to protect her from this moral condemnation. The effect of this expulsion was twofold: it prevented Edith Sutton from accessing the National Insurance Scheme through this particular Society and it deprived her of the Sickness Benefit to which she was entitled, having paid national insurance contributions for ten years. She appealed to the Ministry of Health. The adjudicator appointed by the Ministry of Health did not hear the case directly but instead referred it to the court for an opinion. The court concluded that the Society did have the right to expel her and that it had the right to define "immoral conduct" according to its own standards. However, the Society did not have the right to refuse her benefit while she was still a member:

> that the status of membership was quite separate and distinct from the right to benefits, and that an approved society was entitled to make a rule to expel a member on the ground of immoral conduct even though the result of the

> expulsion was to deprive that member of future contingent benefits which she might have received had she remained a member of the society, but that the society could not make a rule which would deprive a member of accrued benefits to which she would but for that provision have been entitled. (Sutton v New Tabernacle (Old Street Congregational) Approved Society. (1924) 1 K.B. 494)

The court in this case separated out the questions of membership and benefit entitlement but the effect, for Edith Sutton, was to stop her benefit, and for others, to send a strong message regarding the regulation of women's sexual behaviour. While previous chapters look at the way in which attachment to the labour market and work-seeking conditionality was used as a mechanism for defining incapacity for work, this chapter looks at other measures of social control which were sometimes applied. Insurance-based benefit schemes are often held up in contrast to the moralising assumptions of deservingness associated with means-tested and charitable schemes. However, the roots of the National Health Insurance Scheme in the nineteenth century Friendly Societies meant that some of this moralising continued into the twentieth century. People claiming the new insurance-based Sickness Benefit were expected to meet standards of morality and work-seeking behaviour before being considered deserving of support. The heavily moral conditions, relating to sexual behaviour and alcohol use, became less prominent as the scheme became established, but assumptions about personal responsibility for health and work-seeking behaviour continued. The chapter concludes with a consideration of the extent to which these moral conditionalities continued into the post-war scheme and whether these might be returning today in an increasingly conditional welfare system.

Sanctions

Regulation of incapacity benefit claimants' behaviour has generally fallen into two distinct categories, although these overlap somewhat. These are: regulation of claimants' behaviour *before* a claim and regulation *during* a claim. The misconduct rule prevents claimants from accessing incapacity benefits if their sickness or health issue has been caused by their behaviour or misconduct, while the behaviour during sickness rules result in sanctions or termination of benefit if a claimant fails to conform to expected standards of behaviour once a claim is already in place. These misconduct and behaviour rules date back to the earliest years of the Sickness Benefit scheme, and although they are not used in the same way, still exist today in Employment and Support Allowance regulations.

8 Immoral Conduct: Moral Regulation in Incapacity Benefits

Enforcement of standards of behaviour can be traced back to the rules of Friendly Societies in the nineteenth century. Friendly Societies running their own sickness insurance schemes had their own rules of membership and sanctions for failure to conform to expectations of sobriety and respectability (Cordery 2003, pp. 26–27). Under the 1911 Insurance Scheme, Approved Societies were permitted, in fact encouraged, to continue to have such rules. The 1911 Act provided that:

> an approved society may, with the consent of the Insurance Commissioners, provide for the application of its existing rules or make new rules with regard to the manner and time of paying or distributing, and mode of calculating, benefits, suspension of benefits, notices and proof of disease or disablement, behaviour during disease or disablement, and the visiting of sick or disabled persons, and for the infliction and enforcement of penalties (whether by way of fines or suspension of benefits or otherwise). (National Insurance Act 1911, S14, 2)

While many of the Friendly Societies already had such rules, newer Approved Societies did not. The National Insurance Commission published model rules which Societies were encouraged to use. These included:

> a Member in receipt of Sickness or Disablement Benefit –
>
> - Shall obey the instructions of the doctor attending him;
> - Shall not be absent from home between the hours of *8pm and 8am* from 1st April to 30th September and *5pm and 9am* from October 1st to March 31st, and shall not be absent at any time without leaving word where he may be found, provided that the *committee of management* may if they think fit, exempt the member from operation of this rule upon such conditions as they may impose;
> - Shall not leave the *locality* where he resides without the consent of the *committee of management;*
> - Shall not be guilty of conduct which is likely to retard his recovery.

And the optional rule that

> "No member shall qualify for sickness or disablement benefit in respect of injury or disease caused by his own misconduct"

(NHIC 1912, pp. 11–12, italics in original noting wording which Societies might wish to change according to local needs)

The model rules relating to expulsion from the Society included:

material mis-statement or omission on application for membership, fraudulent claims, serious wilful breach of the Act, conviction for felony or other criminal offence, or other immoral conduct or serious personal misconduct. (NHIC 1912, pp. 18–19)

The guidance on model rules provided details of obligatory procedures to be followed in these cases, including a requirement to give written notice and the right to appeal. The 1911 Act empowered Societies to "inflict and enforce" penalties which could include fines, suspension of benefits "or otherwise". The National Insurance Commission regulated the Approved Societies and ratified the rules. Societies could suspend benefit for up to twelve months, fine members up to ten shillings, or, in the case of repeated breaches of rules, twenty shillings, or expel members from membership for breach of such rules (National Insurance Act 1911, S14, 2).

It is worth noting here that suspension of benefit and the expulsion from membership both amounted to benefit being stopped or suspended. Societies could suspend benefit for up to twelve months, excluding claimants from payment for that period. If a claimant was expelled from membership she or he would have to start join a new Society in order to qualify for benefits. Given that, by definition, these claimants had health issues, had perhaps lost their previous employment and had a question over their respectability, joining a new Society would be difficult. If expelled members were still in work and were unable to find a Society willing to accept them, they were required to contribute to the National Insurance Scheme through the Deposit Contributors system, which operated as a savings bank rather than an a full insurance system. Members of the Deposit Contributors System could access panel doctors but could only claim benefits if they had sufficient deposit in the scheme. People who were not working were not required to pay national insurance and so would effectively be excluded from the scheme if expelled. The usual effect, therefore, of expulsion from a Society, was that a member's entitlement to benefit would stop.

The maximum fine of ten shillings (or twenty in the case of repeated offences) should be considered in relation to the rate of benefit payment. In 1911, the standard rate of Sickness Benefit was ten shillings a week for men, seven shillings and sixpence for women and five shillings for Disablement Benefit for both men and women after twenty-six weeks of claim. At the beginning of the scheme, the maximum fine was therefore roughly equivalent to one week's benefit for men and a week and half's benefit for women or two weeks benefit for Disablement Benefit claimants. Although the rates of benefit changed over the next thirty years, the maximum fines did not.

Misconduct Before a Claim

There is a theoretical distinction between "misconduct" where a claimant would be refused benefit where their medical condition was alleged to be the result of their unacceptable conduct and "behaviour during sickness" where the claimant was awarded benefit but breached a rule while in receipt of benefit. The main categories of misconduct in the early twentieth century related to sexual morality, alcohol use and fighting, although the rules could be used more broadly, to prevent payment to people who had indulged in alleged reckless behaviour of various kinds.

Sexual morality was a concern for some Societies, particularly those based on religious membership. Edith Sutton's dispute with the New Tabernacle Society in the 1920s concerned her status as an unmarried pregnant woman. Rules about unmarried pregnancy were applied only to women but in the early years of the 1911 scheme, some Societies attempted to sanction members, either by refusal of benefit, or expulsion from the Society if claimants' health issues were, or were believed to be, the result of sexually transmitted diseases. These rules could be used against both women and men.

The evidence submitted to the 1914 inquiry into Sickness Benefit provides detail of how the rule was used in practice by some Societies in these early years. Mr Smith of the Co-operative Wholesale Society noted that his Society's rules had an explicit clause denying benefit to claimants whose health issue was the result of venereal disease, whatever the cause and claimed that "it is not necessary to inquire as to how they have contracted it" (NHIJC 1914a appendices, para 12268). In their questions to Mr Smith, the committee members showed some surprise at this statement and asked for further detail regarding how the Society would investigate members who were potentially excluded from benefit by this rule. Mr Smith gave the example of a claimant who had symptoms that might have been consistent with a sexually transmitted disease. The Society refused benefit after a sick visitor noted "from his knowledge of the person he had reason to believe that he was suffering in that way", even when the claimant's doctor had not specified this (para 12308). The claimant apparently accepted the decision. In his description of another case, Mr Smith said "as soon as he [the claimant] felt we knew what the cause was, he realised he had no claim" (para 12313). In this case, it was the threat of sanctions, rather than their use which was used to deter potential claimants.

Several witnesses to the 1914 inquiry noted the difficulties resulting from doctors being evasive about the nature of a patient's condition, often using euphemisms or obscure medical terms, perhaps in an attempt to protect their patients from the misconduct rule. Dr Olive Claydon, representing the Association of Registered Medical Women, discussed at some length the problem with certification in cases of sexually transmitted diseases. Preferring not to make a judgement on a patient's morality, she described how she might deal with the situation from a doctor's perspective: "I would give a confidential certificate to the patients and say "if you like to take this is it is your own affair but they will not pay it"' (para 22593). Societies which had this misconduct rule believed that most claimants would self-regulate in this way by not making claims if they thought they would be refused benefit. If they did claim and were refused benefit, claimants appeared to accept the decision and did not appeal. The evidence provided by witnesses to the inquiry suggests that some Societies were using dubious methods to support allegations of sexual misconduct, relying on reading between the lines of doctors' certificates combined with the hearsay and gossip gleaned by sick visitors.

While these witnesses reported that few claimants would appeal against these allegations of sexual misconduct, there are a couple of examples in the published appeal cases where claimants did appeal. In an early case from 1915, the claimant, Mr L, claimed Sickness Benefit after an accident at work. His Society recommended that he claim for the industrial injury under the Workmen's Compensation Act and gave him a form to fill in but agreed to pay Sickness Benefit in the meantime. The employer's insurers denied liability. At this point, the Society decided that the health problem had arisen as a result of Mr L's own misconduct, the result of a sexually transmitted disease. Subsequently, the Society withdrew the accusation of misconduct and argued that Mr L should pursue a claim against his employers for industrial injury. At Mr L's appeal hearing, the adjudicators refused to accept the Society's withdrawal of the accusation of misconduct on the grounds that the Mr L should be allowed to clear his name. The adjudicators determined that there was no medical evidence of Mr L having a sexually transmitted disease and that it was also unlikely that his health issues were the result of an industrial accident. He was therefore entitled to Sickness Benefit. They concluded that "it appears to us impossible to find appropriate language in which to describe the injustice from which the Appellant has suffered" (Case 13, NHIC 1915a, p. 34).

Mr L's case was rather convoluted but it serves to illustrate how a Society could make an accusation of misconduct, based on scanty and conflicting evidence. Reading between the lines of the case it looks as if this Society had made its decision, partly on the basis of local gossip: "the Manager had received some vague suggestion that there was something about the case in addition to what he knew already". It was only by appealing that Mr L was able to get the benefit to which he was entitled as well as to clear his name of the "grossly offensive accusation" of sexual misconduct.

8 Immoral Conduct: Moral Regulation in Incapacity Benefits

The 1914 inquiry into Sickness Benefit discussed the issue of sexually transmitted diseases at length and, although unwilling to exclude sexually transmitted diseases from the misconduct rule, concluded that there were particular difficulties with medical certification in these cases. The report noted that doctors would often conceal the nature of a health issue, by using euphemisms, leaving the Societies the task of guessing whether or not the claimant had a sexually transmitted disease and whether or not this was the result of misconduct. This would lead to Societies asking "what may frequently be offensive questions" (NHIJC 1914b, p. 43).

The inquiry concluded that doctors should take responsibility for deciding whether or not the health issue was the result of misconduct, suggesting that some doctors and Societies distinguished between cases of "fairly recent misconduct", which they seemed to think would apply mainly to men, and misconduct which had taken place "years previously" which they seemed to think would apply mainly to married women, as a result of their husbands' youthful misdemeanours. Men who had been guilty of this recent misconduct should be told the nature of their condition and the implication was that they would then be deterred from claiming benefit, knowing that they would be refused. Married women, on the other hand, should be protected from this information, and subsequent sanctions, presumably on the assumption that they had contracted the disease from their husbands, who had misbehaved sometime in the past:

> the view was that this should "not be disclosed to her [married woman] owing to the fear of "breaking up the home". because "the disease may be due to infection from a person whose misconduct has taken place years previously". (p. 43)

In their recommendation that doctors should make these moral distinctions, the inquiry attempted to leave the responsibility for sanctions with the Societies while protecting individual claimants from intrusive and insensitive enquiries. The extraordinary distinction between men who were assumed to be guilty of misconduct and who would then self-regulate by not claiming benefit and married women who were assumed to be innocent and should be protected from their husbands' past infidelities to protect the family home shows a clear gendered approach to the issue. This attempt to allocate imagined blame and to protect the family does not fit well with other thinking about sexually transmitted diseases at the time, which often blamed women, and came to a pitch during the First World War (Davis 2011; Lammasniemi 2017). The difference between the condemnation of women for sexual impropriety in other spheres and the Committee's rather prudish assumptions about married women's innocence can probably be explained by an allocation of respectability to married members of the National Insurance scheme in contrast to class-based assumptions about poorer women who might be presumed to be prostitutes (Davis 2011).

The inquiry's recommendations were also incompatible with emerging ideas about public health, which sought to disentangle moral issues from the provision of appropriate treatment for sexually transmitted diseases. This public health approach was supported by Mary Macarthur in her dissenting memorandum to the report. She was utterly scathing of the committee's approach, arguing that it was wholly inappropriate for doctors to be making these moral distinctions. Her memorandum provides a detailed argument for abandoning the misconduct rule on sexually transmitted diseases on public health grounds. Macarthur argued that people (both men and women) should always be informed of the nature of their health condition and should not be deterred from seeking medical treatment. She recommended referring the issue to the Royal Commission on Venereal Diseases which met from 1913 to 1916, and which appeared to support Mary Macarthur's position, although did not cite her memorandum (Clarke 1916, p. 43).

The view that public health was more important than moral concerns was repeated in a review of the National Insurance Scheme in 1917, which recommended that payment of benefit should not be refused for people with sexually transmitted diseases. This review, however, suggested that Societies which required "high standards of personal conduct" should be allowed to expel their members if they felt that they had fallen below these moral standards (NHIJC 1917, p. 233). Amending legislation was introduced in 1918, which excluded sexually transmitted diseases from the misconduct rules (Ministry of Health 1920, p. 26). This exception to the misconduct rule for sexually transmitted diseases continued throughout the twentieth century and is still retained in benefits legislation today.

While the misconduct rules on sexually transmitted diseases before 1918 could be used against both men and women, only women could be refused benefit, sanctioned or excluded from membership if their alleged sexual impropriety led to pregnancy. Some Societies regarded an unmarried woman's pregnancy as misconduct and refused benefit if she claimed Sickness Benefit in relation to the pregnancy or after childbirth. While it is difficult to know how widespread this practice was, the evidence to the 1914 Inquiry gives some information about how it was used in practice. Mr Tuckfield (of the National Deposit Friendly Society) noted that his society would refuse to pay benefit to a single woman if her health issues related to pregnancy or childbirth (para 920) and that there had been no appeals against such decisions (para 1340). Mr J Duncan (of the Rational Association Friendly Society) noted that his

Society would refuse benefit to unmarried women (4073). Mr J Shaw (of the Order of Druids Friendly Society) noted the statutory difference between paying Sickness Benefit and maternity benefit to unmarried women, where the statute did not permit societies to refuse Maternity Benefit but that his Society would refuse Sickness Benefit (para 7065). Mr W Rigby of the Catholic Friendly Societies Association claimed that his Society would refuse benefit to unmarried women who made claims related to complications of pregnancy. He noted that when they were refused, such women would go back to their doctors and get new certificates which did not mention pregnancy, thus attempting to avoid the misconduct rules, giving the example of a woman whose doctor had certified her sickness as "varicose veins" in an apparent attempt to get round the rules. When questioned by the Society, the doctor denied that he knew the claimant was pregnant. The committee asked Mr Rigby if the Society would have paid if the doctor had certified her sickness as "varicose veins and pregnancy". Mr Rigby said "Not in this particular case which was that of a single woman" (para 26816).

Other witnesses, however, said that they would not differentiate between married and unmarried women and would pay benefit to any woman whose sickness was related to pregnancy. Despite Mr Smith (Co-operative Wholesale Society) having strong opinions on sexually transmitted diseases, he claimed that his Society would not refuse benefit to unmarried pregnant woman on the grounds of misconduct (para 12407). However, he also discussed the question of what to do when women made claims for Sickness Benefit where it was suspected that they were experiencing complications after abortions. As abortion was illegal, neither doctors nor patients would be willing to admit this. Mr Smith noted that it was therefore very difficult to refuse benefit on the grounds of misconduct in these cases, although there might be strong suspicions. The committee members reminded Mr Smith that "no court would find her guilty of that except with very clear evidence". Mr Smith responded that he agreed and therefore the Society could not refuse benefit, noting that "my point is that in my opinion we are paying in certain conditions when we do not think that we ought to pay" (para 12497).

These examples of variation between Societies in their treatment of married and unmarried women and complications relating to pregnancy show that some Societies attempted to use the Sickness Benefit rules to regulate the sexual activities of their members. The difficulties of getting doctors to provide certificates which would enable Societies to make these judgements and the associated health implications mirror those of the sexually transmitted diseases cases. The refusal of benefit to unmarried pregnant women on the grounds of immoral behaviour was expressly forbidden as a reason for refusing benefit after amending legislation in 1918 (National Health Insurance Act, 1918, s. 12(3)). As with the sexually transmitted diseases exception, this continues as an exception to the misconduct rules on benefits today. Despite the change in legislation in 1918 some Societies still continued to try and enforce ideas about sexual morality behaviour by using their membership rules to expel unmarried pregnant women, for example, in the case of Edith Sutton, which the court ruled was acceptable. In a telling foreshadowing of the "rape clause" in the current Government's "two child policy" for claimants of Universal Credit (Machin 2017), the court in Sutton v New Tabernacle considered that the Society had the right to expel members "by reason of the pregnancy of a single woman due to intercourse with her consent" (Sutton v New Tabernacle (1924) p. 502), implying that consideration might be different if the pregnancy was the result of rape.

Statistics on Societies' use of rules to regulate sexual behaviour are hard to come by. The English Ministry of Health did not provide statistics in its annual reports, although the Scottish Board of Health did. The Scottish Board of Health reported a change in patterns in the early years of the twentieth century, when it reported that "one large society" had been in the habit of expelling "considerable numbers of women periodically on the grounds of moral misconduct" but had recently changed its policy (Scottish Board of Health 1922, p. 134). Given that Societies also used the misconduct rules to deter claims, it is difficult to know how many people were effectively denied Sickness Benefit.

Refusal of benefit or other sanctions could also be used when claimants' health conditions were alleged to be the result of misuse (or any use) of alcohol. As with the sexual morality allegations, these rules dated in part back to the nineteenth-century Friendly Societies which expected their members to conform to expectations of sobriety and respectability which could lead to expulsion from membership or refusal of benefit if breached (Cordery 2003, pp. 26–27). Some Societies were explicitly based on abstinence and so failure to conform to the rules could lead to expulsion from the Society. The Scottish Board of Health reported that the most common reason for expulsion in the early years of the scheme was "violation of the pledge" among the "total abstinence societies" (Scottish Board of Health 1922, p. 134).

Not all Societies expected total abstinence from alcohol but many had rules which prevented payment of benefit if alcohol use was alleged to be the cause of the claimant's health issue. One of the earliest appeal cases concerned a woman, Mrs R, whose landlady had reported to a sick visitor that Mrs R "went out first thing in the morning and returned home late at night very much the worse for drink". The Society stopped Mrs R's benefit because of her breach of the rules and "your behaviour has not been that of a person unable to work". Mrs R appealed and the adjudicators were unimpressed by the Society's investigation, standards of evidence or procedures and found in favour of the Mrs R, saying that, although her case was "not wholly free from suspicion", "Drunkenness is a very serious charge to make, and if the charge is made, it must be supported by proper evidence" (Case 8, NHIC 1915a, p. 22). This case is important, not so much for the substance of Mrs R's claim or the Society's allegations, but the much higher standards of evidence which the Commissioners expected. It is likely that many other claimants would have been sanctioned in this way on the basis of evidence of a similar standard to that used against Mrs R.

Another example of alleged alcohol misuse can be found in 1917, concerning Mrs P, a married woman who had been claiming benefit as a result of rheumatism. The Society did not believe this diagnosis and organised a medical examination. The doctor who examined her stated that he suspected "malingering and alcoholism. She is an undesirable". Benefit was refused and Mrs P appealed. She was referred to a second doctor for a second examination and this doctor confirmed the suspicion that she was "suffering from chronic alcoholism and will not recover until she gives up drinking". When Mrs P appealed to the National Insurance Commissioners, she produced several witnesses including her own doctor, her local rector, her landlady and others. These witnesses strongly disputed the allegations of alcoholism or undesirability, instead stressing her hard-working character, her respectability and her local reputation. Her own doctor gave evidence that her home was "neat, clean and tidy, and as exhibiting no trace whatever of the characteristics of a drunkard's home". The adjudicators concluded that Mrs P's health issues were not related to alcohol and that she was entitled to benefit (Case 77, NHIC 1917, p. 203). The adjudicators appeared to give as much weight to the evidence of Mrs P's respectability as to the medical evidence regarding her health issues, describing her as "an excellent and hard-working woman who bore an excellent reputation among her neighbours". This demonstrates that the case was not just about alcohol as a medical issue but as a moral one.

A later case, from 1927, concerned Mr M, a man described by the adjudicator as "a person of poor physique and so deaf that he was unable to hear the bulk of the evidence against him". Mr M had been expelled from his Society for drunkenness after a sick visitor had called at his home and "found him to be drunk" It seems that the adjudicator had judged Mr M to be genuinely incapable of work and so the question concerned whether alcohol lay at the heart of health problems. The adjudicator was unconvinced by the Society's evidence and found in favour of the claimant (PIN 63/1/424, 1927). The important issue in this case seems to be the degree of alcohol use, rather than the extent of its effect on Mr M's health. Appeal cases of course only dealt with people who challenged the decisions of the Societies. It is quite likely that many other claimants were refused benefit on the grounds of alcohol use, but like those accused of sexual immorality in the early years of the scheme, did not appeal.

The minute books of the Leek Textile workers (WCML) and the Ideal Benefit Society (PIN 24/74 and PIN 24/80) suggest that it was exactly this kind of local evidence which resulted in regular use of sanctions for alcohol use, varying from fines to suspension of benefit and expulsion from Societies. There was not always a clear line between misconduct (the alleged cause of the health issue) and behaviour (behaving inappropriately while claiming benefit). The line between the health relevance and the moral judgement appears to have been thin. The records of the Ideal Benefit Society show that members continued to be sanctioned for alcohol use in the 1930s. In 1938, a Mr D and a Mr S were fined after being reported by a sick visitor as "being frequent visitors of public houses". Mr S had been claiming Disablement Benefit for nearly ten years and, although no details are given in the minute, he clearly had a long-term impairment that was not itself in dispute. He argued at his appeal that he only went to the pub occasionally on a Sunday evening. The committee seemed to accept this evidence and suspended him from benefit for four weeks as a deterrent to future breach of rules. Mr M was refused benefit after he broke his ankle falling off his bicycle. It was alleged that the accident had happened while he was drunk and that therefore he came within the misconduct rules. At the internal appeal hearing, Mr M brought along a witness and the committee overturned the decision due to a lack of evidence of his alleged drunkenness (cases recorded in PIN 24/74). The Ideal Benefit Society also recorded a case of a woman, Mrs M who was sanctioned after she was seen "coming out of a public house" (PIN24/80).

These cases concerning alcohol use illustrate the boundary between the misconduct rules (where the claimant's health issue was alleged to be the result of his or her misconduct) and the behaviour during sickness rules where a claimant could be fined, or refused benefit for behaving in a way which might delay their recovery, and the general rules of some Societies which might prohibit drinking altogether. People could also be refused benefit if they were considered to have brought about their own misfortune by fighting or reckless behaviour. This was often related to allegations of alcohol consumption. An example from 1916 concerned Mr T, who was unable to work as a result of a broken leg, allegedly incurred in a fight with another man outside a club. The Society refused benefit on the grounds that his injury was the result of misconduct, brought about either by drinking or fighting or both. Mr T claimed that he was the victim of a crime, had not been drunk and therefore that his injury was not the result of misconduct. The Society refused to pay Sickness Benefit unless he was able to prove his innocence, by taking legal action against his alleged assailant. At his appeal hearing, both Mr T and his alleged assailant gave evidence, along with a witness to the incident. Both the witness and the alleged assailant supported Mr T's assertion that the other man had started the fight. The adjudicators upheld Mr T's appeal and also noted that the Society "had no right to impose" the condition that Mr T should prove his innocence by taking legal action against his assailant (Case 62, NHIC 1916, p. 166).

This case is interesting because it focusses on blame. Mr T had originally been accused of misconduct, for, at worst, starting a fight or, at best, for falling over while drunk. Mr T was able to refute this allegation only by providing evidence to support his argument that although he had been in the club and that there had been a dispute, his drinking had been moderate and his behaviour had been justifiable. In a similar case from 1921, the claimant, Mr S, was also injured during a fight and the Society claimed that this was misconduct. At the appeal, the case was decided mainly on the evidence of the other party to the fight who claimed that the Mr S had not started the fight. The evidence was sufficient to persuade the adjudicator that Mr S was not to blame and so eligible for benefit (Case 2/36, Ministry of Health 1923, p. 110). This case relies on a narrative of Mr S as an innocent victim of another man's drinking. Both of these cases concerned men who had acquired injuries in fights; but in both cases, alcohol was also involved. Both men were able to retain their benefits only by proving that they were innocent of starting the fights. It is likely that other people, who were less able to defend themselves against these kinds of allegations, would be refused benefit or deterred from claiming in the first place.

Moral assumptions could also be used to judge a claimant's motives in claiming benefit. In a case from 1929, Mr G appealed against refusal of benefit. The case concerned whether or not Mr G was incapable of work, but much of the argument surrounded his reason for claiming benefits. The Society argued that Mr G's sole reason for claiming benefit was that he was in debt and that so long as he was on benefit his debts would not be pursued. This is an interesting moral argument in its own right but the Society felt the need to explain the nature of his debts:

> he admitted he was separated from his wife who had a magistrate's order for maintenance against him … also that there was an affiliation order against him in respect of a bastard child under which he was in arrear; that as long as he was

incapable of work the magistrates would not commit him to prison in respect of the arrears.

The references to the separated wife and the "bastard child" were completely irrelevant to the medical question of whether or not Mr G was capable of work, but was an approach with which the adjudicator agreed:

> his manner and character were such as to render the appellant an entirely unreliable witness. In my opinion the Appellant is and has been perfectly capable of work and invents these symptoms for ulterior motives. (PIN 63/4/524, 1929)

So, in this case, both the Society and the adjudicator were using wider allegations of the claimant's moral standing, both to evaluate his evidence and to impute a motivation for his actions which was entirely irrelevant to the question at hand.

Another common reason for sanctioning claimants was when they were accused of criminal behaviour, particularly violence and assault. In these examples, the Societies would use the misconduct rules, usually to expel members rather than to refuse benefit directly. There was sometimes a direct connection between the Sickness Benefit claim and the alleged criminal activity, where claimants were alleged to have reacted violently to adverse decisions or perceived excessive intrusion into their private lives (see also Chapter 9). Societies could also expel members for criminal behaviour unrelated to their benefit claims. Several of these are recorded in the minutes of the Ideal Benefit Society where male members were expelled after it came to the Society's attention that they had been convicted of stealing, assaulting a police officer or other violent offences (PIN 24/74). The appeals were usually unsuccessful because it was well within the rules of the Society to expel members who had been convicted of criminal offences. There is one case reported where the claimant's appeal was successful however. This concerned a Mr A who had been convicted and served a prison sentence for robbery and assault. Mr A did not attend the hearing but his son-in-law appeared on his behalf, arguing that Mr A had been "very strange his manner for some little time and in his opinion he was absolutely certain that the member was not fully capable when these actions were performed". The committee decided to seek further medical opinion on Mr A and an entry in the minutes two months later explains that they had received a letter from the prison doctor confirming that "the member was in his opinion insane on reception into prison". On receipt of this evidence, the Society decided not to expel Mr A from membership (PIN 24/74, 1938).

A case which was heard in the Scottish courts in 1928 concerned Hannah O'Brien, who claimed Sickness Benefit from the Scottish Catholic Insurance

Society. When her benefit was stopped a month later, she "created a disturbance" at the Society's office and "maliciously broke the glass of the vestibule door of the office". She was convicted of breach of the peace and the Society then expelled her from membership for having breached the rule forbidding "serious personal misconduct". Hannah O'Brien's case ended up in the court because she appealed against a decision to stop her benefit on the date she was expelled. Her case was considered by an appointee of the Scottish Board of Health, who agreed that the Society was within its rights to expel Ms O'Brien under the behaviour rules but referred the case to the Court of Session for an opinion on the technical question of precisely when the benefit should be stopped. (Stated Case in a dispute under section 90(1) of the National Health Insurance Act 1924 between Hannah O'Brien and the Scottish Catholic Insurance Society for the Opinion and Judgement of the First Division of the Court of Session, copy in CS 251/3283 in National Records of Scotland.)

There are several interesting points arising from this case. First of all, it is another example of a claimant's dissatisfaction with a decision on benefit leading to violence and a criminal conviction. Secondly, the technical question of exactly when the benefit should be stopped is a clear confirmation that expulsion from the Society would lead to a loss of benefit for claimants and that it mattered to this claimant. Finally, there is a note in the case file that Hannah O'Brien's address at the time of the case was the Merryflats unit at the Southern General Hospital in Glasgow, at that time a psychiatric unit (NHS Greater Glasgow and Clyde 2015). Somewhere between her criminal conviction and the case being heard by the court, Hannah O'Brien had been admitted to a psychiatric ward. It is not clear whether her mental health issues predated her outburst at the Society's office or whether her criminal conviction, expulsion from the Society and subsequent loss of income was a factor, but there is at least a possibility that the issues were related.

These sanctions for misconduct illustrate the morally conditional nature of the Sickness Benefit scheme before 1948. In most of these instances, except perhaps the alcohol use cases, the claimants had committed (or were alleged to have committed) breaches of moral codes which had little to do with their claims to incapacity for work. Indeed, in some cases, where the claimants had apparent mental health issues, their behaviour might have supported their claims to incapacity. The Societies, endorsed and encouraged by the state regulators, were able to use moral arguments to determine who was and was not entitled to benefit. While the sanctions of suspending benefit led to a direct denial of benefit, fines and expulsion often had a similar effect. The extreme level of sanctions available, maximum suspension of benefit for up to one year, does not appear to have been very common, although there are certainly early appeal cases where the suspension was for six months or a year. It might seem, as the National Health Insurance Commission thought in 1917 (NHIJC 1917, p. 233) and as the Scottish Board of Health reported in 1922 (Scottish Board of Health 1922, p. 134) that these rules would be used primarily by the more morally or religiously inclined Societies. However, there is no doubt that the trade union societies also had strict moral codes and there is evidence of the Prudential, which had no obvious religious or moral affiliations, suspending and expelling members. These sanctions are noted in the minute books of the Prudential Approved Society but unfortunately they contain no detail of the reasons for the sanctions. (Minute Books of Committee of Management of the Prudential Approved Societies 1912–1942, Prudential archives, box L/2/5).

Behaviour During Sickness Rules

The misconduct rules were intended to regulate claimants' moral behaviour, although this had some overlap with the assessment of their capacity for work. For example, if someone's drinking habits suggested that they were not as ill as they claimed, the misconduct rule could be used to expel, fine or suspend them, without getting into a discussion about their incapacity. The behaviour during sickness rules, however, were much more closely linked to the concept of incapacity for work. These rules were intended, theoretically, to ensure that claimants did not do anything to delay their recovery, although it is clear that they were also used as what Stone has described as revelatory signs to test claimants' capacity for work (Stone 1984). As with the misconduct rules, the behaviour during sickness rules has their roots in nineteenth-century Friendly Society membership rules, which were carried forward into the 1911 Sickness Benefit scheme via S14 of the National Insurance Act 1911 and the model rules provided by the National Insurance Commission and the Ministry of Health. These rules included a general prohibition of behaviour likely to retard recovery and a curfew requiring claimants to stay at home in the evenings and not to leave home without permission. This rule, provided as a model rule by the National Insurance Commission, was adopted by most Societies in their rule books (NHIC 1912, p. 11). The out of hours rule appears to have been commonly used to suspend or fine claimants or as evidence of their capacity for work. Although it is difficult to find evidence of the extent of the use of this rule, it appears frequently in the minutes of Societies such as the Ideal Benefit Society (PIN 24/74 and PIN 24/80), the Tunbridge Wells Equitable Friendly Society (PIN24/153) and the Leek Textile Federation (WCML). These Societies would fine members or suspend them from benefit if found breaching the rule of being out of hours while claiming benefit. In the Leek Textile Federation minute book, claimants were fined for being seen out of their homes after 10 pm but also for being seen "at the theatre", "in the picture house" or, frequently in pubs or clubs. It is not clear from the minutes of the Federation whether these claimants were suspected of not really being sick, or whether it was merely the breach of rule which caused the sanction. At other times, the breach of the out of hours rule coincided with a breach of the drinking rules. So in a case from 1913, Mr P was fined "5/ for playing Bill and Handicap in the Bird-in-Hand also 10/ for dancing at Cheddleton", while Mr D was expelled for "being in a public house and the worse for drink whilst on the funds" (Leek Textile Federation: health insurance minute book).

Sometimes a note in the minute book suggests that the sanction for breach of rule was being used to test a claimant's genuine incapacity. So in 1913, a Miss F was fined five shillings for "dancing while on the funds". The implication here was that Miss F was malingering since there was a note "supposed to have a bad foot", suggesting that it was the evidence contrary to the sick claim rather than the "dancing" as such which caused the problem.

While it is likely that most claimants accepted these sanctions, the archive records show that some claimants did appeal. There is an example of this in the Leek Textile Federation where a Mrs M was suspended from benefit for three months in 1922 for being seen "out of hours". She, or her family, must have challenged this decision as a note in the minute book a month later states that this suspension had been rescinded because "other evidence and development showing that she was not quite capable of understanding rules". The minute does not note what this evidence was but the next entry in the book notes that payment should be made to Mrs M for the period up until her entry into a local psychiatric hospital. Although there is little detail regarding Mrs M, it seems as if the out of hours rule was being used most inappropriately in her case and that she was only able to retain her benefit because of assistance from family members. Cases described in the Ideal Benefit Society minutes suggest that it was very rare for an appeal against an out of hours sanction to be successful. The minutes usually record only that the "excuse offered was not reasonable". This suggests that the rules were enforced quite rigidly.

Appeal cases which reached the National Insurance Commissioners commonly concerned the behaviour during sickness rules. In a very early case concerning the out of hours rules, Mr T had made a claim for Sickness Benefit but was not at home when a representative of the Society called at 6.40 pm and had not returned by 7 pm when the representative left. The Society suspended Mr T from Sickness Benefit for twelve months for this alleged breach of the rules. When Mr T appealed against this sanction, the adjudicators accepted that he had breached the out of hours rule and that it was appropriate for the Society to impose a sanction. However, they considered that a twelve-month suspension was excessive and remitted the case to be reconsidered for a more appropriate sanction. In their defence, the Society said that there were "other things" against the claimant which explained the length of the suspension. The adjudicators were not willing to listen to these other allegations since there was no evidence to support them (Case 14, NHIC 1915a, p. 41). This case is an example of the Society attempting to use the breach of the out of hours rules to impose a long-term sanction on a claimant that they suspected was attempting to cheat in some way.

Another early case concerns Mr F, who had been claiming Sickness and then Disablement Benefit for around six months after a diagnosis of tuberculosis. There was no dispute about his incapacity but the Society attempted to fine him for breach of rules because he had been seen outside the hours allowed by the Society. Mr F's defence was that his doctor had advised him to get out in the fresh air as much as possible. When he failed to pay the fine, the Society suspended his benefit indefinitely. The debate at Mr F's appeal hearing concerned whether the Society had the power to do this (it did) but also whether the use of the out of hours rule was reasonable under the circumstances. The adjudicators felt that it was not, given that Mr F had medical advice to get out and about and preferred this advice to the Society's discretionary powers to adapt their rules (Case 69, NHIC 1916, p. 181).

The out of hours rules were still in place in the 1930s. Guidance to Societies in 1933 said:

> Societies should see that the requirements of their rules relating to behaviour of members during sickness are duly observed… Under the prescribed Rule which fixes the hours between which members who are incapacitated are not to be absent from home, the Society has a discretion to give relief from the operation of the Rule. (Ministry of Health 1933, para 417)

This guidance continues with an explanation of the workings of the "leaving home" rule, whereby claimants were permitted to leave their place of residence so long as they had permission to do so. The guidance explains that Societies should normally grant permission, unless there was "a definitive reason for withholding consent". If a Society believed that a claimant had breached the rule, the Societies were permitted only to fine claimants or suspend benefit for up to twelve months as a penalty, not to stop benefit altogether (Ministry of Health 1933, para 419). This rather subtle distinction between suspension and title to benefit relied on the Society being persuaded of the claimant's continuing incapacity. A short-term suspension of benefit might well cover the period of the claimant's illness, leading to a loss of benefit. If there was doubt about the claimant's continuing incapacity for work, Societies would usually refer them to the Regional Medical Officer before stopping benefit altogether. In practice, the effect of suspension and the effect of denial of benefit could be the same for the claimant if it led to payments being stopped. The rather excessive use of the out of hours rule is illustrated in an application by a member for exemption in 1938. Miss H had applied for permission to be out of hours. This was initially refused and she appealed. The appeal was allowed because Miss H was blind and the only time she could go out was in the evenings when her landlady was available to accompany her. On appeal, the Society agreed to give permission to vary out of hours rules for Miss H (Ideal Benefit Society, PIN 24/80).

Another example from 1936 concerned a Mr P who had been reported as absent from his home at 9.30 pm one evening. In this case, it was decided to "take a lenient view", by imposing a fine of 2/6d, on the grounds that he was a "chronic invalid" but he was warned that future violation would lead to more serious consequences (PIN 24/74). The fact that the Society only reluctantly agreed to waive the out of hours rules after an appeal in the case of Miss H and to fine Mr P, suggests that the rule was being used strictly to regulate the behaviour of claimants in this Society at least.

The out of hours rules appeared to be being used in most cases as an indication that the benefit claimant was not really ill or was not as ill as they claimed. The rules also sent a powerful message that claimants were expected to stay at home and not participate in any work-like or leisure activities. This might seem reasonable for people with short-term illnesses which prevented them from attending their workplace in the short term. However, the rule was also used to control the behaviour of people who had long-term health issues or impairments, for example, in the cases of Mr P and Miss H.

It is clear that the moralising expectations of the nineteenth-century Friendly Societies continued well into the twentieth century and that they were embedded in the model rules suggested by the National Insurance Commission and Ministry of Health. Within this overall guidance, individual Societies may have been more or less likely to apply the strict moral expectations regarding sexual behaviour or alcohol use but the misconduct rules were also used to control access to benefit for people who were considered to be problematic. The behaviour during sickness rules was used both as a form of moral regulation and as a revelatory sign to check on claimants' genuine incapacity for work. These rules were applied also to people with long-term health issues and impairments, as a form of house arrest to ensure that they stayed within expected boundaries of "disabled" behaviour.

Moral Regulation After 1948

The post-war National Insurance Scheme removed most of the moralising that existed in the Approved Societies scheme. There was no provision for expulsion from the scheme or for fining alleged moral offenders except insofar as a claimant could be accused of having caused their own incapacity. The misconduct and behaviour rules were separated out so that a more explicit distinction was made between sickness *caused* by misconduct and behaviour *during* sickness. Regulations provided for suspension of benefit for up to six weeks if sickness was caused by misconduct (National Insurance Act 1946 13(3)(a)). Although misconduct was not defined, regulations continued to exempt health issues caused by sexually transmitted diseases or pregnancy (National Insurance Advisory Committee 1948). The misconduct rule remained the same through the introduction of Invalidity Benefit and other changes in the 1970s. Ogus et al., in their discussion of the misconduct rule as it stood in 1988 noted that there had only been one reported Commissioners' case dealing with the provision (Ogus et al. 1988, p. 159). This was R(S)2/53 which concerned whether or not the claimant's alcoholism amounted to misconduct. Mr R had been a publican who admitted to alcohol problems in the past, had stopped drinking and then started drinking again after the distress of a car accident. He claimed benefit when he stopped work and sought help for his alcohol problems. His benefit was suspended for six weeks on the grounds of misconduct. Mr R appealed to the local tribunal which upheld the original decision. The tribunal felt it necessary to note on the decision form that the suspension of his benefit "makes no imputations against his character, which we believe to be good" (initial tribunal decision on Form LT3, in PIN 62/1398). Mr R appealed again to the Commissioner. The local insurance office, in its statement to the Commissioner, had some sympathy for Mr R and noted that his present incapacity was primarily "psycho neurosis" rather than alcoholism but wished the case to be considered by the Commissioner in order to obtain guidance on dealing with claims from people with alcohol issues (Insurance Officer's written submission to Commissioner, in PIN 62/1398). In his decision, the Commissioner considered the meaning of the misconduct rules and whether or not alcoholism counted:

> In approaching the question whether the incapacitating condition of the claimant was caused by misconduct, regard must be had to the question of whether the condition which has been diagnosed as alcoholism is a disease brought on by the claimant's lack of self-control attributable to a defect in character or by the claimant's lack of control attributable to a disease of the mind or body. (R(S)2/53, para 11)

Here, the Commissioner contrasted a medical condition with a "defect of character". Finding that Mr R had been guilty of misconduct and thus subject to disqualification, the Commissioner concluded:

> unless the claimant had lost control of himself as the result of the disease which destroyed or impaired his will-power, so that he was unable to refrain from excessive drinking they [decision makers] should hold him responsible for his condition and find that he caused his incapacity through his own misconduct. (R(S)2/53 para 16)

This decision sent a clear moral message to potential claimants that they should exercise willpower in avoiding behaviour which might lead to claims for incapacity benefits, distinguishing this from medical conditions which might cause a "lack of control". This distinction marks a key point in assuming that claimants' behaviour can be categorised as innocent or blameworthy. By the 1980s, DHSS guidance suggested that claimants should not be sanctioned for misconduct as a result of "drug addiction and alcoholism" but continued to suggest that it would still be possible to disqualify claimants:

> if incapacity results from excessive drinking on a particular occasion and is not true alcoholism. (DHSS 1981, para 2251)

While recognising drug addiction and alcoholism as medically endorsed conditions, this guidance continued to suggest that it would be possible to distinguish innocent from blameworthy behaviour, based on notions of claimants' free will. Bonner et al., note in the 1990s that R(S)2/53 was still the only reported case on the misconduct rule but consider whether in "the current medical and social climate" the provision could be extended to people whose incapacity was the result of "heavy smoking" or "AIDS" (Bonner et al. 1991, p. 558). I am not aware of any cases where people were sanctioned in relation to these issues. The misconduct rule from 1948 has remained in similar form in regulations for Incapacity Benefit and Employment and Support Allowance although there is little evidence of its use.

The behaviour during sickness rules continued after 1948, enabling sanctions to be imposed for failure without good cause to "observe any rules of behaviour" (National Insurance Act 1946 13(3)(b)). Regulations under the Act contained two rules potentially related to moral conduct:

- to "refrain from conduct calculated to retard his recovery"
- not "to be absent from his place of residence without leaving word where he may be found" (NIAC 1948)

There is little evidence of the extent to which the "conduct calculated to retard recovery" rule was used although there were a couple of early Commissioner's decisions which confirmed key aspects of the rule. In R(S)21/52, Mr M had been claiming Sickness Benefit for a week or so, had gone away for a weekend, intending to return to work on the Monday and had further health problems while away. He was disqualified from benefit for breaching both the conduct rule and the away from home rule. The local office argued that going away from home while ill constituted "conduct calculated to retard recovery". The Commissioner agreed that the disqualification from benefit was appropriate (R(S)21/52, papers in CT 11/209). Another early Commissioner's decision concerned a woman with a visual impairment, Miss H, who had refused to participate in a retraining course organised by the local society for blind people. The local office argued that failure to attend the course constituted "conduct calculated to retard recovery". Miss H appealed to a local tribunal which upheld the decision to disqualify her from benefit and she appealed to the National Insurance Commissioner. The local office argued that the conduct regulation was relevant because the word "recovery" concerned "restoration of working capacity" and therefore that failure to attend the course breached the conduct rule. The Commissioner rejected this claim on the grounds that participating in the training course would make no difference to Miss H's visual impairment and that it was not appropriate to use the conduct regulation. Since there was medical evidence to certify her continuing incapacity for work, Miss H was entitled to benefit (R(S)3/57 case papers in CT/11/161). Miss H's case was also an example of an attempt to enforce women's attachment to the labour market and is discussed in more detail in Chapter 6. However, the case law established by this case concerned the interpretation of the meaning of the conduct rules and continued to be cited by legal analysts into the 1990s (Bonner et al. 1991, p. 599). These two cases established case law on the conduct rules. By the 1980s, detailed DHSS guidance was provided on how to investigate possible cases where conduct calculated to retard recovery was suspected. This involved sick visiting, communication with the claimant's GP and an opportunity for the claimant to explain themselves (DHSS 1981, paras 2271–2274). It is clear from Miss H's case in 1957 that the conduct rule was being used not to control moral behaviour but to test attachment to the labour market and the unwritten expectation that claimants should prepare themselves to return to work.

The absence from place of resident rule, it was argued, was to be used only when a claimant was deliberately avoiding a sick visitor. The National Insurance Advisory Committee noted in 1948 that:

> We are informed that the purpose of this rule of behaviour is to provide against the deliberate and persistent avoidance of the sick visitor by the exceptional

claimant about whose title to continuing benefit there may be some doubt para 28. (NIAC 1948, para 28)

This is quite a change from the practice of Approved Societies, which were likely to suspend benefit or fine claimants merely for being out of the house in the evenings, using the rule as a form of curfew, even for long-term claimants. It seems that the place of residence rule was used primarily to support the sick visiting system for claimants who were considered to be problematic. The rule was discussed in an Commissioner's decision R(S)21/52, discussed above, where a sick visitor had found Mr M to be away when he called and so his benefit was stopped under this rule as well as the conduct rule. In his appeal to the Commissioners, Mr M pled ignorance of the rule. The Commissioner found that this was insufficient and upheld the decision to suspend benefit (R(S)21/52, papers in CT 11/209). In 1955, another Commissioner's decision considered the meaning of the rule. In this case, the claimant's benefit had been suspended for breach of rules because he was not in the house on three occasions when a sick visitor called. The claimant had been claiming benefit since 1940 on the basis of a spinal disorder and there seemed to be no dispute as to his incapacity for work. The claimant argued that he "went out" on medical advice because he had been advised to get as much fresh air as possible and that he had no way of "leaving word" as to where he was since there was no one at home during the day. The Commissioner accepted this explanation and upheld the appeal. In this case, the test as to the applicability of the suspension was worded within a moral discourse of the claimant's trustworthiness:

> The claimant had been incapable of work for many years. He was in a bona fide difficulty in leaving word where he might be found. He had not gone away. He was only away from for a few hours. (R(S)6/55 papers in CT11/134)

In this case, the Commissioner agreed that the claimant had good cause to be away from home and that it was impractical for him to "leave word". The rules in these cases were used to test claimants' authenticity as genuinely incapable of work.

The behaviour during sickness rules established in 1948 were confirmed by similar regulations in 1975 (The Social Security [Unemployment, Sickness and Invalidity Benefit] Regulations 1975, 1975, SI 1975/564). By 1991, however, Bonner et al., refer to two Commissioners' decisions where the place of residence rule was still being used in the 1980s. R(S)7/83 and R(S)1/87 concerned the definition of a place of residence (Bonner et al. 1991, p. 599). These decisions suggest that the rule was indeed being used to support the sick visiting system rather than to act as a curfew on claimants.

ESA and Moral Conditionality Today

Employment and Support Allowance brought a whole new package of conditions and sanctions relating to work-seeking behaviour but has also continued to include the clause allowing suspension of benefit for up to six weeks where a claimant's "limited" capability for work is caused by his or her misconduct or where a claimant fails to "refrain from behaviour calculated retard recovery to health, or is absent from place of residence". The exceptions to the misconduct rules still include sexually transmitted diseases but pregnancy is no longer explicitly mentioned (ESA Regulations 2013, reg 93). Bonner et al. (2013) note that the provisions for misconduct under Incapacity Benefit and ESA were essentially the same as those under previous sickness benefit regimes, again citing R(S)2/53 (Bonner et al. 2013, p. 1038). As in previous decades, there is little evidence of the extent to which the rule has been used. For example, recent DWP statistics on sanctions do not include any examples of sanctions for misconduct for claimants of Employment and Support Allowance (DWP 2018). Misconduct sanctions reported in the Gregg Report in 2008 included only those applying to people claiming Jobseeker's Allowance (Gregg 2008, p. 70). The Welfare Reform Act 2009 proposed to introduce compulsory drug testing and treatment for claimants' addictions but these proved to be impractical and to have ethical challenges (Harris 2010; Wincup and Monaghan 2016). Both Harris and Wincup and Monaghan discuss the possible moralising and conditionality of these proposals. They argue that the UK's increasing policies aimed at drug and alcohol users are related to labour market conditionality, rather than moralising ideas about drink or drug dependency as such. However, the definition of limited capability for work within ESA leads to exclusion from benefit for many people with health issues which once would have been excluded for moral reasons. For example, many drug or alcohol users would not qualify for ESA in the first place because of the narrow definitions of limited capability for work and would instead be subjected to the strict labour market conditionality in the Jobseeker's Allowance. Others may qualify for ESA if they have other impairments, whether related or not to drug or alcohol use, but may find themselves sanctioned under work-seeking conditionality rules. While the moralising of the early twentieth century applies in different ways to people today, the practical effect of much labour market conditionality on people with drug or alcohol problems is still that they are denied access to benefits. Today, instead, is a focus on work-related conditionality. There is a subtle distinction here but current welfare reform policies rely, not on moral arguments about behaviour but on moral arguments about the necessity to engage with the labour market. This means that people who have health conditions which might be considered to be self-inflicted, such as drug or alcohol use, are not sanctioned under the misconduct rules, but instead are vilified by a discourse which portrays them as not making sufficient effort to get to work and are sanctioned under the work-seeking behaviour rules.

Conclusions

This chapter has considered the ways in which moralistic attitudes were used to control claimants' behaviour in the early twentieth century. It is clear that assumptions about sexual behaviour, drinking, fighting and criminal activity were all used to deny benefit to some claimants or to deter people from claiming. These tactics were firmly grounded in the Friendly Society tradition of respectability but were used also by the trade union Societies and by the Prudential Approved Society. The more extreme moral tactics relating to sexual behaviour were largely outlawed on public health grounds by the early 1920s, although Societies could (and did) continue to use their right to expel members for breaches of moral codes. Other tests of respectability, particularly drinking and criminal activity continued to be used by Societies to deny benefit, impose fines or expel members until the introduction of a fully state run scheme after 1948. The post-war scheme dispensed with most of this moralising but retained the power to sanction claimants for misconduct, particularly in relation to alcohol use or evidence of behaviour which could delay recovery. These sanctions became much more closely related to questions of labour market attachment and have evolved into a new moralising over work readiness today. Control of moral behaviour requires methods of surveillance to identify wrongdoers and to deter others from prohibited behaviour. The next chapter considers the techniques of surveillance which were used to achieve this control.

References

Bonner, David, Ian Hooker, and Robin White, eds. 1991. *Non-means Tested Benefits: The Legislation 1991 Edition*. London: Sweet and Maxwell.
Bonner, David, Ian Hooker, Richard Poynter, Robin White, Nick Wikeley, and Penny Wood. 2013. *Social Security Legislation 2013/14: Non-means-Tested Benefits and Employment and Support Allowance*. London: Sweet and Maxwell.
Clarke, George Sydenham. 1916. *Royal Commission on Venereal Diseases. Final Report of the Commissioners*. Cd. 8189. London: H.M.S.O.
Cordery, Simon. 2003. *British Friendly Societies 1750–1914*. Basingstoke: Palgrave Macmillan.

Davis, Gayle. 2011. 'Health and Sexuality'. In *The Oxford Handbook of the History of Medicine*, edited by Mark Jackson. Oxford: Oxford University Press.

Department for Work and Pensions. 2018. 'Stat-Xplore'. 2018. https://stat-xplore.dwp.gov.uk.

Department of Health and Social Security. 1981. *Sickness Benefit Law and Procedure. Code SB 1969, as Amended, 1981*. London: HMSO.

NHS Greater Glasgow and Clyde. 2015. 'Celebrating a Proud History: The Southern General Hospital 1922–2015'. http://www.nhsggc.org.uk/media/232799/history_southern_1922-2015.pdf.

Gregg, Paul. 2008. *Realising Potential: A Vision for Conditionality and Support*. London: DWP.

Harris, Bernard. 2010. 'Reducing Dependency? Conditional Rights, Benefit Reform and Drugs'. *Journal of Law and Society* 37: 233–63.

Lammasniemi, Laura. 2017. 'Regulation 40D: Punishing Promiscuity on the Home Front During the First World War'. *Women's History Review* 26 (4): 584–96.

Machin, Richard. 2017. 'The Professional and Ethical Dilemmas of the Two-Child Limit for Child Tax Credit and Universal Credit'. *Ethics and Social Welfare* 11 (4): 404–11.

Ministry of Health. 1920. 'First Annual Report of the Ministry of Health 1919–1920. Part IV.–Administration of National Health Insurance (1917 to 31st March, 1920). Welsh Board of Health.' Cmd. 913. London: HMSO.

———. 1923. *Reports of Decisions on Appeals and Applications Under Section 67 of the National Insurance Act 1911 and Section 27 of the National Insurance Act 1913, Vol 2—Part I*. London: HMSO.

———. 1933. *Approved Societies Handbook: Being a Revised Handbook for the Guidance of Approved Societies in Their Administration of Benefits Under the National Health Insurance Acts, 1924 to 1932*. London: HMSO.

National Health Insurance Commission. 1912. *National Insurance Act 1911 Model Rules*. London: HMSO.

National Health Insurance Commission (England). 1915a. *Reports of Decisions on Appeals and Applications Under Section 67 of the National Insurance Act 1911 and Section 27 of the National Insurance Act 1913*. Cd. 7810.

———. 1916. *Reports of Decisions on Appeals and Applications Under Section 67 of the National Insurance Act 1911 and Section 27 of the National Insurance Act 1913 Part III*. Cd. 8239. London: HMSO.

——— 1917. *Reports of Decisions on Appeals and Applications Under Section 67 of the National Insurance Act 1911 and Section 27 of the National Insurance Act 1913 Part IV*. Cd. 8474. London: HMSO.

National Health Insurance Joint Committee. 1914a. *National Health Insurance. Appendix to the Report of the Departmental Committee on Sickness Benefit Claims Under the National Insurance Act. Volume I*. [Cd. 7688, 7689, 7690, 7691]. London: HMSO.

———. 1914b. *National Health Insurance. Report of the Departmental Committee on Sickness Benefit Claims Under the National Insurance Act.* Cd. 7687. London: HMSO.

National Health Insurance Committee (Joint Committee). 1917. *National Health Insurance. Report on the Administration of National Health Insurance During the Years 1914–1917.* Cd. 8890. London: HMSO.

National Insurance Advisory Committee. 1948. *National Insurance Act, 1946. National Insurance (Unemployment and Sickness Benefit) Regulations, 1948. Report of the National Insurance Advisory Committee in Accordance with Section 77 (4) of the National Insurance Act, 1946.* London: HMSO.

Ogus, Anthony, Eric Barendt, Trevor Buck, and Tony Lynes. 1988. *The Law of Social Security.* 3rd ed. London: Butterworths.

Scottish Board of Health. 1922. 'Third Annual Report of the Scottish Board of Health.' Cmd. 1697. Edinburgh: HMSO.

Stone, Deborah. 1984. *The Disabled State.* Philadelphia: Temple University Press.

Wincup, Emma, and Mark Monaghan. 2016. 'Scrounger Narratives and Dependent Drug Users: Welfare, Workfare and Warfare'. *Journal of Poverty and Social Justice* 24 (3): 261–75.

9

Unacceptable Snooping: Sick Visitors and Other Methods of Surveillance

Introduction

Mrs C was a married woman in her late fifties who had worked in the weaving trade since she was eleven. In the 1920s, she developed rheumatoid arthritis, was no longer able to continue in this work and so claimed Sickness and then Disablement Benefit. Her Approved Society sent a sick visitor to check up on her claim. After three separate visits, the sick visitor reported that Mrs C had been observed "preparing meals" and that, despite her claimed arthritis, Mrs C had "opened the door with her own hands". The Society interpreted these observations as evidence that Mrs C's arthritis was less severe than she was claiming, referred her to a medical referee and subsequently stopped her benefit. Mrs C appealed. At her appeal, the adjudicator found Mrs C to be incapable of work, preferring the evidence of her own doctor and that of a specialist that she was "incapacitated to a serious extent" (PIN 63/1/404, 1927).

Mrs C was fortunate that she was able to appeal, was able to gather additional evidence from a specialist and that the adjudicator in her case preferred this evidence to that of the sick visitor. Mrs C's case is an example of the practice of using sick visitors to check up on claimants, which was widespread in the early twentieth century and continued well into the late twentieth century. Writers on social control usually note that intense levels of surveillance and intrusion are associated with means-tested welfare systems and with particularly stigmatised claimants, such as unemployed people and lone mothers. Sick or disabled people claiming benefits through a social insurance system have usually been assumed to be less closely monitored. However, the medical mechanisms for confirming people's status as sick or disabled involve intrusion at a most personal level. Additional checks against possible cheating or malingering have involved surveillance in the form of sick visitors, who, as in the case of Mrs C, would carry this surveillance into claimant's homes. Recent research on welfare in the UK (Fletcher and Wright 2017) and the United States (Gilliom 2001; Wacquant 2009) has looked at the role of technology in social control of benefit claimants. Gilliom's observation that surveillance "reflects the political social and technological conditions of the era" (p. 19) is important in acknowledging that the highly technical mechanisms of surveillance used in the twenty-first century reflect the technology of the twenty-first century rather than necessarily being new in the level and content of surveillance. Welfare programmes depend on mechanisms of surveillance in order to categorise claimants and assess their claims. Surveillance mechanisms might also be used to provide support or education to potential recipients of welfare programmes, and they can play a role in deterring potential claimants. The early twentieth-century rise of the "friendly visitor" (Gilliom p. 23) is an example of this dual role. These friendly visitors could be seen as benign, checking on claimants' welfare in order to offer support, but they also acted as a reminder to welfare claimants that they were being watched, keeping them within Foucault's "disciplinary net" (Foucault 1977, p. 306). This chapter looks beyond the evidence gathering function of sick visitors and considers the way in which they were used as mechanisms of surveillance.

Sick Visitors as Detectives

Friendly Societies had used sick visitors since the eighteenth century to control access to incapacity benefits but the use of these visitors increased in the late nineteenth century amid concerns about growing numbers of claims (Cordery 2003, p. 150). With the introduction of state regulated incapacity benefits, the 1911 Act encouraged this practice as a means of controlling claims. The 1911 legislation did not specify how sick visitors should operate but did require that female visitors should be used when checking up on claims by women (NHI Act 1911, 14(2)(c)). This principle was reinforced in the earliest guidance on the running of the scheme (National Health Insurance Commission 1912, p. 12). The inquiry into excessive claims in 1914 gathered evidence about the use of sick visitors and showed that many Societies were using sick visitors to keep claims in check, although there was considerable variation in how this was done in practice, with some Societies using paid visitors, while others used volunteers. Concern was expressed that volunteer sick visitors might become over-friendly with claimants and were not trained to carry out the role effectively. Sometimes visitors, while having a surveillance role, were also responsible for making payments of benefit. This meant that claimants could anticipate visits and could therefore "assume the sick manner". It was recommended that this should be avoided by ensuring that visits took place at unpredictable times. The inquiry also noted a concern that some sick visitors were overstepping the mark and attempting to provide medical advice to claimants (NHIJC 1914b, p. 74). Mary Macarthur's dissenting memorandum to the inquiry report noted that sick visitors were "often untrained, inexperienced and inefficient and, in cases known to the committee, offensively and indelicately inquisitorial in the methods they employ" (NHIJC 1914b, Macarthur dissenting memorandum, p. 80).

There was no doubt that the sick visitors could be intrusive and certainly saw their role as detecting and preventing inappropriate claims for benefit. This role was emphasised repeatedly in reports by the National Health Insurance Commission and, subsequently, the Ministry of Health. There is a reference to this detecting role in an early report on the scheme in Scotland, with advice that sick visitors should "pay visits at irregular intervals, during the day as well as in the evening, and to furnish written reports of visits in a form containing specific questions" (NHIC [England] 1917, p. 116).

This advice to make visits at unexpected times was a key aspect of the detective role of sick visitors. Peel has discussed the way in which early twentieth century social welfare workers often thought of themselves as detectives, seeking to uncover the suspected game-playing strategies of poor people in order to reveal the truth (Peel 2012). Sick visitors were advised to use similar tactics to catch out malingering benefit claimants in order to reveal the true nature of their health issues. Sick visitors were also used to identify claimants who might fail to meet the moral standards set by some Societies. Some of the evidence to the 1914 inquiry confirms this role. For example, in a discussion about Societies' approaches to sexually transmitted diseases (see also Chapter 8), Mr Fletcher of the Great Western Railway Staff Friendly Society gave an example of how his Society might use sick visitors to deal with cases of suspected misconduct. Describing a medical certificate where the doctor had used "a Latin term" that he did not understand, Mr Fletcher looked up a dictionary to find out what it meant and discovered that it "came under a branch of disease which would come under the head of misconduct" (NHIJC 1914a appendices, para 21,477). Mr Fletcher explained that he would use his sick visitor to provide evidence in these cases "I should be all at sea but is quite possible that the sick visitor would find out more" (para 21,478). Clearly, Mr Fletcher did not have much confidence in his own understanding of sexually transmitted diseases but thought that sick visitors' investigations, presumably asking intrusive questions, would be able to uncover evidence of immoral activity. The implication here was that the sick visitors would have local knowledge of claimants' sexual and moral behaviour and they would be able to use their detective skills to investigate and advise the Society of this kind of gossip.

It was a sick visitor who brought Edith Sutton's pregnancy to the attention of her Approved Society, leading to one of the key court cases on sexual morality and incapacity benefits (see Chapter 8). Apart from these severely moralistic Societies, many others would sanction claimants for other misdemeanours such as drinking, fighting or being seen "out of hours". These behavioural sanctions were often applied to men and were often made on the basis of sick visitors' evidence, following the guidance to visit at unexpected times of day and night.

If sick visits were intended merely for welfare or advisory purposes, this detective role would be unnecessary. There is little evidence that the sick visitors used for the control of incapacity benefits were social workers in the sense usually understood by writers looking at the origins of social work in organisations such as the Charity Organisation Society (see Lewis 1995; Peel 2012). They were not motivated by assumptions about charity. This may have been because of the sick visitors' origins in Friendly Societies which prided themselves as rights-based, self-help organisations rather than charitable institutions, although some societies did also have charitable purposes beyond their membership, for example in providing payments to widows and orphans or making payments when members were not strictly entitled (Cordery, pp. 110, 133). Societies themselves sometimes preferred to describe the sick visiting service as supportive. For example, the annual reports of the National Amalgamated Approved Society provide a more positive view of sick visitors, noting their welfare role in highlighting the difficult social circumstances of members. The Society's annual report for 1922 noted that:

> These visits of the sickness visitors are revealing to the committee the distressing conditions under which large numbers of members are living. The unsatisfactory housing conditions of many families produce sickness and disablement claims on the funds which could and should be remedied not only in the interests of the funds but also in the interests of the individuals.

While noting this welfare role, the annual report also suggested that there may have been problems with sick visitors in the past when it noted:

> The committee desire to thank the sickness visitation staff for the greatly improved judgment and tact shown by a very high percentage of staff. (Annual Report of the National Amalgamated Approved Society 1922, in London Metropolitan Archives CLC/B/017/MS292820)

This reference to most staff showing "greatly improved judgment", suggests that there had been a problem with some sick visitors overstepping their role. By 1936, this Society noted "the excellent and discreet manner in which this work is carried out by the members of the sickness visitation staff" (Annual Report of the National Amalgamated Approved Society 1936, in London Metropolitan Archives CLC/B/017/MS292820). This reference to the discreet manner of sick visitors implies that they were learning how to go about their work in a less heavy handed way than in the past but discretion might also imply more subtle forms of surveillance. There is another example of one Society's view of sick visitors in the report in a local paper of a branch meeting of local Approved Societies in Bristol, in 1934. In this newspaper report, Brother Adams described the history of sick visiting in the nineteenth-century friendly society scheme, arguing that its main purpose was to make payments and support members but that, over time, sick visiting was also necessary to guard against "unfair claims". While describing this as a "perfect system", which the societies had developed before the introduction of National Insurance, Brother Adams went on to ask:

> What is visiting meant to be? Is it to be a casual call in an indifferent way usually at the same time on a certain day of the week, is it to be a simple method for the payment of benefit, or is it to be a fraternal visit by a person who has the ability to detect. No one desired to see every sick visitor a suspicious person with the crime detecting ability of a detective but a person whose visit would cheer the sick, but at the same time quickly discover the malingerer. (*Western Daily Press*, 27 December 1934, p. 6)

Despite his concern that sick visitors should "cheer the sick", in his description of some sick visitors as having "crime detecting" abilities, and the powers to "discover malingerers", Brother Adams demonstrated the key purpose of the sick visiting scheme as surveillance. In the early appeal hearings, sick visitors' evidence was often cited by Societies, showing the activities of sick visitors in some detail. In 1914, Mrs R, described in the appeal case as, "a comber tenter, engaged in hard and laborious employment" had been claiming Sickness Benefit for around six months. A sick visitor visited Mrs R at home and observed that she was "upstairs and her daughter was spring cleaning. I do not know what she [Mrs R] was doing". The sick visitor had not actually observed Mrs R doing any cleaning but assumed that she must be working alongside her daughter in this task. Since this appeared to be evidence of capacity for work, the Society stopped her benefit. The adjudicators at Mrs R's appeal were not impressed by the sick visitor's evidence and allowed the appeal (Case 39, NHIC [England] 1915b, p. 109). Despite this result, Mrs R's case exemplifies the way in which sick visitors' invasive surveillance could lead to an initial refusal of benefit, particularly for female claimants. Not all claimants would have exercised their right of appeal.

In a case from 1917, the adjudicators discussed the balance between the sick visitor's observations and medical evidence. In this case, the claimant, Mrs S, had been claiming Sickness and then Disablement Benefit for over a year because of a back problem and suspected cancer. While her medical certificates clearly stated that she was incapable of work, and this had been confirmed by a medical referee, benefit was stopped after a sick visitor observed her "in the streets, shopping". The Society argued that this was evidence of her capacity for light work. The adjudicators disagreed, preferring the evidence from the doctor, confirmed by the medical referee and by evidence from a local hospital. In this case, the sick visitor was not only visiting the claimant at home but was also keeping an eye on her activities outside of the home, reaching well beyond the role of a "visitor" (Case 110, NHIC [England] 1919, p. 266).

Appeal cases from the 1920s show further examples of sick visitors going beyond any kind of welfare role and using detective skills to catch out claimants. In the case of Mrs W, a married woman with a visual impairment, the sick visitor's evidence was considered, in particular in relation to Mrs W's ability to carry out housework. The sick visitor noted having "seen the claimant in the street" and had observed her hanging out her washing, noting in particular that "the washing had been done well". Mrs W was unsuccessful at her appeal, as the adjudicator found that she was capable of some work (63/1/414, 1927). The sick visitor here had clearly been watching Mrs W, using covert methods of surveillance, both in the street and on approach to Mrs W's house, where she noted not only the fact of the washing but its quality. In another, related case, concerning the same Approved Society, a surprisingly detailed report by the sick visitor showed that she saw herself as a detective, looking out for opportunities to catch the claimant out. This case concerned Mrs B, another married woman, who had had a series of claims for Sickness Benefit, the most recent being the result of influenza. The sick visitor's evidence was detailed:

> as she passed the Appellant's window she saw the Appellant standing on the table fastening newly washed clothes on to a line in the front room of her house. She entered the house and by that time the Appellant, who had seen her passing, had seated herself in a chair; the Appellant was wearing a course washing apron, had her sleeves rolled up and her hands were soft and crinkled as if she had been washing; there were two rows of clothes pegged to the line and there was a large basket of newly washed clothes in the room. The sick visitor charged the Appellant with washing the clothes but the Appellant denied it and said that the lodger, who was upstairs sitting with the Appellant's sick child, had done the

washing. The Appellant brought this lodger downstairs and the latter said she had done the washing. The sick visitor replied that she did not believe it as the lodger was wearing a white blouse and a skirt and her hands did not look as if she had been washing. A fortnight later the sick visitor saw the Appellant again pegging out clothes – this time on a line in the back yard. (PIN 63/1/416, 1927)

The adjudicator accepted this evidence as evidence of Mrs B's capacity for work and rejected the appeal. These two cases concerned the same Approved Society and probably concerned the same sick visitor, who carried out detailed surveillance of the claimants under her supervision. Sick visitors were used in this way to investigate claims by married women and to check up on their capacities to carry out domestic work.

Sick visitors continued to be used for surveillance well into the 1920s and 1930s, with Ministry of Health guidance providing detailed advice as to how sick visitors should go about their duties. This guidance attempted to standardise the activities of sick visitors, clarifying their role. The Ministry of Health advised that sick visitors should visit at unpredictable times, including during the day and in the evenings, and should make written reports of their visits. The 1933 Handbook provided a model report form. On this form, sick visitors were asked to record a series of indicators of claimants' activities, along with basic information about health issues, recent contacts with doctors and plans for returning to work. These included

> How does the Member occupy their time?
> What were they doing at the time of the visit?
> Do they appear to have been working?
> Does the Member look ill?
> Do you think the Member is doing what he can to enable him to get back to work?
> Do you think the Member has been out after hours? (Ministry of Health 1933, p. 327, Model Form)

The questions beginning "Do you think.." are clear recommendations to the sick visitors to make value judgements. Other questions appear to be invitations to sick visitors to use surreptitious methods of inquiry, such as checking what claimants are doing when they visit. Combining these observations with visiting at unpredictable times is compelling evidence of the sick visitors' surveillance role.

Local Knowledge and Acting on Tip-Offs

While guidance on sick visitors activities was mostly focussed on the act of visiting, Societies also relied on local knowledge and tip-offs from neighbours in monitoring the activities of claimants. In an early case from 1914, Mrs R, a laundry worker, had claimed Sickness Benefit. Her benefit was stopped after the Society decided that she was "a drunkard". The evidence for this came initially from Mrs R's landlady, who reported her to the sick visitor. The sick visitor duly attempted to visit Mrs R but, discovering that she had moved house, tracked her down to her new address and visited Mrs R at six-thirty in the evening, finding that she was out. Mrs R appealed against the decision to refuse benefit. Mrs R's appeal was eventually successful, mainly because the adjudicators did not accept that there was evidence that her illness was caused by alcohol (Case 8, NHIC [England] 1915a, p. 22). The case is important as an example of the use of tip-offs to sick visitors at this early stage in the scheme. The example of the nine herring workers in 1915 (discussed in Chapter 4) was also one where the Society was acting on information from a local informant.

There are also later examples of this kind of tip-off, for example in 1928, the claimant, Mrs D, was another married woman. The Society had been paying benefit for five years but had received anonymous letters that Mrs D was doing housework. The Society sent a sick visitor to check up on Mrs D's activities. Mrs D was caught buying sugar and butter, was alleged to be breaching the rule on working and was expelled from the Society. The evidence of the sick visitor was key in the Society's decision making. At her appeal, Mrs D produced evidence, from her own doctor, her husband and her sister, which contradicted the sick visitor's evidence. She also explained that she was shopping for small groceries such as butter and sugar in order to get out of the house. Mrs D's doctor argued that it was "was essential to her health that she should go out for walks whenever she could". The adjudicator found in Mrs D's favour, arguing that the rules had been misinterpreted and that they could not be intended to include this kind of low level housework (PIN 63/4/516, 1928).

Another example in an appeal hearing from 1928 concerned Miss N. Miss N had mental health issues, and the discussion at her appeal hearing was focussed on whether or not her ability to go out and about in the evenings was evidence of capacity for work. The Society had given Miss N permission to attend Salvation Army meetings in the evenings, and it had also been accepted that she could break the curfew by going to her mother's house every night because her mental health issues resulted in difficulty sleeping. The Society's sick visitor had clearly been keeping a close eye on Miss N's activities and had "frequently seen the respondent at open air Salvation Army meetings, not always in the best weather, and on some occasions in the street in the evenings". These activities were confirmed by witnesses, described as "Mrs D and Mrs M" who had seen Miss N "alone out of doors in the evenings". It is not clear who Mrs D and Mrs M were but it seems likely that they were neighbours who were being used by the Society in the wider surveillance of this claimant. The sick visitor had been watching Miss N's activities very closely, despite, or perhaps, because of, the agreement that she should be allowed to go out in the evenings (PIN 63/3/500).

Although there appears to be a gendered pattern of sick visitors' evidence, with women mainly being caught doing housework and men mainly being caught breaching rules of behaviour, sick visitors could also be used to catch men working or showing evidence of capacity for work. There is an example from 1929, concerning Mr R who was a former dock labourer who had bronchitis, asthma and a heart condition. A male sick visitor from his Society, which was linked to a trade union, and who was described as "one of the men" and so presumably a former colleague of Mr R, had "caused the man to be sent to the RMO". The RMO found him fit for work. In this case, the adjudicator preferred the evidence of Mr R's doctor and upheld his appeal, finding that he was "in a very frail state of health" (PIN 63/4/523, 1929). This is an example of a trade union Society using local gossip to monitor its members.

Although adjudicators in appeal hearings were usually unwilling to value such evidence without supporting medical statements, in an appeal hearing from 1928, the adjudicator noted the value of surveillance evidence in assessing capacity for work. This case concerned Mrs D, a married woman who was described as "suffering from neurosis" brought about by her experience of air raids during the First World War. She had been claiming benefit for around ten years. The adjudicator weighed up various sources of evidence, including that of Mrs D's own doctor and Regional Medical Officer but noted also that:

> It appears to me that the best means of judging of an appellant's capacity as distinguished from her desire to make the necessary effort of will is to observe the conduct of her life. (PIN 63/3/484, 1928)

Evidence of the "conduct" of Mrs D's life came from several sources, including staff from a convalescent home where she had recently stayed. The matron of the home and a doctor had observed her being able to walk about the grounds, make her own bed and walk up a steep hill to the nearby village. On one occasion, she was observed "hastening up the hill" when she thought she was about to miss a bus. It is clear that Mrs D was being watched at all times while in this home, perhaps unaware that this evidence would be used to support the Society's case that she was fit for work.

In one case, where the Society suspected that the claimant was working while claiming benefit, the sick visitor acted as an agent provocateur. The claimant, Mr S, was alleged to have been running a small business as a second-hand furniture salesman while claiming benefit. Mr S had admitted that he did buy second-hand goods but they were for his own use. In the process of checking up on him, the sick visitor observed Mr S buying items at an auction sale. Then, "acting on instructions", the sick visitor went to Mr S's home, observed that "his house was unusually crowded with furniture and other articles" and attempted to make a purchase, asking the price of various articles. He continued to engage Mr S in conversation, asking him "where he got all the stuff". Mr S cheerfully told him that he bought it at auction sales and provided more detailed information about how he bought and transported the goods and other aspects of his living arrangements. At his appeal, the adjudicator accepted the sick visitor's evidence and upheld the Society's decision that Mr S had breached the Society's rules by working while claiming. As a result, Mr S expelled from the Society It is not entirely clear from the report of the appeal whether the sick visitor had been incognito while carrying out this investigation, but it seems unlikely that Mr S would have provided this level of information had he realised that the purpose of the visit was for the Society to check up on the validity of his claim (PIN 63/2/441, 1928).

This case may have been unusual. However, it is in line with the general detective work which sick visitors were expected to carry out. Sick visitors were sometimes despatched to claimants' homes to check up on knowledge which had been obtained through neighbours, gossip and other hearsay methods, particularly in relation to claimants who were thought to be breaching the out of hours rules or carrying out worklike activities. This kind of surveillance also had parallels in the Unemployment Benefit "genuinely seeking work" test in the 1920s, where home visits were encouraged to assess claimants' honesty and "general demeanour" (Deacon 1976, p. 60). It is clear that sick visitors played a key role in monitoring the behaviour of incapacity benefit claimants in this Approved Society period.

Some claimants reacted violently to sick visitors' intrusions. There are examples in some of the appeal hearings and in reports in local newspapers of men accused of assaulting sick visitors when they were unhappy with information that the visitors had provided to their local Societies. An example from 1919 concerns Mr C who, despite being "an old soldier" with several years of war service to his credit, had been refused benefit on a particular occasion. He assaulted an official of the Society and was convicted of a criminal offence. On another occasion, he "used bad language and threats". The Society expelled him from membership. Mr C appealed against the expulsion. The adjudicators found in favour of the Society, suggesting that Mr C should "apologise for his misconduct and undertake to behave properly in future, but this, the Appellant absolutely declined to do" (Case 2(4), Ministry of Health 1923, p. 9). In a case from 1927, Mr T was expelled from the Society for allegedly using "abusive language" and "threatening behaviour" towards a sick visitor. When he appealed, Mr T gave a different version of events and the adjudicator concluded that the "disagreement" which had occurred between Mr T and the sick visitor did not amount to "serious personal misconduct" and so overturned the expulsion (PIN 631/1/413).

In 1922, a defendant at the Bristol police court was charged with assaulting a sick visitor who had previously reported him for "driving about in a pony and trap" while "on the funds", leading to the defendant's expulsion from his Society. Although the defendant said it was "a tissue of lies", it was alleged that he called the sick visitor "offensive names (such as spy and sneak) and assaulted him" (reported in *Western Daily Press*, 28 November 1922). In a later report of an assault on a sick visitor in Burnley, the magistrate's court heard that a sick visitor had reported a claimant for being out of the house out of hours while claiming benefit. When the sick visitor returned to the defendant's house the next day, the defendant allegedly threatened him with a chair and a poker if he did not pay his benefit (reported in *Burnley Express*, 27 August 1932).

These may have been isolated incidents, but they provide further evidence of sick visitors carrying out a surveillance role and of some resistance from claimants to this "spying and sneaking".

Sick Visiting in the 1930s

Reports of internal appeals to the Societies such as the Ideal Benefit Society in the late 1930s and early 1940s (in PIN 24/74 and PIN 24/80), the Tunbridge Wells Equitable Friendly Society (PIN 24/153) and the Leek Textile Federation (WCML) provide examples of the use of sick visitor evidence, usually of women doing housework and of men or women drinking or being out at night. These cases provide an insight into the frontline decision making in cases which did not reach the independent appeal hearings, but where claimants, nevertheless, had challenged the decision. A late example of this was reported in a letter to a local paper in 1941, headed "Sickness is no Crime". Rev W Rowland Jones reported that he had visited a parishioner who was angry about a recent sick visitor's visit "She had asked him innumerable questions filled up endless forms and imposed restrictions upon him as to what he must and must not do while he was not at work". "She treated me as if I had done something wrong. Is it a crime to be sick?" (Rev W Rowland Jones, vicar of Denton Manchester, *Daily Herald*, 27 January 1941).

It is quite likely that there were many more cases where benefits were stopped or claimants were sanctioned on the basis of sick visitor evidence. Equally, this level of surveillance would also be used to deter claimants from claiming in the first place if they thought they would be watched in this way. Successful benefit claimants would be deterred from indulging in the morally loaded activities such as drinking or being seen in public, which might threaten their claims if caught by sick visitors or other local networks.

The 1940s and the Transition to a State System

Before 1948, the organisation of sick visiting was entirely up to individual Approved Societies, although subject to guidance from the Ministry of Health. From 1948, the Ministry of Pensions and National Insurance continued the practice of sick visiting following the advice in the pre-war Ministry of Health Handbook "as a matter of expediency". By 1949, the Ministry was preparing its own guidance and forms (memo dated 8 March 1949 in PIN 35/37). This memo shows the clear link between the Approved Society system and the plans being made under the new National Insurance system. A subsequent memo to all local offices suggested that sick visiting should be increased (memo to all regional controllers, dated 17 June 1949). Further papers in this file show that there was a concern about the balance between welfare and surveillance functions of sick visitors. This was noted in the record of a meeting with local insurance office managers:

> Some concern was expressed lest the Home Visiting arrangements should develop into a police service. The Controller explicitly denied that anything of the sort was contemplated and promised that the important welfare aspect of Sick Visiting should be emphasized in the instructions he was going to issue. (Notes of meetings of North Western Region Managers, dated 19 August 1949)

An undated memo in this file from 1949 refers to the sick visiting system being attacked in the press as "a particularly objectionable example of unacceptable snooping by government officials" (undated memo, Headed "Sick visiting (General Policy)" in PIN 35/37). The memo then went on to explain that this concern about "unacceptable snooping" had to be assessed in the context of other reports of "abnormal increases in absenteeism allegedly due to sickness". The file continues with a draft circular on the "control of claims" which outlines the role of the sick visiting service:

In addition to the prompt payment of sickness or injury benefit in all proper cases, Local Offices have an equally important duty to perform, to which much greater attention must now be paid than has hitherto been possible. This duty is the adequate supervision and control of claims to benefits, both in the claimant's interest and for the protection of the Insurance Funds from possible abuse. This can only be done by systematic scrutiny of claims, supported by an efficient system of "sick visiting" at the home and reference to the RMO(H) where there is doubt as to the claimant's incapacity. (Draft Circular on the Control of Claims to Sickness or Injury Benefit, dated 25 November 1949)

The reference here to paying "much greater attention" to the control of claims that had been possible in the past suggests that the move from the Approved Society system to a state system was not going to lead to decreased surveillance.

Professionalisation of Sick Visitors and Training in the 1950s

Further files from this early post-war period include detailed training materials for sick visitors from the early 1950s. These stress the role of the sick visitor as an initial step in the control of claims. The training materials reinforce in the minds of sick visitors that they will somehow be able to distinguish between "genuine" and malingering claimants:

> In genuine cases the Home Visit is welcomed and appreciated, and encourages a sense of responsibility among insured persons. (Ministry of National Insurance Home Visiting course for Clerical Officers Instructor's Brief, para 5 in PIN 35/38)

By suggesting that "genuine" claimants would welcome the sick visitor and, presumably that malingerers would not, these training materials support Stone's view of the home visit as a means of uncovering "revelatory signs" (Stone 1984, p. 101) encouraging sick visitors to make subjective judgements about who is, and is not, genuine. The instructions also reinforce the sick visitor's role in providing a reminder to claimants to self-regulate, by "encouraging a sense of responsibility". Detailed instructions in the training materials included continuing advice to sick visitors to use their detective skills to expose any signs of malingering:

> The insured person has a right to know the reason for your visit and you should as far as possible satisfy him without boldly telling him e.g. that you have come to find out whether he is obeying the rules as to behaviour during sickness. In

> such a case you will usually be able to veil the real reason for the visit by some initial enquiry as to how the claimant is progressing
> <u>Watch what the claimant is doing on your entry and make a note of it later</u>
> Listen and observe rather than talk. (Ministry of National Insurance Home Visiting course for Clerical Officers Students Notes, 1951 in PIN 35/38, [underlining in original])

These notes continue the advice from the Approved Societies' scheme that sick visitors should use covert methods to monitor claimants' behaviour, including making careful notes on what the claimant was doing at the time of the visit. The specific instruction to "veil the real reason for the visit" is further evidence of the sick visitor as a detective. The training notes stress that the sick visitor is not to give medical advice and also that the sick visitor is not a fraud officer. There is some advice that sick visitors should be alert to claimants' possible need for further welfare advice and should carry information about "local Welfare Organisations" but this is described as a secondary object of the visit.

Actions of sick visitors are revealed in some of the case files for post-1948 Commissioners decisions. Sick visitors' evidence was the prompt for several key cases, including R(S)11/51, where it was a sick visitor who had caught Mrs E scrubbing the front path (see Chapter 1). In a statement the sick visitor detailed her observations:

> I visited Mrs E at her home today. The household consists of herself and husband only and they occupy a Ground floor flat consisting of kitchen, scullery, bedroom and sitting room. The house is very clean and tidy and gives the appearance of being regularly cleaned. All meals are taken at home by Mrs E and her husband, which Mrs E prepares, she also does her own shopping, although she states that this is mainly a weekly visit to the grocers to place her order and anything else is obtained from a shop, just across the back lane. I asked Mrs E about the housework she does and she gave me to understand that she was not able to do heavy work, such as scrubbing or brushing, or any that required strenuous effort, but she can do dusting, washing dishes, making beds and "tidying up". When asked about washing she said her sister-in-law does her washing "sometimes", if not, Mrs E sends it to the laundry. As Mrs E does not have regular help in the house, and the house appears so very clean, it would seem that Mrs E is able to do normal household duties. (Sick visitor statement, 18/4/51 in PIN 62/1354)

This detailed description of Mrs E's house, including the sick visitor's observation that it is "so very clean", is a good example of the covert detective skills which sick visitors were advised to develop. After the flurry of activity on women and domestic duties, following the cases of Mrs E in R(S)11/51 and Mrs B in R(S)17/51 (see Chapter 6), there was a drive to increase sick visiting of married women to check up on their capacity for domestic duties outside the home. The sick visitors' forms were amended to include specific questions for women about domestic duties:

> If claimant is domestic head of household,
> How much domestic work does she do?
> Does she do it without frequent periods of rest? (Form BF32, copy in PIN 35/41)

Although this addition to the form was to be used where women were the "domestic head of household", this kind of intrusion on women's activities was also applied to single women. An example is the case of Miss F, whose case was reported as R(S)20/52 (see also Chapter 9 for a discussion of this case). Miss F was an unmarried woman who lived with her mother and brother. She had been diagnosed as having agoraphobia and was unable to leave her home unaccompanied. There is a copy of sick visitor's report in the case file. Miss F was not the "domestic head of household" and the sick visitor had not ticked that box on the form. However, the form includes a question about whether there is any evidence of the claimant working. The sick visitor's response is:

> As there were some visitors in the house, the possibility cannot be ruled out.
> (copy of sick visitor's report on R(S)20/52, filed in PIN 62/1383)

This reference to "visitors" in the house related to the allegation that Miss F was capable of working by assisting her mother in running a boarding house. Miss F strongly denied this allegation, claiming instead that she sometimes helped in the kitchen and that the visitors were relatives. The Commissioners found that Miss F was fit for work. Although the decision to refuse benefit was based primarily on the Regional Medical Officer's report, the comment from the sick visitor is evidence of sick visitors following the advice to use detective skills in their visits. The sick visitor on this occasion chose to interpret the presence of visitors in the house as evidence of Miss F's capacity to contribute to housework and therefore to the possibility of her ability to work from home.

During the 1950s, sick visitors became less important in the gathering of evidence of capacity for work, as the medical evidence from the Regional Medical Officer service took precedence (see Chapter 3). However, they continued as a first step in the control mechanism and as a mechanism of surveillance. Detailed instructions to sick visitors continued into the 1980s, with advice to carry out visits at unpredictable times, and to ask surreptitious questions about claimants' lives and activities. An example from the 1980s includes the following advice:

> He [the sick visitor] should ascertain whether the claimant can go out unaccompanied, how far he can walk. How far he can travel on public transport or, if he has a car, whether he is able to drive it. He should also take into consideration anything the claimant may tell him, any information given in confidence by a relative and what he has observed for himself. Any inconsistency between the claimant's activities at the time of the visit and the certified cause of incapacity should be reported. (DHSS 1981, para 5131)

Further detailed advice was provided for checking up on claimants who were considered to be particularly problematic: married women, self-employed people, people with a history of frequent short-term claims, claims during national holidays or sporting events, claims from people on strike, claimants with medical certificates from non-conventional sources, claims relating to alcohol where "there is not true alcoholism" and claimants where the GP has indicated some doubt about the claimant by making a special reference on the sick note (DHSS 1981, para 5221). The 1981 guidance also noted that sick visits should also be initiated where "information has been received from an outside source, e.g. an anonymous letter" (para 4884). Other than some updating of language, the guidance on the value of sick visits in 1981 is almost identical to that in 1960 and to that of similar guidance in 1949. This guidance shows that the role of the sick visitor, while declining as a main source of evidence of capacity for work, was still being used to watch claimants for signs of failure to conform to expectations of behaviour during sickness. This period in the history of social security brought a new authoritarianism in the form of increased fraud investigations which seem to have taken the place of sick visitors as the main form of social control of benefit claimants (Dominelli 1988, McKeever, 1999). Much of the use of sick visitors as investigators might overlap with the activities of fraud officers, but it is important to note that most of the claimants in the cases discussed here were not accused of fraud but of malingering or of failing to follow rules of behaviour while on benefit. This level of scrutiny suggests a detailed surveillance of claimants of incapacity benefits which is often forgotten in the narratives today regarding the welfare state of the late twentieth century.

Medical Surveillance

The preceding discussion looks at the role of sick visitors in the governance of incapacity benefit claimants, but incapacity benefits, by definition, have always relied on heavy medical surveillance. Claimants cannot even begin to make a claim, let alone sustain one over time, without endorsement by medical professionals. Claimants must subject themselves to what has been termed "the medical gaze" (Foucault, 1977, p. 184). Every claim requires this basic medical endorsement but, as discussed in Chapter 4, this has not usually been sufficient for a claim of incapacity, and claimants have been subject to medical examinations and tests of all kinds to ensure that their claim is valid, from a medical perspective. Surveillance has taken the form of the requirement to submit regular medical certificates from General Practitioners and the requirement to attend medical examinations by specialists, state officials and experts of various kinds. Failure to attend medical examinations is assumed to be an admission of malingering, leading to benefit being refused. This assumption has been consistent in decision making across the twentieth and twenty-first centuries. An example of this kind of assumption can be found in discussions by the Ministry of Pensions in the 1950s, where a civil servant argued, in relation to the increase in referrals to the Regional Medical Service:

> You asked specifically whether we could say how effective the new system was as a deterrent against the would be offender. We feel that we are not able to express a precise view on this somewhat imprecise problem. Since, however, a doctor is asked to furnish a report on his patient every time a reference is made and since a patient who tends to malinger soon learns that he will inevitably be referred for examination, we think that the increase in the number of references must create a healthier attitude to certification. (Letter dated 12/1/56 from MJ Hewitt (MoH) to Gr Ashford at the Treasury, in PIN 35/125)

The use of the term "would be offender" and the reference to the efficiency of the system as a "deterrent" clearly marks the Regional Medical Service in its role as part of the disciplinary mechanism in preventing perceived unwarranted claims.

When claimants challenge adverse decisions, they are more likely to be successful if they can also provide additional evidence, requiring them to subject themselves to the wider gaze of experts and specialists, who may be willing to provide evidence to support their claim. Claimants are required to subject themselves to the "network of writing" which Foucault describes as resulting from capturing records of examinations (1977, p. 189) as they become dependent on the documents which define them as being sufficiently disabled to qualify for benefits. The major change in the assessment of incapacity for work in 1995 led to changes in the mechanisms for surveillance. Since long term claims of incapacity were no longer dependent on a classification of incapacity alone and were dependent instead on a combination of a medical certificate of incapacity and a medical assessment under the Incapacity Benefits points' rules, surveillance became even more medicalised. Under Incapacity Benefit and Employment and Support Allowance, claimants are required to fill in endless forms, describing their health issues and daily struggles, bringing the medical gaze into the most minute and personal details of claimants' lives. In her discussion of a similar procedure for claiming Disability Living Allowance, Shildrick has described this as being "controlled not by a display of external coercion but by continuous surveillance and by the insistent demand for a personal accounting" (Shildrick 1997, p. 49). Similarly, in the United States, the increasing difficulties of poor people to access welfare have led to the medicalisation of poverty (Hansen et al. 2014). The claim forms are not sufficient however and most claimants for Employment and Support Allowance must subject themselves to further surveillance through medical examinations by "experts" of various kinds. Ironically, these experts have themselves been questioned for having the wrong kind of expertise, making this intrusion even more offensive to many claimants. (See Chapter 4 for a discussion of medical evidence.)

Conclusions

The twentieth-century incapacity benefit schemes included surveillance as a mechanism of controlling claims and of deterring undesirable behaviour in benefit claimants. Medical surveillance has always been a key part of this mechanism, but the sick visitors were used as a means of watching claimants' everyday lives throughout the twentieth century. Although some of these visitors had a general welfare role, they operated primarily as detectives, seeking to enforce rules of behaviour, uncover malingerers and supervise the activities of married women suspected of being housewives. Surveillance of incapacity benefit claims since the introduction of ESA in 2008 has reached extreme levels, with the formal introduction of work-related conditionality. This means that claimants must subject themselves not only to the medical gaze of the medical professionals but also day-to-day surveillance of their work-seeking activities. The stigma of being a benefits claimant also leads people to self-regulate their daily lives for fear of their benefits being cut or of being labelled as a "scrounger" (Fletcher and Wright 2017; Manji 2016). These findings from current benefit claimants' experiences have echoes in the experiences of claimants in the interwar period, who were required to curtail their activities to avoid being reported by sick visitors or neighbours.

References

Cordery, Simon. 2003. *British Friendly Societies 1750–1914*. Basingstoke: Palgrave Macmillan.

Deacon, Alan. 1976. *In Search of the Scrounger*. Leeds: University of Leeds.

Department of Health and Social Security. 1981. *Sickness Benefit Law and Procedure. Code SB 1969, as Amended, 1981*. London: HMSO.

Dominelli, Lena. 1988. 'Thatcher's Attack on Social Security: Restructuring Social Control'. *Critical Social Policy* 8 (23): 46–61.

Fletcher, Del Roy, and Sharon Wright. 2017. 'A Hand Up or a Slap Down? Criminalising Benefit Claimants in Britain via Strategies of Surveillance, Sanctions and Deterrence'. *Critical Social Policy*. https://doi.org/10.1177/0261018317726622.

Foucault, Michel. 1977. *Discipline and Punish: The Birth of the Prison*. Translated by Alan Sheridan. London: Allen Lane.

Gilliom, John. 2001. *Overseers of the Poor: Surveillance, Resistance, and the Limits of Privacy*. Chicago: University of Chicago Press.

Hansen, Helena, Philippe Bourgois, and Ernest Drucker. 2014. 'Pathologizing Poverty: New Forms of Diagnosis, Disability, and Structural Stigma Under Welfare Reform'. *Social Science & Medicine*, Structural Stigma and Population Health, 103 (Supplement C): 76–83.

Lewis. 1995. *The Voluntary Sector, the State and Social Work in Britain: The Charity Organisation Society/Family Welfare Association since 1869*. Aldershot: Edward Elgar.

Manji, Kainde. 2016. 'Social Security Reform and the Surveillance State: Exploring the Operation of "Hidden Conditionality" in the Reform of Disability Benefits Since 2010'. *Social Policy and Society* 16 (2): 1–10.

McKeever, Gráinne. 1999. 'Fighting Fraud: An Evaluation of the Government's Social Security Fraud Strategy'. *Journal of Social Welfare and Family Law* 21 (4): 357–71.

Ministry of Health. 1923. *Reports of Decisions on Appeals and Applications Under Section 67 of the National Insurance Act 1911 and Section 27 of the National Insurance Act 1913, Vol 2—Part I*. London: HMSO.

———. 1933. *Approved Societies Handbook: Being a Revised Handbook for the Guidance of Approved Societies in Their Administration of Benefits Under the National Health Insurance Acts, 1924 to 1932*. London: HMSO.

National Health Insurance Commission. 1912. *National Insurance Act 1911 Model Rules*. London: HMSO.

National Health Insurance Commission (England). 1915a. *Reports of Decisions on Appeals and Applications Under Section 67 of the National Insurance Act 1911 and Section 27 of the National Insurance Act 1913*. Cd. 7810. London: HMSO.

———. 1915b. *Reports of Decisions on Appeals and Applications Under Section 67 of the National Insurance Act 1911 and Section 27 of the National Insurance Act 1913 Part II*. Cd. 8040. London: HMSO.

———. 1917. *Reports of Decisions on Appeals and Applications Under Section 67 of the National Insurance Act 1911 and Section 27 of the National Insurance Act 1913 Part IV.* Cd. 8474. London: HMSO.

———. 1919. *Reports of Decisions on Appeals and Applications Under Section 67 of the National Insurance Act 1911 and Section 27 of the National Insurance Act 1913 Part V.* Cmd. 134. London: HMSO.

National Health Insurance Joint Committee. 1914a. *National Health Insurance. Appendix to the Report of the Departmental Committee on Sickness Benefit Claims Under the National Insurance Act. Volume I.* Cd. 7688, 7689, 7690, 7691. London: HMSO.

———. 1914b. *National Health Insurance. Report of the Departmental Committee on Sickness Benefit Claims Under the National Insurance Act.* Cd. 7687. London: HMSO.

Peel, Mark. 2012. *Miss Cutler and the Case of the Resurrected Horse: Social Work and the Story of Poverty in America, Australia and Britain.* Chicago: University of Chicago Press.

Shildrick, Margrit. 1997. *Leaky Bodies and Boundaries: Feminism, Postmodernism and (Bio)Ethics.* London: Routledge.

Stone, Deborah. 1984. *The Disabled State.* Philadelphia: Temple University Press.

Wacquant, Loïc J. D. 2009. *Punishing the Poor: The Neoliberal Government of Social Insecurity.* English edition. Durham, NC and London: Duke University Press.

10

Conclusion

When I started the research that led to this book, I thought I was investigating the definition of incapacity for work and how it had changed across the first century of the welfare state in the UK. I thought it was about how medical evidence was used to come to conclusions about people's capacity for work and how medical models of disability defined people as incapable. Capacity and incapacity for work are usually presented as something which can be assessed objectively, although perhaps open to degrees of difference in professional interpretation: differences which can be resolved through the collection of better evidence or better regulation and monitoring of decision making. I knew from preliminary research (Gulland 2012, 2013) that this was strongly gendered: men were treated differently from women, and that deep-seated notions of deservingness pervaded decision making across the twentieth century and into the twenty-first century. The research, and therefore the book, would be about how these themes developed, how they changed and how they operate today. It took me rather longer to realise that the book is really about work: what work is, what it is not, who should do it, who should be compensated when work does not provide a sufficient income and who should be exempted from any requirement to look for it. Incapacity benefits are not just about who can work but also about who should. They are also about what counts as work and how that work is valued. This means that the book is as much about work as it is about medical ideas about incapacity. These are moral issues, deeply infused with assumptions about gender, age, social class, ethnicity and disability. They are about social control.

Decision making on incapacity benefits for most of the twentieth century was heavily influenced by gendered assumptions about what men and women could and should be doing with their time. Incapacity benefits have been based on a model of a typical worker, a person, usually a man, who would leave school, find a job and work full time until retirement. Gaps in this working life caused by illness or impairment would be covered by incapacity benefits. There was an assumption that this typical person would recover, retrain if necessary and get back to work. Feminists have long criticised this perspective as being based on male patterns of labour market participation and have argued for women's domestic roles to be recognised as work. Early models of incapacity did recognise women's domestic activities as work but this did not help women in their claims for income maintenance. Instead, this recognition of domestic labour as work served to mark them as being outside the labour market, denying them a right to benefit. Gender roles have changed since the early twentieth century. Although working-class women have always engaged in the paid labour market, it has now become the expectation and the norm that all women will do so. Women's patterns of work continue to be different from men's, as responsibilities for childcare, housework and family care still remain heavily gendered. Domestic duties have changed. The work of cleaning and cooking has become much less labour intensive, but this work still needs to be done by someone. Caring responsibilities for other family members, children and adults seemed to be almost invisible from benefit decision making in the early twentieth century. Caring responsibilities are now more visible and social security policies acknowledge some childcare responsibilities, if inadequately. Childcare is commodified by nursery provision or childcare allowances, enabling mothers to do "real work" in the labour market, while other low paid women look after the children, thus allowing both groups of women to have the moral status of "working" (Levitas 2001). Gendered patterns of part-time working are evidence that women still take the major responsibility for fitting their working lives around children. Today's welfare state has not been able to find a way of commodifying other aspects of women's unpaid caring and domestic work, although the growth of a care industry has led to significant numbers of low paid women working as paid carers (Hayes 2017). The tightening of eligibility rules for means-tested benefits for lone parents, bringing work-seeking conditionality to all parents whose youngest children are more than one year old, means that many lone parents with health issues seek to claim Employment and Support Allowance instead. They then risk their caring responsibilities being used as evidence of capacity for work (Gulland 2011).

Today some of the assumptions about gender and disability in incapacity benefit decision making have changed. Equalities legislation means that benefits can no longer be explicitly gendered, and yet gender inequality continues in patterns of claims for benefit, with social security systems built on unequal access to the labour market and distribution of domestic and caring responsibilities. The social model of disability shows that the concept of incapacity for work is meaningless outside its social context. Despite this important insight and campaigning by disability organisations, assessments for incapacity for work have become increasingly medicalised since 1995 and the introduction of Incapacity Benefit closely followed by Employment and Support Allowance. The points systems now used for assessing incapacity mean that most social aspects of work are ignored in decision making. Meanwhile, the quantitative nature of these points systems gives them a veil of objectivity.

Incapacity benefits in the UK have depended on a binary distinction between capacity and incapacity for work. ESA changed the language so that now nobody is "incapable of work" and everyone is either capable of work, or has limited capacity for work or has limited capacity for work-seeking activities. This Orwellian shift may have introduced a third dimension to the binary capable/incapable divide but decision makers must still place individual claimants in one of these three categories. What matters with a decision is who makes it, how they make it, how they justify it and whether or not there is any opportunity for challenging it.

Such decision making depends on knowledge, on the collection and assessment of evidence, on the value of different types of evidence. It is clear that medical knowledge has always been key to incapacity benefit decision making. Despite its elevated status, medical knowledge is not neutral. There has been a continuing thread through the incapacity benefit schemes that an individual claimant's doctor cannot be fully trusted to provide "objective" evidence on questions of capacity for work. As a result, there have been efforts to find sources of independent medical evidence to justify claims, initially through the Regional Medical Service and more recently through the use of outsourced private companies such as ATOS and Maximus. There has always been debate about the balance between the claimant's doctor's deeper, but allegedly subjective, knowledge of people's lives and health issues, compared with the independent but shallower knowledge of these Policy makers and legal decision makers have repeatedly stressed that benefits decisions should be made using both sources of evidence, rather than relying on one or the other. In practice, decision makers have usually preferred the evidence of second level assessors, except on appeal. However, decision making has also depended on more informal knowledge and common-sense ideas of "work" and by "incapacity".

Incapacity benefits were created as part of a welfare state which depends on the work ethic and an expectation of attachment to the labour market. Monitoring this work ethic depends on systems of surveillance. This surveillance begins with a minimum requirement that claimants seek endorsement of their claims from medical professionals of various kinds. This level of medical surveillance is taken for granted and is a daily reality for people with impairments and chronic health conditions. Medical surveillance may be acceptable, but it can also include much more intrusive judgement by doctors as to claimants' motives and morals. In the early years of the twentieth century, some doctors thought it was appropriate to make judgements about people's sex lives and the extent of their blameworthiness in contracting sexually transmitted diseases. This was extreme but medical surveillance has been, and continues to be, fundamental to the decision making apparatus of incapacity benefits. Refusal or failure to participate in this medical surveillance has been consistently judged as an admission of malingering or feigned sickness and leads to automatic refusal of benefit. These mechanisms for medical surveillance depend on an assumption that medical evidence will provide objective statements about people's impairments and capacities.

Social control of claimants has led to sick visitors watching people going about their daily lives, looking for clues as to their possible malingering, morally unacceptable behaviour, or evidence of working. Women have been observed hanging out their washing, scrubbing their front steps and carrying heavy shopping. Farmers have been judged to be working because they were wearing wellington boots. I have found at least one example of a sick visitor acting as an agent provocateur, attempting to buy second-hand goods from a claimant, suspected of running a business. In the early twentieth century, benefit claimants were subject to curfews and close monitoring of their social lives.

Behavioural conditionality has been a hidden conditionality in incapacity benefit schemes until very recently. However, since 2008, people claiming Employment and Support Allowance and deemed to have "limited capability for work" are expected to account for their daily activities and to show that they are carrying out appropriate work-seeking behaviour. The introduction of explicit work-seeking conditionality under Employment and Support Allowance and the limitation of non-means-tested ESA to one year for most claimants mean that benefits for people claiming incapacity for work will become increasingly means-tested and conditional. The principle of a national insurance-based Sickness Benefit introduced in 1911 has almost disappeared in practice. The introduction of Universal Credit, as a means-tested umbrella benefit for all working age claimants, will become the main benefit available to disabled people and those with long term health conditions. Universal Credit blurs many of the traditional distinctions between incapacity, unemployment and underemployment. However, these distinctions will still be important in defining the amount of benefit available to claimants and in setting the work-seeking conditions that claimants must fulfil. The combination of increased means-testing and conditionality suggests that social control of claims for those with restricted capacity for work will increase. The recent introduction of a two-child limit into the UK means-tested benefits harks back to early twentieth century ideas about moral responsibility. Although the policy is not specifically targeted at claimants of incapacity benefits, people claiming Universal Credit on the basis of limited capability for work are subject to this control of their private lives. The wording of the two-child limit, and the categories of exemption from it, place responsibility for reproduction clearly on mothers, implying that women are guilty if they have too many children. O'Brien has described the two-child limit as 'the most significant violation of human rights that has yet been written into the fabric of the UK social security system' (O'Brien 2018, p. 701). The wording of the "rape clause" whereby women are entitled to claim benefits for more than two children if a child is conceived as a result of a "non-consensual sexual act" is dangerously reminiscent of the discussions in Sutton v New Tabernacle in 1922.

The history of policy and decision making on incapacity benefits shows a continuous search for objectivity in assessing people's claims. Policy discourse has often harked back to golden ages, when claimants were more responsible, doctors were more reliable or circumstances allowed more generous interpretation of the rules. The most recent policy discourse has been that the state has let claimants down by allowing them to stay on benefits for too long, creating dependency and stifling people's natural desire to get back to work. This is not new.

In 1976, the disability activist organisation, Union of Physically Impaired Against Segregation (UPIAS), predicted that any disability benefit scheme which required assessment of impairment would lead to:

> an army of experts… armed with the latest definitions and tests for measuring, will prod and probe into the intimate details of our lives. They will bear down on us with batteries of questions, and wielding tape measures will attempt to tie down the last remaining vestige of our privacy and dignity as human beings. (UPIAS and Disability Alliance 1976, p. 18)

Forty years on, instead of the comprehensive income scheme which the Disability Alliance proposed, there is a much reduced and oppressive benefits system but complete with the army of experts with their tape measures. Control and surveillance has been, and continues to be, central to the system. Medical surveillance is at its heart but is combined with other forms. The endless search for objective assessments, culminating in the current ESA medical test is trying to do something which cannot be done. The mechanisms required to sort people into categories of eligibility and conditionality are expensive, but carry an even greater human cost. Subjecting people to the levels of surveillance, testing and conditionality that has occurred across the twentieth century and continuing in ever harsher and uncompromising forms is inhumane and demeans us all. When I began the research for this book, I wondered whether assessment systems in the past had been more humane than the points-based systems under ESA today. I conclude that they were, in principle. The definition of incapacity described in Mrs E's case, R(S)11/51, seems to be more humane and seems to take better account of the social structures which constrain people's access to the labour market. However, the mechanisms for making these assessments were intrusive and depended on social assumptions about who could or should work. They did not, in themselves, create any jobs or make it any easier for people to find work, whatever side of the capacity/incapacity line they fell.

This begs the question as to whether there is a system of assessing people's capacity for work which would be more humane. My conclusion, in the end, is that there is not. Systems of assessment rely on more or less explicit assumptions about who can or should work. They also rely on assumptions about what "work" is and how it should be recompensed. Feminists have long noted the volume of unpaid labour carried out by women. Disability theorists have shown that disabled people are prevented from accessing the labour market or from earning a decent living by the barriers created by society rather than by their impairments. Levels of compensation for paid work are heavily structured by gender, social class, ethnicity, disability, caring responsibilities and the state of the labour market. So any system which attempts to categorise people as able to work or not is bound to become caught up in these structural inequalities. A solution, perhaps, is a citizens' income which does not rely on categorising people as capable or incapable of work. Post-work theorists such as Frayne (2015) and Weeks (2011) have promoted this idea as way of disentangling social security schemes from gendered expectations of labour market participation. While these ideas are sometimes considered to be utopian, policy makers and governments have begun to take them more seriously in recent years. Citizens' income schemes of course carry their own problems but would be a useful alternative to the impossible task of attempting to classify people in the way that incapacity benefits schemes have tried to do.

References

Frayne, David. 2015. *The Refusal of Work: The Theory and Practice of Resistance to Work*. London: Zed Books.

Gulland, Jackie. 2011. 'Ticking Boxes: Understanding Decision Making in Employment and Support Allowance'. *Journal of Social Security Law* 18: 69–86.

———. 2012. '"Fitting Themselves to Become Wage-Earners": Conditionality and Incapacity for Work in the Early 20th Century'. *Journal of Social Security Law* 119: 51–70.

———. 2013. 'Extraordinary Housework: Women and Claims for Sickness Benefit in the Early 20th Century'. *Women's History Magazine* 71: 23–30.

Hayes, Lydia. 2017. *Stories of Care: A Labour of Law: Gender and Class at Work*. London, UK: Palgrave.

Levitas, Ruth. 2001. 'Against Work: A Utopian Incursion into Social Policy'. *Critical Social Policy* 21 (4): 449–65.

O'Brien, Charlotte. 2018. "Done Because We Are Too Menny". *The International Journal of Children's Rights* 26 (4): 700–739.

Union of Physically Impaired Against Segregation, and Disability Alliance. 1976. *Fundamental Principles of Disability*. London: UPIAS. http://disability-studies.leeds.ac.uk/files/library/UPIAS-fundamental-principles.pdf.

Weeks, Kathi. 2011. *The Problem with Work: Feminism, Marxism, Antiwork Politics, and Postwork Imaginaries*. Durham: Duke University Press.

Appendix Sources and Methods

Archives

All archive records referred to in the text are from The National Archives in London, unless otherwise specified. The following is a list of all archive sources cited, with their approximate dates.

The National Archives, London

ACT 1/582 Joint Committee sub-committee to consider increase in disablement benefit first investigation (1930s)
BN36/58 DHSS Sickness Benefit Law and Procedure. Code SB 1981
CT11 National Insurance Commissioners' files (1948–1960s)
MH 62/201 Incapacity for work: consideration of 'fitness for other work' in cases of temporary unfitness only for ordinary occupation (1930)
PIN 4/5 Ministry of Health National Health and Pension Insurance appeals and disputes Appointment of panel of Referees (1920s)
PIN 8/106 Beveridge Report—sick visitors—functions (1940s)
PIN 13/941 Liability for fire watching of insured persons certified as incapable of work and in receipt of sickness or disablement benefits (1940s)
PIN 24/153 Minute book of Tunbridge Wells Equitable Friendly Society (1912–21)
PIN 24/74 Ideal Benefit Society Minute Book Appeals sub-committee Men (1935–1941)
PIN 24/80 Ideal Benefit Society Minute Book Appeals sub-committee Women (1935–1941)

PIN 35/7 Incapacity borderline cases (1940s)
PIN 35/37 Supervision of claims to SB—organisation of sick visiting (1940s)
PIN 35/38 Supervision of claims to SB—organisation of sick visiting (includes training materials for sick visitors) (1950s)
PIN 35/41 supervision of claims to SB—housework references (1950s)
PIN 35/72 Medical certification: comment in the medical and national journals (1960s)
PIN 35/78 Incapacity for work interpretation and policy (1940–1970s)
PIN 35/86 Sickness benefit—local appeal tribunals' attitude toward RMO (H) Reports (1950s)
PIN 35/123 Sickness Benefit for Home Workers: Survey of General Position (including voluntary organisations) (1948–1949)
PIN 35/125 Supervision of claims to SB—organisation of sick visiting—revision (1950s)
PIN 35/392 Therapeutic Earnings (1960s)
PIN 35/394 Permitted work and earnings while drawing Sickness Benefit (1970s)
PIN 35/405 Control of claims—revised proposals for 1967
PIN 35/491 HNCIP Amendment of regulation 13A of the NCIP regulation 1975
PIN 35/657 Severe Disablement Allowance policy (1980s)
PIN 62 Ministry of Pensions and National insurance files relating to National Insurance Commissioners' decisions (1948–1960s)
PIN 63 National Health Insurance Appeals: court of referees (1927–1929).

London Metropolitan Archive, London

CLC/B/017/MS292820 Records of the National Amalgamated Approved Society.

National Records of Scotland, Edinburgh

CS 251/3283 papers relating to Stated Case in a dispute under section 90(1) of the National Health Insurance Act 1924 between Hannah O'Brien and the Scottish Catholic Insurance Society for the Opinion and Judgment of the First Division of the Court of Session
HH 3/9 Department of Health for Scotland Morbidity Statistics Scheme (1930s).

Prudential Assurance Company Archive, London

L/2/5 Minute books and annual reports of the Committee of Management of the Prudential Approved Societies.

Public Record Office of Northern Ireland, Belfast (PRONI)

D1929/3/1/2 papers relating to Watson and O'Neill solicitors, Lurgan.

Working Class Movement Library, Salford (WCML)

TU/SILK/7/3 Leek Textile Federation: health insurance minute book.

British Newspaper Archive (Online)

References to, Burnley News, Burnley Express, Chichester Observer, Hull Daily Mail, Daily Herald, Lancashire Evening Post, Lancashire Evening Post (full references provided where cited in the text)

Sources for Appeal Cases

The appeal cases referred to in the book can be found in the following places:

Published Appeal Cases

- Published, anonymised, appeal decisions from England and Wales between 1913 and 1923. These were published in two volumes. For ease of reference, I have labelled these as cases 1–140 and 2(1)–2(40) and have provided full publication details, where cited.
- Published anonymised appeal decisions from Ireland between 1913 and 1916. For ease of reference, I have labelled these as cases Ir1–Ir44 and have provided full publication details, where cited.
- Published anonymised reported National Insurance Commissioners decisions between 1948 and 2001. I have labelled these according to the labelling system used in the published decisions, usually in the format R(S)number/date, although some earlier appeals took the form C(S) or C(W)(S). Very early reported decisions have an additional label "K" or "KL". According to Micklethwait, "The meaning of these letters has now been for-

gotten" (1976, p. 76). Where I have also consulted the case papers relating to these decisions, I have referred to their archive record in the National Archives, which usually bears no relationship to the reported numbering system.
- There are very few court cases relating to the concept of incapacity for work. Where I have referred to these, I have used their full legal record.

Archived Appeal Cases

- Archived appeal decisions between 1927 and 1929, National Archives. These are all filed in PIN 63, and I have cited these according to their numbering in these files.
- Miscellaneous appeal decisions, referred to or included in civil service files in the National Archives or the National Records of Scotland. The Public Record Office of Northern Ireland contains files relating to a particular solicitor's firm which represented people at early appeal hearings. I have cited these according to their archive record.
- Records of internal appeals to individual Approved Societies are all cited according to their archive record.
- Archived papers relating to National Insurance Commissioners' decisions in the 1950s and 1960s in the National Archives. The case papers for these decisions are filed in two places: PIN 62 which contains the Ministry of National Insurance papers and CT11 relating to the Office of the National Insurance Commissioner. Where I have found both files for the same decision, the two files are almost identical, both containing copies of all the relevant papers submitted to the Commissioners. In the book, I have cited these according to their official number, whether or not reported, and by their archive record.

Analysis, Ethics and Anonymity

It was not possible to make digital scans of many of the documents I consulted. Instead, I stored partial transcriptions and my notes from all of the documentary sources, either published or archive, in an NVivo database to enable more detailed analysis. This enabled me to search and analyse the material using a variety of approaches, including case analysis by gender, age, marital status, date, Approved Society, decision maker, representation and advocacy at appeal hearings and length of time on benefit. I stored these elements of each case as attributes in the NVivo database, recognising that these aspects of a person's life or claim are also social constructions and would not always represent a claimant's own view of their experience. Some of this information was often missing and so could only be inferred from the narrative. An example of this is marital status. Men's marital status is rarely mentioned in appeal records, whereas for women it often is, either in the narrative of the case or in the use of the title Mrs or Miss. Age is sometimes mentioned but not always. Initially, I attempted to classify cases by the claimant's occupation and impairment. This proved to be impossible, either because the information was missing or because the references to early twentieth-century occupations or use of medical terms were beyond my knowledge. These documents nevertheless would provide a rich source for medical or labour historians. The use of NVivo enabled me to explore concepts such as work, conditionality, incapacity, morality, references to sick visitors, housework, self-employment and the use of evidence across all of the sources. I was also able to carry out specific searches, for example on cases concerning people with epilepsy, references to claimants' caring responsibilities for children or other relatives or to their physical appearance. In a light-hearted moment, I searched on references to Christmas in order to write a seasonal blog post.

All the sources that I have used for this project come from documentary sources, available in the public domain in published form or in publicly accessible archives. I have therefore not sought the consent of any of the people concerned for the use of their experiences. This does not exempt me from an ethical approach to the use of this material. All of the material in these sources is personal, often highly moralised in tone and often referring to detailed aspects of people's medical conditions, personal lives and work histories. Although the material is openly accessible and most of the people can be assumed to have died, I have tried to treat their experiences with respect and, in most cases, to preserve their anonymity.

Ethical practices and the use of real names in research vary across disciplines. Social scientists usually anonymise as standard practice. Historians and legal scholars, on the other hand, are more likely to use real names. The material in this book consists of some sources where the names are already anonymised (the published early twentieth-century appeal cases and post-war Commissioners' decisions), those where the names are available but only in archives (the appeal cases from the 1920s, the case papers for the post-war Commissioners' decisions, the appeal records of individual Approved Societies and some references to individual claimants in the civil service records). In a very few cases, the names of claimants are fully in the public domain (legal cases and newspaper reports). In order to protect anonymity of those not fully in the public domain and to provide some consistency for the reader, I have adopted the following practices in naming claimants.

Where the case is already anonymised, I have assigned a title and initial to the claimant (e.g. Mr B, Mrs C). After careful consideration on the use of titles, I have used the twentieth-century tradition of marking gender and women's marital status by the use of Mr/Mrs/Miss, rather than twenty-first-century traditions of Mr/Ms or adopting a non-gendered lack of titles. I believe that this best reflects the usage in the sources and reflects the marking of gender and marital status which was clearly important to decision makers at the time. I recognise that this may not always reflect the titles that claimants themselves would have used but also that, for many working-class people for much of the twentieth century, the use of a title was a mark of respect.

Where I have been able to identify the real name of a claimant, for example in the archive files, I have preserved the initial of their surname (Mr W, Mrs S) and have followed the same approach to titles as for the anonymised cases. I hope that this strikes a balance between preserving anonymity and paying attention to the historian's expectation of not changing the historical record. Where the claimant's name is unquestionably in the public domain, (mostly in court cases) I have used their real name (e.g. Edith Sutton). Similarly, I have used the real names of public figures, civil servants and representatives of Approved Societies where these are known.

Reference

Micklethwait, Robert. 1976. *The National Insurance Commissioners*. Hamlyn Lectures. London: Stevens. https://socialsciences.exeter.ac.uk/law/hamlyn/lectures/archive.

References

Adler, Michael. 2018. *Cruel, Inhuman or Degrading Treatment? Benefit Sanctions in the UK*. Basingstoke: Palgrave Pivot.
Adler, Michael, and Jackie Gulland. 2003. *Tribunal Users' Experiences, Perceptions and Expectations: A Literature Review*. London: Council on Tribunals. http://webarchive.nationalarchives.gov.uk/20100910235604/, http://www.council-on-tribunals.gov.uk/publications/577.htm.
Baldwin, Sally, and Jane Falkingham. 1994. *Social Security and Social Change: New Challenges to the Beveridge Model*. Hemel Hempstead: Harvester Wheatsheaf.
Bambra, Clare. 2011. *Work, Worklessness, and the Political Economy of Health*. Oxford: Oxford University Press.
Barnes, Colin. 1991. *Disabled People in Britain and Discrimination*. London: Hurst and Company/BCODP.
———. 2000. 'A Working Social Model? Disability, Work and Disability Politics in the 21st Century'. *Critical Social Policy* 20 (4): 441–57.
———. 2012. 'Re-thinking Disability, Work and Welfare'. *Sociology Compass* 6 (6): 472–84.
Barnes, Colin, and Geof Mercer. 2005. 'Disability, Work and Welfare: Challenging the Social Exclusion of Disabled People'. *Work, Employment & Society* 19 (3): 527–45.
Barnes, Colin, and Alan Roulstone. 2005. '"Work" Is a Four-Letter Word; Disability, Work and Welfare'. In *Working Futures? Disabled People, Policy and Social Inclusion*, edited by Alan Roulstone and Colin Barnes. Bristol: Policy Press.
Bauman, Zygmunt. 2005. *Work, Consumerism and the New Poor*. 2nd ed. Buckingham: Open University Press.

Beatty, Christina, Steve Fothergill, Donald Houston, and Ryan Powell. 2010. 'Bringing Incapacity Benefit Numbers down: To What Extent Do Women Need a Different Approach?' *Policy Studies* 31: 143–62.

Beatty, Christina, Steve Fothergill, Donald Houston, Ryan Powell, and Paul Sissons. 2009. 'A Gendered Theory of Employment, Unemployment and Sickness'. *Environment and Planning C: Government and Policy* 27 (6): 958–74.

Becker, Howard. 1998. *Tricks of the Trade: How to Think About Your Research While You're Doing It*. Chicago and London: University of Chicago Press.

Beveridge, Sir William. 1942. *Social Insurance and Allied Services*. Cmd. 6404. London: HMSO.

Black, Carol. 2008. *Working for a Healthier Tomorrow Dame Carol Black's Review of the Health of Britain's Working Age Population*. London: TSO.

Bonner, David. 1995. 'Incapacity for Work: A New Benefit and New Tests'. *Journal of Social Security Law* 2 (2): 86–112.

———. 2008. 'Employment and Support Allowance: Helping the Sick and Disabled to Return to Work?' *Journal of Social Security Law* 15 (4): 123–50.

Bonner, David, Ian Hooker, and Robin White, eds. 1991. *Non-means Tested Benefits: The Legislation 1991 Edition*. London: Sweet and Maxwell.

Bonner, David, Ian Hooker, Richard Poynter, Robin White, Nick Wikeley, and Penny Wood. 2013. *Social Security Legislation 2013/14: Non-Means-Tested Benefits and Employment and Support Allowance*. London: Sweet and Maxwell.

Borsay, Anne. 2004. *Disability and Social Policy in Britain since 1750: A History of Exclusion*. Basingstoke: Palgrave Macmillan.

Braithwaite, William. 1957. *Lloyd George's Ambulance Wagon: Being the Memoirs of William J Braithwaite 1911–1912*. London: Methuen.

Brodie, Douglas, Nicole Busby, and Rebecca Zahn, eds. 2016. *The Future Regulation of Work: New Concepts, New Paradigms*. London: Palgrave.

Brodkin, Evelyn, and Malay Majmunder. 2010. 'Administrative Exclusion: Organizations and the Hidden Costs of Welfare Claiming'. *Journal of Public Administration Research and Theory* 20: 827–48.

Brodkin, Evelyn, and Gregory Marston. 2013. *Work and the Welfare State: Street-Level Organisations and Workfare Politics*. Washington: Georgetown University Press.

Buck, Trevor, David Bonner, and Roy Sainsbury. 2005. *Making Social Security Law: The Role and Work of the Social Security and Child Support Commissioners*. Aldershot: Ashgate.

Busby, Nicole. 2011. *A Right to Care? Unpaid Work in European Employment Law*. Oxford: Oxford University Press.

Butler, Judith. 2006. *Gender Trouble*. Abingdon: Routledge.

Child Poverty Action Group. 1984. 'Work within Limits'. *Welfare Rights Bulletin* (61, August): 10–11.

Citizens Advice Scotland. 2017. *Burden of Proof: The Role of Medical Evidence in the Benefits System*. Edinburgh: Citizens Advice Scotland.

Clarke, George Sydenham. 1916. *Royal Commission on Venereal Diseases. Final Report of the Commissioners*. Cd. 8189. London: HMSO.

Clasen, Jochen, and Daniel Clegg. 2007. 'Levels and Levers of Conditionality: Measuring Change Within Welfare States'. In *Investigating Welfare State Change: The Dependent Variable Problem in Comparative Analysis*, edited by Jochen Clasen and Nico Siegel. Cheltenham: Edward Elgar.
Conaghan, Joanne. 2013. *Law and Gender*. Oxford: Oxford University Press.
Cordery, Simon. 2003. *British Friendly Societies 1750–1914*. Basingstoke: Palgrave Macmillan.
Daly, Mary, and Katherine Rake. 2003. *Gender and the Welfare State*. Oxford: Polity.
Davis, Gayle. 2011. 'Health and Sexuality'. In *The Oxford Handbook of the History of Medicine*, edited by Mark Jackson. Oxford: Oxford University Press.
Deacon, Alan. 1976. *In Search of the Scrounger*. Leeds: University of Leeds.
Deacon, Sarah, Pamela Fitzpatrick, Marilyn Howard, and Hilary Land. 2007. *Women and Incapacity Benefits*. London: CPAG in Association with Women's Budget Group.
Dean, Hartley. 2000. 'Managing Risk by Controlling Behaviour: Social Security Administration and the Erosion of Welfare Citizenship'. In *Risk, Trust and Welfare*, edited by Peter Taylor-Gooby. Basingstoke: Macmillan.
Department for Work and Pensions. 2018. 'Stat-Xplore'. https://stat-xplore.dwp.gov.uk.
Department for Work and Pensions, and Department of Health. 2017. *Improving Lives: The Future of Work, Health and Disability CM 9526*. London: HMSO.
Department of Health and Social Security. 1981. *Sickness Benefit Law and Procedure. Code SB 1969, as Amended, 1981*. London: HMSO.
Department of Social Security. 1993. *A Consultation on the Medical Assessment for Incapacity Benefit*. London: Department of Social Security.
———. 1994. *The Medical Assessment for Incapacity Benefit*. London: HMSO.
———. 1996. *Social Security Committee Incapacity Benefit Minutes of Evidence*. London: The Stationery Office.
Disability Alliance. 1983. *Invalid Procedures? A Study of the Control System for Invalidity Benefit*. London: Disability Alliance Educational Research Association.
———. 1987. *Poverty and Disability: Breaking the Link. The Case for a Comprehensive Disability Income Scheme*. London: Disability Alliance Educational Research Association.
———. 1994. *Response to 'A Consultation on the Medical Assessment for Incapacity Benefit'*. London: Disability Alliance Educational Research Association.
Disney, Richard, and Steven Webb. 1991. 'Why Are There so Many Long Term Sick in Britain'. *Economic Journal* 101: 252–62.
Dominelli, Lena. 1988. 'Thatcher's Attack on Social Security: Restructuring Social Control'. *Critical Social Policy* 8 (23): 46–61.
Dwyer, Peter. 2016. 'Citizenship, Conduct and Conditionality: Sanction and Support in the 21st Century UK Welfare State'. In *Social Policy Review 28: Analysis and Debate in Social Policy, 2016*, edited by Menno Fenger, John Hudson, and Needham Catherine, 41. Bristol: Policy Press.

Dwyer, Peter, and Sharon Wright. 2014. 'Universal Credit, Ubiquitous Conditionality and Its Implications for Social Citizenship'. *Journal of Poverty and Social Justice* 22 (1): 27–35.

Dwyer, Peter, Katy Jones, Jenny McNeill, Lisa Scullion, and Alisdair Stewart. 2018. 'Welfare Conditionality: Sanctions, Support and Behaviour Change'. *Final Findings: Disabled People*. www.welfareconditionality.ac.uk.

Epps, George Selby Washington. 1937. *National Health Insurance. Report by the Government Actuary on the Fourth Valuation of the Assets and Liabilities of Approved Societies*. Cmd. 5496. London: HMSO.

Fletcher, Del Roy, and Sharon Wright. 2017. 'A Hand Up or a Slap Down? Criminalising Benefit Claimants in Britain via Strategies of Surveillance, Sanctions and Deterrence'. *Critical Social Policy*. https://doi.org/10.1177/0261018317726622.

Fletcher, Del Roy, John Flint, Elaine Batty, and Jennifer McNeill. 2016. 'Gamers or Victims of the System? Welfare Reform, Cynical Manipulation and Vulnerability'. *Journal of Poverty and Social Justice* 24 (2): 171–85.

Foster, William Justus, and F. G. Taylor. 1937. *National Health Insurance*. 3rd ed. London: Sir Isaac Pitman and Sons Ltd.

Foucault, Michel. 1972. *The Archaeology of Knowledge*. Translated by Alan Sheridan. London: Tavistock.

———. 1973. *The Birth of the Clinic: An Archaeology of Medical Perception*. Translated by Alan Sheridan. London: Routledge.

———. 1977. *Discipline and Punish: The Birth of the Prison*. Translated by Alan Sheridan. London: Allen Lane.

Frayne, David. 2015. *The Refusal of Work: The Theory and Practice of Resistance to Work*. London: Zed Books.

French, Sally, and John Swain. 2012. *Working with Disabled People in Policy and Practice*. Basingstoke: Palgrave Macmillan.

Fudge, Judy. 2016. 'A New Vocabulary and Imaginary for Labour Law'. In *The Future Regulation of Work New Concepts, New Paradigms*, edited by Douglas Brodie, Nicole Busby, and Rebecca Zahn. London: Palgrave.

Geiger, Ben Baumberg. 2017. 'Benefits Conditionality for Disabled People: Stylised Facts from a Review of International Evidence and Practice'. *Journal of Poverty and Social Justice* 25 (2): 107–28.

Gilliom, John. 2001. *Overseers of the Poor: Surveillance, Resistance, and the Limits of Privacy*. Chicago: University of Chicago Press.

Glendinning, Caroline, and Disability Alliance. 1980. *'After Working All These Years': A Response to the Report of the National Insurance Advisory Committee on the 'Household Duties' Test for Non-contributory Invalidity Pension for Married Women*. London: Disability Alliance.

Glucksmann, Miriam. 2000. *Cottons and Casuals: The Gendered Organisation of Labour in Time and Space*. Durham: Sociology Press.

Gregg, Paul. 2008. *Realising Potential: A Vision for Conditionality and Support*. London: DWP.

Grint, Keith, and Darren Nixon. 2015. *The Sociology of Work*. 4th ed. Cambridge: Polity Press.
Grover, Chris. 2017. 'Ending Reassessment for Employment and Support Allowance for Some Disabled People in the UK'. *Disability & Society* 32 (8): 1269–74.
Grover, Chris, and Linda Piggott. 2010. 'From Incapacity Benefit to Employment and Support Allowance: Social Sorting, Sickness and Impairment, and Social Security'. *Policy Studies* 31: 265–82.
Grue, Jan. 2015. *Disability and Discourse Analysis*. Farnham: Ashgate.
Gulland, Jackie. 1996. *Weighing Up the Bag of Potatoes Test: Tribunals and Incapacity Benefit* (Unpublished MSc dissertation). Edinburgh: University of Edinburgh.
———. 2011. 'Ticking Boxes: Understanding Decision Making in Employment and Support Allowance'. *Journal of Social Security Law* 18: 69–86.
———. 2012. '"Fitting Themselves to Become Wage-Earners": Conditionality and Incapacity for Work in the Early 20th Century'. *Journal of Social Security Law* 119: 51–70.
———. 2013. 'Extraordinary Housework: Women and Claims for Sickness Benefit in the Early 20th Century'. *Women's History Magazine* 71: 23–30.
———. 2017. 'Working While Incapable to Work? Changing Concepts of Permitted Work in the UK Disability Benefit System'. *Disability Studies Quarterly* 37 (4). http://dsq-sds.org/article/view/6088.
———. 2018. 'Appellant Knowledge and Representation in Early Twentieth Century Sickness Benefit Tribunals' (Unpublished paper).
———. 2019. 'Conditionality and Social Security: Lessons from the Household Duties Test'. *Journal of Social Security Law* 26 (2): 60–76.
Hampton, Jameel. 2016. *Disability and the Welfare State in Britain: Changes in Perception and Policy 1948–79*. Bristol: Policy Press.
Handler, Joel F. 2004. *Social Citizenship and Workfare in the United States and Western Europe*. Cambridge: Cambridge University Press.
Hansen, Helena, Philippe Bourgois, and Ernest Drucker. 2014. 'Pathologizing Poverty: New Forms of Diagnosis, Disability, and Structural Stigma Under Welfare Reform'. *Social Science & Medicine*, Structural Stigma and Population Health, 103 (Supplement C): 76–83.
Harrington, Malcolm. 2010. *An Independent Review of the Work Capability Assessment*. London: The Stationery Office.
———. 2011. *An Independent Review of the Work Capability Assessment—Year Two*. London: The Stationery Office.
———. 2012. *An Independent Review of the Work Capability Assessment—Year Three*. London: The Stationery Office.
Harris, Bernard. 2004. *The Origins of the British Welfare State: Society, State, and Social Welfare in England and Wales, 1800–1945*. Basingstoke: Palgrave Macmillan.
Harris, Neville. 2000. 'Beveridge and Beyond: The Shift from Insurance to Means-Testing'. In *Social Security Law in Context*, edited by Neville Harris. Oxford: Oxford University Press.

———. 2010. 'Reducing Dependency? Conditional Rights, Benefit Reform and Drugs'. *Journal of Law and Society* 37: 233–63.

Hayes, Lydia. 2017. *Stories of Care: A Labour of Law: Gender and Class at Work.* London, UK: Palgrave.

Hochschild, Arlie. 1989. *The Second Shift: Working Parents and the Revolution at Home.* London: Piatkus.

Holmes, Phil, Mauricea Lynch, and Ian Molho. 1991. 'An Econometric Analysis of the Growth in Numbers Claiming Invalidity Benefit: An Overview'. *Journal of Social Policy* 20 (1): 87–105.

Hooker, Ian, Richard Poynter, Robin White, Nick Wikeley, John Mesher, and Edward Mitchell. 2017. *Social Security Legislation 2017/18 Non-Means-Tested Benefits and Employment and Support Allowance. Vol. 1.* London: Sweet and Maxwell.

House of Commons. 1974. *Social Security Act 1973. Social Security Provision for Chronically Sick and Disabled People.* HC 274. London: HMSO.

House of Commons Work and Pensions Committee. 2014. *Employment and Support Allowance and Work Capability Assessments First Report of Session 2014–15.* HC 302. London: HMSO.

Houston, Donald, and Colin Lindsay. 2010. 'Fit for Work? Health, Employability and Challenges for the UK Welfare Reform Agenda'. *Policy Studies* 31: 133–42.

Hughes, Bill. 2015. 'What Can a Foucauldian Analysis Contribute'. In *Foucault and the Government of Disability*, edited by Shelley Tremain, 2nd ed. Ann Arbor: University of Michigan Press.

Hunter, Rosemary. 2013. 'The Gendered "Socio" of Socio-Legal Studies'. In *Exploring the 'Socio' in Socio-Legal Studies*, edited by Dermot Feenan. Basingstoke: Palgrave Macmillan.

Jay, Douglas. 1951. *National Insurance Act, 1946. First Interim Report by the Government Actuary for the Period 5th July, 1948 to 31st March, 1950.* London: HMSO.

Jones, Margaret, and Rodney Lowe. 2002. *From Beveridge to Blair: The First Fifty Years of Britain's Welfare State 1948–98.* Manchester: Manchester University Press.

Kemp, Peter, and Jacqueline Davidson. 2009. 'Gender Differences Among New Claimants for Incapacity Benefit'. *Journal of Social Policy* 38: 589–606.

Lammasniemi, Laura. 2017. 'Regulation 40D: Punishing Promiscuity on the Home Front During the First World War'. *Women's History Review* 26 (4): 584–96.

Land, Hilary. 1978. 'Who Cares for the Family?' *Journal of Social Policy* 7 (3): 257–84.

———. 1994. 'The Demise of the Male Breadwinner—In Practice but Not in Theory: A Challenge for Social Security Systems'. In *Social Security and Social Change: New Challenges to the Beveridge Model*, edited by Sally Baldwin and Jane Falkingham. Hemel Hempstead: Harvester Wheatsheaf.

———. 2009. 'Slaying Idleness Without Killing Care: A Challenge for the British Welfare State'. In *Social Policy Review 21*, edited by K. Rummery, Ian Greener, and Chris Holden. Bristol: The Policy Press.

Lawrence, Charles. 1926a. *Report of the Royal Commission on National Health Insurance.* Cmd. 2596. London: HMSO.

———. 1926b. *Report of the Royal Commission on National Health Insurance Cmd. 2596 Appendices to Minutes of Evidence Vols. 1–4*. Cmd. 2596. London: HMSO.
Lens, Vicki. 2015. 'Welfare Law'. In *The Handbook of Law and Society*, edited by Austin Sarat and Patricia Ewick. Chichester: Wiley Blackwell.
Lesser, Henry. 1939. *The National Health Insurance Acts 1936-1938 with Explanatory Notes, Reported Cases, Decisions of the Minister of Health and Statutory Rules and Orders*. London: Stone and Cox Ltd.
Levine-Clark, Marjorie. 2015. *Unemployment, Welfare and Masculine Citizenship: So Much Honest Poverty in Britain 1870–1930*. Basingstoke: Palgrave Macmillan.
Levitas, Ruth. 2001. 'Against Work: A Utopian Incursion into Social Policy'. *Critical Social Policy* 21 (4): 449–65.
Lewis, Jane. 1983. 'Dealing with Dependency: State Practices and Social Realities 1870–1945'. In *Women's Welfare Women's Rights*, edited by Jane Lewis. London: Croom Helm.
———. 1995. *The Voluntary Sector, the State and Social Work in Britain: The Charity Organisation Society/Family Welfare Association since 1869*. Aldershot: Edward Elgar.
Lipsky, Michael. 2010. *Street Level Bureaucracy: Dilemmas of the Individual in Public Services*. 30th Anniversary Expanded Edition. New York: Russell Sage Foundation.
Lister, Ruth. 1994. '"She Has Other Duties"—Women, Citizenship and Social Security'. In *Social Security and Social Change: New Challenges to the Beveridge Model*, edited by Sally Baldwin and Jane Falkingham. Hemel Hempstead: Harvester Wheatsheaf.
———. 2003. *Citizenship: Feminist Perspectives*. 2nd ed. Basingstoke: Palgrave Macmillan.
Litchfield, Paul. 2013. *An Independent Review of the Work Capability Assessment—Year Four*. London: TSO.
———. 2014. *An Independent Review of the Work Capability Assessment—Year Five*. London: TSO.
Loach, Irene, and Ruth Lister. 1978. *Second Class Disabled—A Report on the Non-contributory Invalidity Pension for Married Women*. London: Equal Rights for Disabled Women Campaign.
Loach, Ken. 2016. *I, Daniel Blake*. Sixteen Films.
Lonsdale, Susan. 1993. *Invalidity Benefit an International Comparison*. London: DSS Analytical Services Division, Social Research Branch.
Low, Lord, Baroness Meacher, and Baroness Grey-Thompson. 2015. *Halving the Gap? A Review into the Government's Proposed Reduction to Employment and Support Allowance and Its Impact on Halving the Disability and Employment Gap*. London: Royal Mencap Society. mencap.org.uk/esa-review.
Lowe, Rodney. 1993. *The Welfare State in Britain since 1945*. Basingstoke: Macmillan.
Luckhaus, Linda. 1986. 'Severe Disablement Allowance: The Old Dressed Up as New?' *Journal of Social Welfare and Family Law* 8 (3): 153–69.
Machin, Richard. 2017. 'The Professional and Ethical Dilemmas of the Two-Child Limit for Child Tax Credit and Universal Credit'. *Ethics and Social Welfare* 11 (4): 404–11.

Macnicol, John. 2013. 'The History of Work Disability'. In *Disability Benefits, Welfare Reform and Employment Policy*, edited by Colin Lindsay and Donald Houston. London: Palgrave.

Manji, Kainde. 2016. 'Social Security Reform and the Surveillance State: Exploring the Operation of "Hidden Conditionality" in the Reform of Disability Benefits Since 2010'. *Social Policy and Society* 16 (2): 1–10.

Martin, Jean, Howard Meltzer, and David Elliot. 1988. *The Prevalence of Disability Among Adults OPCS Surveys of Disability in Great Britain Report 1*. London: HMSO.

Mashaw, Jerry. 1983. *Bureaucratic Justice: Managing Social Security Disability Claims*. New Haven: Yale University Press.

McKeever, Gráinne. 1999. 'Fighting Fraud: An Evaluation of the Government's Social Security Fraud Strategy'. *Journal of Social Welfare and Family Law* 21 (4): 357–71.

Mesher, John. 1986. 'Recent Social Security Commissioners' Decisions'. *The Journal of Social Welfare Law* 8 (1): 52–64.

Micklethwait, Robert. 1976. *The National Insurance Commissioners*. Hamlyn Lectures. London: Stevens. https://socialsciences.exeter.ac.uk/law/hamlyn/lectures/archive.

Ministry of Health. 1920. *First Annual Report of the Ministry of Health 1919–20. Part IV.–Administration of National Health Insurance (1917 to 31st March, 1920). Welsh Board of Health*. Cmd. 913. London: HMSO.

———. 1921. *Second Annual Report of the Ministry of Health, 1920–1921*. Cmd. 1446. London: HMSO.

———. 1923. *Reports of Decisions on Appeals and Applications Under Section 67 of the National Insurance Act 1911 and Section 27 of the National Insurance Act 1913, Vol 2—Part I*. London: HMSO.

———. 1933. *Approved Societies Handbook: Being a Revised Handbook for the Guidance of Approved Societies in Their Administration of Benefits Under the National Health Insurance Acts, 1924 to 1932*. London: HMSO.

———. 1946. *Report of the Ministry of Health for the Year Ended 31st March 1946 Including the Report of the Chief Medical Officer on the State of the Public Health for the Year Ended 31st December 1945*. Cmd. 7119. London: HMSO.

Ministry of National Insurance. 1950. *Report of the Ministry of National Insurance for the Period 17th November, 1944, to 4th July, 1949*. Cmd. 7955. London: HMSO.

Ministry of Pensions and National Insurance. 1953. *National Insurance Act, 1946 National Insurance (Industrial Injuries) Act 1946 Medical Certification: Notes for Chairmen and Members of Local Tribunals L.T. Memo No. 4*. London: HMSO.

———. 1960. *Instructions to National Insurance Offices on Law and Procedure Relating to Sickness Benefits under the National Insurance Acts Code SB*. London: HMSO.

Mullen, Tom. 2016. 'Access to Justice in Administrative Law and Administrative Justice'. In *Access to Justice: Beyond the Policies and Politics of Austerity*, edited by Ellie Palmer, Tom Cornford, Yseult Marique, and Marique Guinchard. Oxford: Hart Publishing.

Munger, Frank. 2004. 'Rights in the Shadow of Class'. In *The Blackwell Companion to Law and Society*, edited by Austin Sarat. Oxford: Blackwell.

National Audit Office. 1989. *Invalidity Benefit: Report by the Comptroller and Auditor General HC 91.* London: HMSO.

———. 2001. *The Medical Assessment of Incapacity and Disability Benefits Report by the Comptroller and Auditor General.* HC 280. London: HMSO.

———. 2010. *Support to Incapacity Benefits Claimants Through Pathways to Work.* London: TSO.

———. 2012. *Contract Management of Medical Services HC 627.* London: The Stationery Office.

———. 2016. *Contracted-Out Health and Disability Assessments.* HC609. London: House of Commons.

National Health Insurance Commission. 1912. *National Insurance Act 1911 Model Rules.* London: HMSO.

———. 1915. *National Insurance Acts Handbook for the Use of Approved Societies.* English edition. London: HMSO.

National Health Insurance Commission (England). 1915a. *Reports of Decisions on Appeals and Applications Under Section 67 of the National Insurance Act 1911 and Section 27 of the National Insurance Act 1913.* Cd. 7810. London: HMSO.

———. 1915b. *Reports of Decisions on Appeals and Applications Under Section 67 of the National Insurance Act 1911 and Section 27 of the National Insurance Act 1913 Part II.* Cd. 8040. London: HMSO.

———. 1916. *Reports of Decisions on Appeals and Applications Under Section 67 of the National Insurance Act 1911 and Section 27 of the National Insurance Act 1913 Part III.* Cd. 8239. London: HMSO.

———. 1917. *Reports of Decisions on Appeals and Applications Under Section 67 of the National Insurance Act 1911 and Section 27 of the National Insurance Act 1913 Part IV.* Cd. 8474. London: HMSO.

———. 1919. *Reports of Decisions on Appeals and Applications Under Section 67 of the National Insurance Act 1911 and Section 27 of the National Insurance Act 1913 Part V.* Cmd. 134. London: HMSO.

National Health Insurance Commission (Ireland). 1916. *Reports of Decisions on Appeals and Applications Under Section 67 of the National Insurance Act, 1911 and Section 27 of the National Insurance Act, 1913.* Dublin: A Thom.

National Health Insurance Committee (Joint Committee). 1917. *National Health Insurance. Report on the Administration of National Health Insurance During the Years 1914–17.* Cd. 8890. London: HMSO.

National Health Insurance Joint Committee. 1914a. *National Health Insurance. Appendix to the Report of the Departmental Committee on Sickness Benefit Claims Under the National Insurance Act. Volume I.* [Cd. 7688, 7689, 7690, 7691]. London: HMSO.

———. 1914b. *National Health Insurance. Report of the Departmental Committee on Sickness Benefit Claims Under the National Insurance Act.* Cd. 7687. London: HMSO.

National Insurance Advisory Committee. 1948. *National Insurance Act, 1946. National Insurance (Unemployment and Sickness Benefit) Regulations, 1948. Report of the National Insurance Advisory Committee in Accordance with Section 77 (4) of the National Insurance Act, 1946.* London: HMSO.

———. 1976. *Social Security Act 1975 Social Security (Medical Evidence) Regulations 1976 (S.I. 1976 No. 615). Report of the National Insurance Advisory Committee.* HC 349. London: House of Commons. 1975-065773.

———. 1977. *Social Security Act 1975, Social Security (Non-contributory Invalidity Pension) Amendment Regulations 1977 (S.I. 1977 No. 1312). Report of the National Insurance Advisory Committee.* Cmd. 6900. London: HMSO.

———. 1980. *Report of the National Insurance Advisory Committee on a Question Relating to the Household Duties Test for Non-contributory Invalidity Pension for Married Women.* Cmd. 7955. London: HMSO.

NHS Greater Glasgow and Clyde. 2015. *Celebrating a Proud History: The Southern General Hospital 1922–2015.* http://www.nhsggc.org.uk/media/232799/history_southern_1922-2015.pdf.

O'Brien, Charlotte. 2018. "Done Because We Are Too Menny". *The International Journal of Children's Rights* 26 (4): 700–739.

Ogus, Anthony, and Eric Barendt. 1978. *The Law of Social Security.* London: Butterworths.

Ogus, Anthony, Eric Barendt, Trevor Buck, and Tony Lynes. 1988. *The Law of Social Security.* 3rd ed. London: Butterworths.

Orloff, Ann Shola. 2010. 'Gender'. In *The Oxford Handbook of the Welfare State*, edited by Francis G. Castles, Stephan Liebfried, Jane Lewis, and Christopher Pierson. Oxford: Oxford University Press.

Pahl, Ray. 1984. *Divisions of Labour.* London: Blackwell.

Patrick, Ruth. 2011. 'Disabling or Enabling: The Extension of Work-Related Conditionality to Disabled People'. *Social Policy and Society* 10 (3): 309–320.

Patrick, Ruth. 2016. 'Living with and Responding to the "scrounger" Narrative in the UK: Exploring Everyday Strategies of Acceptance, Resistance and Deflection'. *Journal of Poverty and Social Justice* 24 (3): 245–59.

Patrick, Ruth, Patience Seebohm, and Lawrence M. Mead. 2011. 'The Wrong Prescription: Disabled People and Welfare Conditionality'. *Policy & Politics* 39 (2): 275–91.

Paz-Fuchs, Amir. 2008. *Welfare to Work Conditional Rights in Social Policy.* Oxford: Oxford University Press.

Pedersen, Susan. 1993. *Family, Dependence, and the Origins of the Welfare State: Britain and France, 1914–1945.* Cambridge: Cambridge University Press.

Peel, Mark. 2012. *Miss Cutler and the Case of the Resurrected Horse: Social Work and the Story of Poverty in America, Australia and Britain.* Chicago: University of Chicago Press.

Phillips, Melanie. 1978. 'Minister Blocks "loophole" in Disabled Pensions'. *The Guardian* (14, September edition).

Piven, Frances Fox, and Richard A. Cloward. 1972. *Regulating the Poor: The Functions of Public Welfare.* New York: Vintage.

Prideaux, Simon, Alan Roulstone, Jennifer Harris, and Colin Barnes. 2009. 'Disabled People and Self-directed Support Schemes: Reconceptualising Work and Welfare in the 21st Century'. *Disability & Society* 24 (5): 557–69.

Pryma, Jane. 2017. '"Even My Sister Says I'm Acting Like a Crazy to Get a Check": Race, Gender, and Moral Boundary-Work in Women's Claims of Disabling Chronic Pain'. *Social Science & Medicine* 181 (Supplement C): 66–73.

Rahilly, Simon. 2010. 'Employment and Support Allowance: More Fine Tuning of the Incapacity Tests and the End of Incapacity Benefit'. *Journal of Social Security Law* 17: 137–40.

Ritchie, J., K. Ward, and W. Duldig. 1993. *GPs and Invalidity Benefit: A Qualitative Study of the Role of GPs in the Award of Invalidity Benefit DSS Report No. 18*. London: HMSO.

Robinson, Emily. 2010. 'Touching the Void: Affective History and the Impossible'. *Rethinking History: The Journal of Theory and Practice* 14: 503–20.

Roulstone, Alan. 2012. 'Disabled People, Work and Employment'. In *Routledge Handbook of Disability Studies*, edited by Nick Watson, Alan Roulstone, and Carol Thomas. Abingdon: Routledge.

———. 2015. 'Disability, Work and Welfare'. In *Disabled People, Work and Welfare Is Employment Really the Answer?* edited by Chris Grover and Linda Piggott. Bristol: Policy Press.

Roulstone, Alan, and Simon Prideaux. 2012. *Understanding Disability Policy*. Bristol: Policy Press.

Rowlingson, Karen. 2009. 'From Cradle to Grave: Social Security and the Lifecourse'. In *Understanding Social Security*, edited by Jane Millar, 2nd ed. Bristol: Policy Press.

Safford, Archibald. 1954. 'The Creation of Case Law Under the National Insurance and National Insurance (Industrial Injuries) Acts'. *Modern Law Review* 17: 197–210.

Sainsbury, Diane. 1996. *Gender, Equality and Welfare States*. Cambridge: Cambridge University Press.

Scottish Board of Health. 1922. *Third Annual Report of the Scottish Board of Health*. Cmd. 1697. Edinburgh: HMSO.

———. 1923. *Fourth Annual Report of the Scottish Board of Health*. Edinburgh: HMSO.

Shah, Sonali, and Mark Priestley. 2011. *Disability and Social Change: Private Lives and Public Policies*. Bristol: Policy Press.

Shakespeare, Tom, Nicholas Watson, and Ola Abu Alghaib. 2017. 'Blaming the Victim, All Over Again: Waddell and Aylward's Biopsychosocial (BPS) Model of Disability'. *Critical Social Policy* 37 (1): 22–41.

Sherry, Mark. 2016. 'A Sociology of Impairment'. *Disability & Society* 31 (6): 729–44.

Shildrick, Margrit. 1997. *Leaky Bodies and Boundaries: Feminism, Postmodernism and (Bio)Ethics*. London: Routledge.

Shildrick, Margrit, and Janet Price. 1999. 'Breaking the Boundaries of the Broken Body'. In *Feminist Theory: A Reader*, edited by Janet Price and Margrit Shildrick. Edinburgh: Edinburgh University Press.

Smith, Roger, and Mark Rowland. 1986. *Rights Guide to Non-Means-Tested Social Security Benefits*. 9th ed. London: Child Poverty Action Group.

Sohrab, Julia. 1994. 'An Overview of the Equality Directive on Social Security and Its Implications for Four Social Security Systems'. *European Journal of Social Policy* 4: 263–76.

Stone, Deborah. 1984. *The Disabled State*. Philadelphia: Temple University Press.

Thane, Pat. 1991. 'Visions of Gender in the Making of the British Welfare State: The Case of Women in the British Labour Party and Social Policy 1906–1945'. In *Maternity and Gender Policies: Women and the Rise of the European Welfare States 1880s–1950s*, edited by Gisela Bock and Pat Thane. London: Routledge.

———. 1996. *Foundations of the Welfare State*. 2nd ed. London: Longman.

Thomas, Carol. 2007. *Sociologies of Disability and Illness: Contested Ideas in Disability Studies and Medical Sociology*. Basingstoke: Palgrave Macmillan.

———. 2011. 'Disability: Prospects for Inclusion'. In *Fighting Poverty, Inequality and Injustice: A Manifesto Inspired by Peter Townsend*, edited by Alan Walker, Adrian Sinfield, and Carol Walker. Bristol: Policy Press.

Timmins, Nicholas. 1995. *The Five Giants: A Biography of the Welfare State*. London: HarperCollins.

Tomlinson, J. 1984. 'Women as "Anomolies": The Anomolies Regulations of 1931, Their Background and Administration'. *Public Administration* 62: 423–37.

Turner, Angela, and Arthur McIvor. 2017. '"Bottom Dog Men": Disability, Social Welfare and Advocacy in the Scottish Coalfields in the Interwar Years, 1918–1939'. *The Scottish Historical Review* 96 (2): 187–213.

Union of Physically Impaired Against Segregation, and Disability Alliance. 1976. *Fundamental Principles of Disability*. London: UPIAS. http://disability-studies.leeds.ac.uk/files/library/UPIAS-fundamental-principles.pdf.

Valverde, Mariana. 2003. *Law's Dream of a Common Knowledge*. The Cultural Lives of Law. Princeton: Princeton University Press.

———. 2009. 'Jurisdiction and Scale: Legal 'Technicalities' as Resources for Theory'. *Social & Legal Studies* 18 (2): 139–57.

Wacquant, Loïc J. D. 2009. *Punishing the Poor: The Neoliberal Government of Social Insecurity*. English edition. Durham, NC and London: Duke University Press.

Walker, Alan. 2010. 'Disability'. In *The Peter Townsend Reader*, edited by Alan Walker, David Gordon, Ruth Levitas, Peter Phillimore, Chris Phillipson, Margot Salomon, and Nicola Yeates. Bristol: Policy Press.

Watson, Alfred W. 1922. *National Health Insurance. Report by the Government Actuary on the Valuations of the Assets and Liabilities of Approved Societies as at 31st December 1918*. Cmd. 1662. London: HMSO.

———. 1929. *National Health Insurance. Report by the Government Actuary on an Examination of the Sickness and Disablement Experience of a Group of Approved Societies in the Period 1921–27*. Cmd. 3548. London: HMSO.

———. 1931. 'National Health Insurance Report by the Government Actuary on the Third Valuation of the Assets and Liabilities of Approved Societies'. Cmd. 3978. London: HMSO.

———. 1932. *National Health Insurance and Contributory Pensions Bill, 1932. Report by the Government Actuary on the Financial Provisions of the Bill.* Cmd. 4073. London: HMSO.

Watts, Beth, Suzanne Fitzpatrick, Glen Bramley, and David Watkins. 2014. *Welfare Sanctions and Conditionality in the UK.* York: Joseph Rowntree Foundation.

Webster, David, James Arnott, Judith Brown, Ivan Turok, Richard Mitchell, and Ewan Macdonald. 2010. 'Falling Incapacity Benefit Claims in a Former Industrial City: Policy Impacts or Labour Market Improvement'. *Policy Studies* 31: 163–85.

Weeks, Kathi. 2011. *The Problem with Work: Feminism, Marxism, Antiwork Politics, and Postwork Imaginaries.* Durham: Duke University Press.

Whiteside, Noel. 1983. 'Private Agencies for Public Purposes: Some New Perspectives on Policy Making in Health Insurance Between the Wars'. *Journal of Social Policy* 12: 165–94.

———. 1987. 'Counting the Cost: Sickness and Disability Among Working People in an Era of Industrial Recession, 1920–1939'. *Economic History Review* XL: 228–46.

———. 2014. 'Constructing Unemployment: Britain and France in Historical Perspective'. *Social Policy & Administration* 48 (1): 67–85.

Wiggan, Jay. 2012. 'Telling Stories of 21st Century Welfare: The UK Coalition Government and the Neo-liberal Discourse of Worklessness and Dependency'. *Critical Social Policy* 32 (3): 383–405.

Wikeley, Nick. 1995. 'The Social Security (Incapacity for Work) Act 1994'. *Modern Law Review* 58 (4): 523.

Wikeley, Nick, Anthony Ogus, and Eric Barendt. 2002. *The Law of Social Security.* 5th ed. London: Butterworths/LexisNexis.

Willott, Sarah, and Christine Griffin. 1996. 'Men, Masculinity and the Challenge of Long-Term Unemployment'. In *Understanding Masculinities*, edited by Mairtin Mac an Ghaill. Buckingham: Open University Press.

Wincup, Emma, and Mark Monaghan. 2016. 'Scrounger Narratives and Dependent Drug Users: Welfare, Workfare and Warfare'. *Journal of Poverty and Social Justice* 24 (3): 261–75.

Work and Pensions Committee. 2009. 'Decision Making and Appeals in the Benefits System Second Report of Session 2009–10'. HC 313. London: HMSO.

———. 2017. *ATOS, Maximus and Capita Questioned on "Gruelling" Medical Assessments.* http://www.parliament.uk/business/committees/committees-a-z/commons-select/work-and-pensions-committee/news-parliament-2017/atos-maximus-capita-medicals-17-19/.

Wright, Sharon. 2003. 'The Street-Level Implementation of Unemployment Policy'. In *Understanding Social Security*, edited by Jane Miller. Bristol: Policy Press.

———. 2012. 'Welfare to Work, Agency and Personal Responsibility'. *Journal of Social Policy* 41 (2): 309–28.

Index

A

Abortion 163. *See also* Moral conditionality
Adaptations. *See* Equipment and adaptations
Addictions. *See* Alcohol, Drugs
Age, relevance of in assessing incapacity 1, 7, 143. *See also* Retirement pensions
Age rules in benefit entitlement 24
Alcohol 3, 159, 164–174, 178, 179, 190, 198. *See also* Moral conditionality
All work test. *See* Incapacity Benefit
Amalgamated Association of Card, Blowing and Ring Room Operatives 112
Amalgamated Society of Woodworkers 66
Appeal hearings 15, 205
Appeal hearings, appointment of adjudicators 25
Appeal hearings, lay members 25
Appeal hearings, medical assessments during 61
Appeal hearings, medical assessors 26, 61
Appeal hearings, representation 26, 95, 141
Appeals, Approved Society internal procedures 25
Appeals, procedures 25
Approved Society 24, 57, 84, 85, 137, 143, 155, 183, 186, 188, 189. *See also* Names of particular societies
Approved Society, definition of 24
Approved Society, model rules for 25, 119, 157–158, 169–173
Approved Society, records of 14
Archival research 3, 14, 15, 211
Association of Registered Medical Women 160
ATOS 72, 73, 205
Attendance Allowance 5

B

BAMS. *See* Benefits Agency Medical Service

Index

Barriers to inclusion 6, 28, 45, 46. *See also* Models of disability
Behaviour during sickness 65, 67, 156, 159, 166, 170–177. *See also* Misconduct rule
Benefits Agency Medical Service 46, 72
Beveridge Report 15, 26, 37, 42
Beveridge, William 9, 37, 119
Blind people. *See* Visual impairments
Board of Health, Scottish 25, 59, 164
Body work 12
Braithwaite, William 137
Breach of rules 125, 145. *See also* Behaviour during sickness, Domestic work, Moral conditionality
British Medical Association 63
Businesses, small. *See* Self-employment

Care, of adults. *See* Carers
Care, of children. *See* Childcare
Carers 13, 124, 152, 204
Case law, status of appeal cases as 14, 26
Catholic Friendly Societies Association 163
Chartered Accountants Benevolent Association 151
Child Poverty Action Group 37, 95
Childcare 125, 152, 204. *See also* Domestic work and children
Chronic illness 7, 35
Citizens' income 208
Claim forms 54, 71–73
Claims, deterring 37, 114
Class K contributors 114, 118
Claydon, Olive 159
Cohabiting. *See* Housewives Non-contributory Invalidity Pension (HNCIP)

Conditionality, forms of 13, 24, 28–29. *See also* Moral conditionality, Work-seeking conditionality
Contributory benefits. *See* National insurance, Non-contributory benefits
Control measures 39, 42, 44, 53, 197
Co-operative Wholesale Society 112, 159, 163
Criminal convictions 168
Curfews. *See* Out of hours rule

Dancing 171
Deaf people. *See* Hearing impairments
Department of Health and Social Security 43–45, 64, 67, 70, 95, 125, 126, 129, 141, 150, 175, 176, 198
Dependency 11, 128, 151, 207
Deposit contributors 158
Deservingness 7, 12, 156, 203
DHSS. *See* Department of Health and Social Security
Disability. *See* Models of disability
Disability Alliance 6, 7, 64, 207
Disability benefits 5. *See also* Incapacity benefits
Disability category, in benefits decision making 5, 7, 12. *See also* Incapacity for work
Disability, distinction between sickness and. *See* Sickness
Disability income scheme 6, 37, 207
Disability Living Allowance 200
Disablement Benefit (Approved Societies scheme) 24, 34–45, 110, 114, 157
Disablement Income Group 38, 129
Disablement resettlement officers 91

Discrimination, disability 6, 28, 36, 91, 96, 105
Discrimination, sex 117, 131
Doctors' certificates. *See* Medical certificates
Doctors, independence of 53–73, 205
Doctors, panel doctor system 34, 114, 158
Doctors, role of GP 57, 70, 71
Domestic labour. *See* Domestic work
Domestic service. *See* Domestic work, paid
Domestic work 3, 11, 67, 109–131, 204. *See also* Housewives Non-contributory Invalidity Pension (HNCIP)
Domestic work and children 112, 113, 152, 204
Domestic work, and unmarried women 117, 124, 126, 144, 197
Domestic work as a second shift 111
Domestic work, as evidence of capacity for work 118, 121, 122
Domestic work, commodification of 204
Domestic work, common knowledge of 70, 124
Domestic work, evidence of married women's attachment to the labour market 110–131, 143
Domestic work, guidance regarding 116, 124, 126
Domestic work, lack of value of 10, 152
Domestic work, men 112, 116–118, 123, 125, 126, 128
Domestic work, paid 11, 110, 123, 130, 144
Domestic work reference 125, 126. *See also* Control measures
Drugs, addictions 175, 179
Drunkenness. *See* Alcohol

Earnings, low pay 90
Earnings, sufficiency of 33, 136–143
Education, relevance of in assessing capacity for work 1, 50
Employment. *See* Work
Employment and Support Allowance (ESA) 1, 38, 73–75
Employment and Support Allowance, and work-seeking conditionality 11, 13, 28. *See also* Conditionality, forms of
Employment and Support Allowance, definition of incapacity for work 35
Employment and Support Allowance, introduction of 15, 28, 47
Employment and Support Allowance, limited capability for work 48, 73
Employment and Support Allowance, limited capability for work-related activities 28
Employment and Support Allowance, medical tests for 48, 73
Employment and Support Allowance, support group in 38
Employment and Support Allowance, work capability assessment 47, 49, 74
Employment law 9
Epilepsy 40, 69, 90, 96–98, 101, 104
Equipment and adaptations, relevance of in assessing capacity for work 49, 129
Ethics, research ethics 16, 215
Evidence 53–76. *See also* Knowledge, Medical evidence
Evidence, adjudicators' observations of claimants 67–70
Evidence, of local informants 53, 54, 58, 190
Excessive claims. *See* Inquiry into Sickness Benefit 1914

Expert knowledge. *See* Knowledge

F

Family. *See* Carers, Domestic work, Work
Feminisation of incapacity benefits 9
Fighting 159, 166, 167
Fines. *See* Sanctions
First World War 15, 98, 146, 161
Fit notes 74. *See also* Medical certificates
Foucault, Michel 8, 53, 55, 184, 199. *See also* Medical gaze
Fraud 39, 145, 198
Friendly societies, history of 24, 57, 156, 164. *See also* Approved Society

G

Gender. *See also* Domestic work, Housewives Non-Contributory Invalidity Pension (HNCIP), Women etc.
Gender and alternative work 88–91
Gender and social security 8, 9, 36, 111, 127. *See also* Domestic work, Housewives Non-Contributory Invalidity Pension (HNCIP), Women etc.
Gender and work 9, 89, 109–131, 146, 203. *See also* work
Gender categories 10
General Practitioner (GP). *See* Doctors
Great Western Railway Staff Friendly Society 185

H

Hague, William 47
Harrington review 74
Healthcare professional, as assessors for ESA 74
Hearing impairments, assessment of in incapacity benefits 46
HNCIP, abolition of 129
HNCIP and cohabiting women 127
HNCIP, claim procedure 128
HNCIP, definition of incapacity for work in 128
HNCIP, housework rule 126–130. *See also* Domestic work
HNCIP, introduction of 27, 127
HNCIP, reported in the press 129
Homeworking 89–90, 146
Horsbrugh, Florence, MP 114
Hospital, evidence from 66, 188
Hospital inpatients, and capacity for work 48, 90
Housekeepers. *See* Domestic work
Housewives. *See* Domestic work
Housewives Non-Contributory Invalidity Pension. *See* HNCIP
Housewives Non-Contributory Invalidity Pension (HNCIP) 27, 127–131
Housing conditions, relevance of in assessing capacity for work 46

I

I Daniel Blake (film) 74
Ideal Benefit Society 25, 119, 193
Illness. *See* Chronic illness, Sickness
Immoral conduct. *See* Moral conditionality
Impairment. *See* Models of disability
Incapacity Benefit 13, 28, 44–47. *See also* Disablement Benefit, Employment and Support Allowance, Housewives Non-contributory Invalidity Pension (HNCIP), Invalidity Benefit, NCIP, Severe Disablement

Allowance, Sickness Benefit, Statutory Sick Pay
Incapacity benefit, all work test in 46, 71
Incapacity benefit, definition of incapacity in 35
Incapacity benefit, exemption from medical testing 47
Incapacity benefit, medical tests for 2, 28, 34, 46, 47
Incapacity benefits and the social model of disability 7
Incapacity for work, definition of 2, 33, 34, 42
Incapacity for work, deemed incapacity 34
Incapacity for work, social construction of 8, 33
Incapacity for work, social elements in 28, 33, 44–48, 103–105, 150
Income Support 27
Individual model of disability. *See* Models of disability
Industrial injury benefits 80, 92, 93, 160. *See also* Workmen's Compensation Scheme
Infectious diseases 34
Inquiry into Sickness Benefit 1914 3, 33, 39, 56, 59, 65, 155–179, 183. *See also* Macarthur, Mary
Inquiry into Sickness Benefit 1914, as a source of evidence 14
Inquiry into Sickness Benefit 1914, evidence on appeal procedures 25
Intersectionality 8
Invalidity Benefit 27
Invalidity Benefit, definition of incapacity for work in 34
Invalidity Benefit, rising number of claims for 28
Ireland 14. *See also* Northern Ireland

J
Jobseeker's Allowance. *See* Unemployment benefits
Juvenile Improved Order of the Total Abstinent Sons of the Phoenix Sick and Burial Friendly Society 24

K
Knowledge 205
Knowledge, administrative 55
Knowledge, as objective 8, 63, 203, 205
Knowledge, claimants' 8, 55, 56, 69, 71, 74
Knowledge, common-sense 55, 69, 71, 205
Knowledge, expert 54
Knowledge, legal 55
Knowledge, medical 8, 53, 54, 74, 76, 198–200

L
Labour, division of 10
Labour market, attachment to 36, 176. *See also* Married women
Labour market, exclusion from 37, 49, 80
Labour market, relevance of in deciding incapacity for work 81, 121, 136, 139
Learning disabilities, exemption from medical testing 47
Leek Textile Federation 113, 166, 171, 193
Leek Textile Federation, internal appeal procedures 25
Light work 84–96
Limited capability for work. *See* Employment and Support Allowance (ESA)

Limited capability for work-related activities. *See* Employment and Support Allowance (ESA)
Lipsky, Michael 13
Litchfield review 74
Lodgers, letting rooms to 148, 197

M

Macarthur, Mary 15, 111, 112, 162, 185
Male breadwinner model 9, 110, 119
Malingering 43, 80, 151
Malingering, mechanisms to detect 8, 67
Mandatory reconsideration 27
Married women. *See also* Domestic work, Housewives Non-Contributory Invalidity Pension (HNCIP)
Married women, and national insurance contributions 24, 109–111, 119–120, 127–129
Married women, attachment to the labour market 4, 104, 109, 114, 117, 125
Masculinity 9
Maternity Benefit 114, 163
Maximus 73, 205
Means-testing 13, 27, 29, 135, 204. *See also* Income Support, National Assistance, Supplementary Benefit, Universal Credit
Medical assessment 1, 34, 53–75, 199–200, 203, 205
Medical assessors. *See* Appeal hearings
Medical certificates 53–74
Medical certificates and moral conditionality 159
Medical certificates, as claims mechanisms 34, 46, 72, 73
Medical certificates, lax certification 53, 56, 58, 66

Medical conditions and increased surveillance 39
Medical evidence, case law concerning 56, 62, 64
Medical evidence, conflicting 40, 56, 57, 59
Medical evidence, value of 57
Medical gaze 8, 53, 54, 199
Medical model of disability. *See* Models of disability
Medical opinions, second 53. *See also* Regional Medical Service
Medical referees 57. *See also* Regional Medical Service
Medical tests. *See* Medical assessment
Men. *See also* Domestic work and men, Male breadwinner model, Masculinity
Men, and claims for Invalidity Benefit 28
Men, as typical workers 36
Mental health, exemptions from medical testing 47
Ministry of Health 14, 25, 40, 53, 59, 61
Ministry of Labour (Northern Ireland) 25
Ministry of National Insurance 2, 42
Ministry of Pensions 62, 64, 70, 121, 123, 135, 199
Ministry of Pensions and National Insurance 123
Misconduct rule 185–193. *See also* Moral conditionality
Misdemeanours. *See* Moral conditionality
Models of disability, British model 5
Models of disability, individual model 44, 93
Models of disability, medical model 5, 34, 47, 48
Models of disability, social model 5–7, 35, 46, 96–105, 205

Moral conditionality 155–179, 206. *See also* Alcohol, Criminal convictions, Drugs, Fighting, Sanctions, Sexual behaviour
Moral conditionality and ESA 178
Moral conditionality, after 1948 174
Moral conditionality, conduct calculated to retard recovery 176
Mrs 'E' 1–5, 122, 136, 196–197, 208. *See also* R(S)11/51 in table of cases

National Amalgamated Approved Society 186
National Assistance 135
National Audit Office 47, 64, 67
National Deposit Friendly Society 162
National Farmers Union 141
National Health Service 26
National insurance 2, 23–27, 206
National Insurance Advisory Committee (NIAC) 128, 129
National Insurance Appeal Tribunals 27
National Insurance Commission 14, 25
National Insurance Commissioners, appeals to after 1948 27
National Insurance Commissioners, decisions after 1948 as sources 15
National Insurance Commissioners, in the Approved Society scheme. *See* National Insurance Commission
National Union of Mineworkers 80
NCIP. *See* Non-contributory Invalidity Pension
Neurasthenia 98, 99, 117

New Tabernacle (Old Street Congregational) Approved Society 155, 159, 164
NHS. *See* National Health Service
Non-contributory benefits 27, 37. *See also* Housewives Non-contributory Invalidity Pension (HNCIP), NCIP, Severe Disablement Allowance
Non-Contributory Invalidity Pension 37, 127, 130. *See also* Housewives Non-Contributory Invalidity Pension (HNCIP)
Normal work rule. *See* Own occupation test
Northern Ireland 25–26, 66

Office of Population Censuses and Surveys 46
Old age pensions. *See* Retirement pensions
OPCS. *See* Office of Population Censuses and Surveys
Order of Druids Friendly Society 163
Out of hours rule 170, 177, 205
Own occupation test 39–46

Paid work 136–143. *See also* Earnings, Unpaid work
Panel doctor system 34, 158. *See also* Doctors
Partially fit for work 44
Pay. *See* Earnings
Penalties. *See* Sanctions
Period of interruption in employment 36
Permitted work 146–147, 149
Personal Independence Payments 5
PIP. *See* Personal Independence Payments

Points systems, in assessing capacity for work 34, 46, 72, 75, 205. *See also* Employment and Support Allowance (ESA), Incapacity Benefit
Post-work theory 11, 152, 208
Pregnancy 102, 103, 159, 162–164, 174, 178, 186. *See also* Maternity benefit, Moral conditionality
Pregnancy and unmarried women 159, 162, 163
Prudential Approved Society 24, 116, 170

R

Rape, pregnancy as a result of 164, 207
Rational Association Friendly Society 162
Reasonable adjustments 49
Regional Medical Officer. *See* Regional Medical Service
Regional Medical Service, Approved Societies scheme 59, 62
Regional Medical Service, establishment of 59
Regional Medical Service, 1948 scheme 55–63, 70
Regulation, of Approved Societies 23, 24
Regulation, of behaviour. *See* Conditionality
Regulation, of decision making 23, 62, 203
Rehabilitation 146. *See also* Training
Remuneration. *See* Earnings
Remunerative work. *See* Paid work
Report of the Departmental Committee on Sickness Benefit Claims under the National Insurance Act. *See* Inquiry into Sickness Benefit 1914

Representation. *See* Appeal hearings
Reserve army of labour 12
Reserved occupations 91
Retirement, early 28
Retirement pensions 13, 24
Revelatory signs 54, 82, 88, 195
RMO. *See* Regional Medical Officer
Royal Commission 1926 15, 41, 59, 65
Royal Commission 1926, evidence on appeals procedures 25
Royal Commission on Venereal Diseases 162. *See also* Sexually transmitted diseases

S

Safford, Archibald 4
Sanctions 156–159
Sanctions, in ESA 28
Scotland 14, 59, 66, 67, 94, 162–169, 185
Scotland, appeals procedures in 25–26
Scottish Board of Health. *See* Board of Health, Scottish
Scottish Catholic Insurance Society 169
SDA. *See* Severe Disablement Allowance
Second World War 119, 146
Second World War, fire-watching duties as evidence of capacity for work 62
Second World War, regional medical service during 61
Self-directed support 12
Self-employment 139–143. *See also* Work
SEMA Group 72
Severe Disablement Allowance 27, 37, 130
Sexual behaviour 3, 156, 158–179. *See also* Moral conditionality

Sexually transmitted diseases 157–162. *See also* sexual behaviour
Sexually transmitted diseases, and public health 161–162
Sexually transmitted diseases, attitudes of Approved Societies 159–161, 185
Sexually transmitted diseases, doctors' certificates 159–162
Sickness. *See also* Chronic illness
  long term 36, 38, 41, 43, 50
  short term 35, 38, 44
  six month rule 35–39
Sickness Benefit (Approved Society Scheme), claim process 34, 55
Sickness Benefit (Approved Society Scheme), contribution conditions for 36, 110, 114
Sickness Benefit (Approved Society Scheme), definition of incapacity in 33
Sickness Benefit (Approved Society Scheme), introduction of 24–29
Sickness Benefit, (post-war scheme) contribution conditions for 26, 111
Sickness Benefit (post-war scheme), introduction of 26
Sickness, distinction between disability and 7, 35, 36
Sick notes. *See* Medical certificates
Sick pay. *See* Statutory Sick Pay
Sick visitors 2, 55, 183–200, 206
Sick visitors and curfews 176, 177
Sick visitors as detectives 54, 192
Sick visitors as part of the control system for incapacity benefits 64, 197, 198
Sick visitors, decline in the use of 67, 198
Sick visitors, guidance on the use of 66, 150, 184–189, 198
Sick visitors, in Northern Ireland 66
Sick visitors, in the nineteenth century 184
Sick visitors, reactions to the use of 192
Sick visitors reports as a source of evidence 65, 124, 187
Sick visitors, training 195–198
Sick visitors, welfare role of 186, 196
Small stamp 111
Social assistance. *See* Means-testing
Social control 12–14, 203–207. *See also* Surveillance
Social insurance. *See* National insurance
Social issues in definition of incapacity. *See* Incapacity for work, definition of
Social model of disability. *See* Models of disability
Statutory Sick Pay 27, 38, 73
Stone, Deborah 8, 13, 75. *See also* Disability category
Street level bureaucracy 13, 14, 35, 53, 69
Supplementary Benefit 27, 145
Supplementary Benefits Commission 151
Support Group. *See* Employment and Support Allowance (ESA)
Surveillance 183–200, 205, 207
Surveillance and atypical claimants 39, 196, 198
Surveillance, and long term claims 37
Surveillance and married women 39, 123, 148
Surveillance, forms of 183–200
Surveillance, sick visitors 4, 155, 184
Suspension of benefit. *See* Sanctions
Suspension of membership. *See* Sanctions

T

Tate, Mavis, MP 115
Therapeutic earnings. *See* Permitted work
Townsend, Peter 6
Trade unions, as Approved Societies 24
Trade unions, as representatives 95
Trade unions, role in rising claims for in the 1970s 28
Training, relevance in decisions on incapacity for work 123. *See also* Conditionality
Tribunals. *See* Appeal hearings
Tribunals, upper tier. *See* National Insurance Commissioners
Tunbridge Wells Equitable Friendly Society 170–193
Two child rule 164, 207

U

Unemployable 98, 100, 151
Unemployment 36
Unemployment benefits 12, 28, 80, 83, 92, 113, 114, 140, 192
Unemployment, relationship between unemployment and incapacity 28, 45, 80, 81, 206
Union of Physical Impaired Against Segregation (UPIAS) 6, 11, 207
Universal basic income. *See* Citizens' income
Universal Credit 29, 35, 164, 206
Unpaid work 143. *See also* Domestic work, Paid work
UPIAS. *See* Union of Physical Impaired Against Segregation
Usual occupation. *See* Own occupation

V

Validating device 54

Venereal disease. *See* Sexually transmitted diseases
Violence. *See* Moral conditionality
Visual impairments, assessment of incapacity benefits 46, 47
Visual impairments, pensions for blind people 24

W

Wages for housework 10
Wales 25–26
War pensions, as evidence of impairment 85
Watson, Alfred, government actuary 113
WCA. *See* Employment and Support Allowance (ESA), Work Capability Assessment
Webb, Sidney 33, 44, 49
Welfare rights advisers 15, 94
Women. *See* Domestic work, Gender, Married women
Women and the welfare state 9, 111
Women, patterns of work in the past 11, 111
Women's Trade Union League 15
Work 135–153, 204, 205. *See also* Domestic work, Light work, Homeworking, Letting rooms to lodgers, Permitted work, Post-work theory, Self-employment
Work, alternative work 79–81, 88–94
Work, barriers to 12. *See also* Models of disability
Work and disabled people 11
Work as an individual activity 147
Work Capability Assessment. *See* Employment and Support Allowance (ESA)
Work, definition of for benefits purposes 135–153

Work, definition of for census purposes 11
Work ethic 205
Work, family as employers 98, 99, 144–146
Workhouse test 53
Worklessness 151. *See also* Unemployment
Work/life balance 11
Workmen's compensation scheme 92, 160
Work, moral superiority of 10, 11, 151–153, 203–207
Work, part-time 136
Work-seeking behaviour 73, 92. *See also* Work-seeking conditionality
Work-seeking conditionality 28, 80, 178, 206
Work, sociology of 10, 11

Young, Hilton 115

Lightning Source UK Ltd.
Milton Keynes UK
UKHW021812300719
347113UK00002B/58/P